Queenship an

Series editors
Charles Beem
University of North Carolina
Pembroke
NC, USA

Carole Levin
University of Nebraska–Lincoln
Lincoln
NE, USA

This series focuses on works specializing in gender analysis, women's studies, literary interpretation, and cultural, political, constitutional, and diplomatic history. It aims to broaden our understanding of the strategies that queens—both consorts and regnants, as well as female regents—pursued in order to wield political power within the structures of male-dominant societies. The works describe queenship in Europe as well as many other parts of the world, including East Asia, Sub-Saharan Africa, and Islamic civilization.

More information about this series at
http://www.springer.com/series/14523

Estelle Paranque · Nate Probasco
Claire Jowitt
Editors

Colonization, Piracy, and Trade in Early Modern Europe

The Roles of Powerful Women and Queens

Editors
Estelle Paranque
New College of the Humanities
London, UK

Claire Jowitt
University of East Anglia
Norwich, UK

Nate Probasco
Briar Cliff University
Sioux City
IA, USA

Queenship and Power
ISBN 978-3-319-86091-6   ISBN 978-3-319-57159-1 (eBook)
DOI 10.1007/978-3-319-57159-1

© The Editor(s) (if applicable) and The Author(s) 2017
Softcover reprint of the hardcover 1st edition 2017
This work is subject to copyright. All rights are solely and exclusively licensed by the Publisher, whether the whole or part of the material is concerned, specifically the rights of translation, reprinting, reuse of illustrations, recitation, broadcasting, reproduction on microfilms or in any other physical way, and transmission or information storage and retrieval, electronic adaptation, computer software, or by similar or dissimilar methodology now known or hereafter developed.
The use of general descriptive names, registered names, trademarks, service marks, etc. in this publication does not imply, even in the absence of a specific statement, that such names are exempt from the relevant protective laws and regulations and therefore free for general use.
The publisher, the authors and the editors are safe to assume that the advice and information in this book are believed to be true and accurate at the date of publication. Neither the publisher nor the authors or the editors give a warranty, express or implied, with respect to the material contained herein or for any errors or omissions that may have been made. The publisher remains neutral with regard to jurisdictional claims in published maps and institutional affiliations.

Cover credit: © World History Archive/Alamy Stock Photo

Printed on acid-free paper

This Palgrave Macmillan imprint is published by Springer Nature
The registered company is Springer International Publishing AG
The registered company address is: Gewerbestrasse 11, 6330 Cham, Switzerland

To Michelle Bonche, my Mimi, may you rest in peace.
Estelle Paranque

This book is dedicated to Sir Walter Raleigh (c.1552–1618), explorer, courtier, writer, iconoclast.
Claire Jowitt

Acknowledgements

We are delighted to pay tribute here to the colleagues, friends, and family that have sustained us during the development and realization of this project. Our greatest debt is to Carole Levin and Charles Beem, Series Editors of Queenship and Power, whose belief in the project, intellectual generosity, and friendship have been instrumental in bringing this book to fruition. It has also been a delight to work with such intellectually stimulating material and such professional contributors. Our authors' diligence and their patience in responding to editorial suggestions have made our work both so much easier and a real pleasure. We thank the anonymous reviewer for thoughtful suggestions that helped reshape the collection and further develop its intellectual coherence. We also gratefully acknowledge the team at Palgrave Macmillan for all they did to support the project from inception to realization, and every step in between.

Claire Jowitt would like to acknowledge the financial support of the Faculty of Arts and Humanities at the University of East Anglia for the fees and reproduction costs for images in her essay.

Contents

1   Introduction to Colonization, Piracy, and Trade in Early Modern Europe: The Roles of Powerful Women and Queens   1
    Nate Probasco, Estelle Paranque and Claire Jowitt

Part I Demonstration of Power

2   Mary I, Mary of Guise and the Strong Hand of the Scots: Marian Policy in Ulster and Anglo-Scottish Diplomacy, 1553–1558   17
    Jonathan Woods

3   Catherine de Medici and Huguenot Colonization, 1560–1567   41
    Nate Probasco

4   Isabel Clara Eugenia, Governor of the Spanish Netherlands: Trade, Politics, and Warfare, Ruling like a King 1621–1633   73
    Estelle Paranque

Part II Diplomatic Strategies

5   Caterina Cornaro and the Colonization of Cyprus   97
    Lisa Hopkins

6   Trade and Piracy: The Role of a Potential Queen
    Consort in the 1620s   117
    Valentina Caldari

7   "The Princesses' Representative" or Renegade
    Entrepreneur? Marie Petit, the Silk Trade, and
    Franco-Persian Diplomacy   141
    Junko Thérèse Takeda

Part III Exotic Encounters

8   "I would not have given it for a wilderness of monkeys":
    Turquoise, Queenship, and the Exotic   169
    Carole Levin and Cassandra Auble

9   A Vision on Queen Elizabeth's Role in Colonizing
    America: Stephen Parmenius's *De Navigatione* (1582) 195
    Erzsébet Stróbl

10 Captains, Kings, Queens: Politics, Piracy, and the
    Sea in Middleton's The Phoenix (c.1603–04)   223
    Claire Jowitt

Index   251

Editors and Contributors

About the Editors

Estelle Paranque is Lecturer in Early Modern History at New College of the Humanities. She completed her Ph.D. at UCL in 2016. Her research focuses on Elizabeth I of England's representations in the French royal correspondence with their ambassadors. She has published several essays on Elizabeth's warlike rhetoric and Henry III of France's father figure. She is currently co-editing with Valerie Schutte a collection on *Forgotten Queens in Medieval and Early Modern Europe: Political Agency, Myth-Making and Patronage* which will be published by Routledge.

Nathan Probasco is Assistant Professor of History at Briar Cliff University in Sioux City, Iowa. He teaches courses in European, Atlantic world, and World History. His research has appeared in Renaissance Quarterly, The Journal of Military History, and Explorations in Renaissance Culture, as well as *The Foreign Relations of Elizabeth I*, edited by Charles Beem.

Claire Jowitt is Professor of English and History at the University of East Anglia, and Associate Dean for Research for Arts and Humanities. She is the author of *Voyage Drama and Gender Politics 1589–1642: Real and Imagined Worlds* (2003) and *The Culture of Piracy, 1580–1630: English Literature and Seaborne Crime* (2010). She has edited a number of volumes including *Pirates? The Politics of Plunder* (2006), and co-edited (with Daniel Carey) *Richard Hakluyt and Travel Writing in Early Modern Europe* (2012).

CONTRIBUTORS

Cassandra Auble is a Ph.D. candidate in the Department of History at West Virginia University. Her current research examines the role of jewelry in particular late medieval and early modern political contexts, specifically in credit relations and gift exchange. She explores how contemporaries utilized jewelry in political settings as a way to construct meaning, represent themselves, and negotiate personal and political relationships. She has published reviews in the *Sixteenth Century Journal* and the Journal of British Studies, and her essay "Bejeweled Majesty: Queen Elizabeth I, Precious Stones and Statecraft," was recently published in *The Emblematic Queen: Studies in Early Modern Visual Culture*.

Valentina Caldari is a Departmental Lecturer in Early Modern History at Balliol College, University of Oxford from 2015–2017. She completed in August 2015 her European-funded joint doctorate at the University of Kent and the Universidade do Porto under the supervision of Prof. Kenneth Fincham and Prof. Fátima Vieira, respectively. She has co-organized three international conferences: Early Stuart Politics (with Dr. Sara Wolfson) held in Canterbury in April 2014; The Black Legend—then and now (with Dr. Elizabeth Evenden) held at the Institute of Historical Research in London in September 2014; and Anglo-Iberian Relations, 1500-1850 (with Dr. Evenden) held in Mértola in April 2015. Her publications include 'Diplomacy and Marriage: Early Stuart Dynastic Politics in their European Context, 1604–1630' (ed. with Dr. Sara Wolfson) (Boydell & Brewer, forthcoming 2016) and 'The Secret Mechanisms of Courts: Factions in Early Modern Europe', (ed. with Rubén González Cuerva), Libros de la Corte, Monográfico 2 (2015).

Lisa Hopkins is Professor of English and Head of Graduate School at Sheffield Hallam University. She is a co-editor of Shakespeare, the journal of the British Shakespeare Association, of the Arden Early Modern Drama Guides, and of Arden Studies in Early Modern Drama. She has written mainly on Marlowe, Shakespeare, and Ford, but her publications also include Goddesses and Queens: The Iconography of Elizabeth I, co-edited with Annaliese Connolly (Manchester University Press, 2007), *Writing Renaissance Queens: Texts by and about Elizabeth I and Mary, Queen of Scots* (University of Delaware Press, 2002), *Women Who Would Be Kings: Female Rulers of the Sixteenth Century* (Vision Press, 1991), and *Elizabeth I and Her Court* (Vision Press, 1990). She co-organizes the annual Othello's Island conference on Cyprus (http://www.othellosisland.org/) and guest-edited a special issue of The Journal of Mediterranean Studies on 'Othello and his Islands': https://www.um.edu.mt/__data/assets/pdf_file/0009/299835/vol25no12016.pdf

Carole Levin is Willa Cather Professor of History at the University of Nebraska, where she specializes in early modern English cultural, political, and women's history. She is the author or editor of seventeen books, including *The Heart and Stomach of a King: Elizabeth I and the Politics of Sex and Power* (2nd ed., 2013), Dreaming the English Renaissance (2008), and (with John Watkins) Shakespeare's Foreign Worlds (2009). Her most recent books are the edited collection, *Scholars and Poets Talk About Queens* (2015) and (with Anna Riehl Bertolet and Jo Eldridge Carney) the editor of *A Biographical Encyclopedia of Early Modern Englishwomen: Exemplary Lives and Memorable Acts, 1500–1650* (2016). She has held long-term fellowships at both the Newberry Library in Chicago and the Folger Shakespeare Library in Washington DC, and in 2015, she was a Fulbright Scholar at the University of York in England.

Erzsébet Stróbl is Senior Lecturer in the Institute of English Studies at Károli Gáspár University of the Reformed Church in Hungary, Budapest. She completed her Ph.D. studies at Eötvös Loránd University, Budapest, in 2010, with the thesis *The Cult of Elizabeth: Ideology, Representation and Ritual*. Her main research interests include early modern cultural history, political theory, and discourses on feminine authority. She published extensively on various aspects of Queen Elizabeth's cult and her summer progresses, the symbolism of the figure of the 'wild man' in Tudor courtly and civic performances, the *dance macabre* motif in radical Protestant rhetoric and devotional works, as well as on works of George Gascoigne and John Lyly.

Junko Thérèse Takeda (Ph.D., Stanford University 2006) is an Associate Professor in early modern French history at Syracuse University. Research and teaching interests include economic globalization and the Enlightenment, political and diplomatic history, migration, and the history of disease. Her first book, Between Crown and Commerce: Marseille and the Early Modern Mediterranean (Johns Hopkins, 2011), explored the political tradition of civic republicanism in the context of French international trade with the Ottoman Empire. She is currently completing her second monograph, *The Other Persian Letters: Globalization and the Failed Franco-Iranian Embassies of 1704–15*. Recent articles include "French Mercantilism and the Early Modern Mediterranean: A Case Study of Marseille's Silk Industry," Special Issue: France and the Mediterranean, French History (March 2015), and "Global Insects: Silkworms, Sericulture and Statecraft in Napoleonic France and Tokugawa Japan," Special Issue: Animals and French History, French History (March 2014).

Jonathan Woods is a Ph.D. candidate at Fordham University, where he studies early modern British and Irish history under Prof. Christopher Maginn. He has taught as a teaching fellow and associate at Fordham since 2011. His dissertation, "Rebellion and Reformation in Scotland: the Rise of the Scottish Congregation and the End of the Auld Alliance, 1547–1561," examines the role of private armies, lordship, and kinship in the reformation rebellion of 1559–1560. Jonathan has published and presented widely on religion and politics in the Tudor and Stuart frontiers and has held fellowships from the Folger and Huntington libraries.

List of Figures

Fig. 10.1	*Sir Walter Raleigh*, by unknown English artist, oil on panel, 1588 © National Portrait Gallery, London	237
Fig. 10.2	Detail, *Sir Walter Raleigh*, by unknown English artist, oil on panel, 1588 © National Portrait Gallery, London	238
Fig. 10.3	Cantino World Map, 1502. Western half of the Cantino map of the world, 1502, showing (at left) the Tordesillas Treaty demarcation line of 1494, which divided the non-Christian "new" lands between Spain and Portugal, 370 leagues west of Cape Verde Islands. Granger Historical Picture Archive/Alamy Stock Photo	241

CHAPTER 1

Introduction to Colonization, Piracy, and Trade in Early Modern Europe: The Roles of Powerful Women and Queens

Nate Probasco, Estelle Paranque and Claire Jowitt

The early modern period was a time of momentous change for Europeans. In the fifteenth century, European population numbers began to recover from the destruction wrought by the Black Plague, but the continent was little more than a backwater to more technologically advanced regions such as China, India, and the Arab world.[1] The Protestant Reformation that swept across Northern Europe in the sixteenth century, and the subsequent Catholic Reformation, created not only religious division but also social, political, and cultural discord, which resulted in a series of both intranational and international wars. Yet simultaneous to the era's conflicts

N. Probasco (✉)
Briar Cliff University, Sioux City, IA, USA

E. Paranque
New College of the Humanities, London, UK

C. Jowitt
University of East Anglia, Norwich, UK

© The Author(s) 2017
E. Paranque et al. (eds.), *Colonization, Piracy, and Trade in Early Modern Europe*, Queenship and Power, DOI 10.1007/978-3-319-57159-1_1

were the intellectual developments of the European Renaissance that spread, in part, due to the introduction of the printing press and moveable type by Johannes Gutenberg in 1439.[2] A new climate of invention and innovation, with its emphasis on the practical benefits of "discovery," resulted in what has been termed a "Scientific Revolution."[3] By the late eighteenth century, Europe had emerged as a major force in global politics.

As this thumbnail history indicates, "discovery" is central to these geopolitical changes and the emergence of a new world order. Perhaps no single early modern event did more to encourage Europeans to reconceptualize their existence than Christopher Columbus's encounter with the Americas in 1492, which brought contact with remarkably diverse cultures previously unknown to Europeans. The Ottoman conquest of Constantinople in 1453, which severed the trading links between Europe and the Silk Road that had stretched across Asia for centuries, forced European rulers to send out diplomats, merchants, and explorers to seek out new markets and routes to acquire Eastern goods. They gradually, and often by force, established commercial links with peoples and nations, and access to markets and goods, from all corners of the world. As the often localized obligations of feudalism gave way to more nationalistic goals of mercantilism, monarchs and rulers began to attempt to colonize new lands.[4] The marked uptick in trade made piracy and other forms of illicit trade more profitable, which created further rivalries and increased tension among Europe's monarchs, particularly as Pope Alexander VI established in 1493 a line of territorial demarcation that excluded Northern Protestant European nations from new territories. This line divided the New World between Spain and Portugal, and the response of excluded nations was to both plunder and seek ways to break the monopoly.

With papal authority behind them, and to consolidate their access to lucrative new resources and markets, sovereigns such as King Ferdinand II of Aragon, John II of Portugal, Manuel I of Portugal, and Holy Roman Emperor Charles V commissioned an increased number of long-range explorations, and, in effect, redrew the map of the world. Other rulers such as William the Silent, Prince of Orange, and King Francis I of France responded by forging trade alliances and by sponsoring privateers. A new and popular genre of writing emerged in the wake of these activities: to announce these aspirations for territory and trade, written accounts of explorations and adventures by participants regularly began to be published either singly or as compendious collections (often in multiple editions and languages), designed to promote and celebrate national achievement.[5]

While male royal champions of exploration and commerce have been studied extensively, yet, with the exception of Elizabeth I, similar women in power are less frequently examined in this context. The objective of this collection is to bring to light these examples in order to more fully understand how prominent women wielded authority in colonization, piracy, and trade, three pursuits traditionally seen and celebrated as masculine spheres of activity.

Much as Europe attained global prominence during the early modern era, it was a time of ascendancy for a number of prominent European women too. The list of scholars who have discussed early modern queenship grows by the day, and the breadth of this research is remarkable.[6] Scholars from several geographic regions and across various disciplines have made groundbreaking findings on the distinctive ways in which women aged, perceived illness, resisted or supported religious reforms, and expressed themselves and their interests through letters.[7] It is not an overstatement to say that our understanding has been revolutionized since Joan Kelly-Gadol provocatively asked in 1977 "Did Women Have a Renaissance?"[8] Examining the roles of female rulers and of other powerful women in what were viewed as exclusively male vocations continues to present thought-provoking contrasts. During the early modern era, women were rarely allowed on ships, especially on pirate vessels, since they were believed to bring bad luck to the voyage, and yet female rulers like Elizabeth encouraged her male subjects at sea to attack and steal from England's enemies.[9] Elizabeth similarly supported England's fledgling colonizing voyages, but the male leaders of these expeditions included only a small number of women among the colonists.[10] Although several female rulers and women in other positions of power sponsored and funded colonizing and exploratory voyages, colonization, piracy, and trade were areas dominated by men and, as such, the roles that women possessed have too often been overlooked.[11] Women might have lacked authority within the patriarchal system that dominated early modern Europe, but they nonetheless influenced how nations, companies, and individuals colonized and traded, sometimes in unexpected ways.

Many scholarly trailblazers have lit the path for the present study. The era in which "gender history" was narrowly understood as referring only to women's or family history has passed: Important work has been undertaken to expand our understanding of the ways early modern male and female identities were socially constructed and men and women's behavior culturally conditioned. Just as studies of early modern femininity are at the vanguard of historical inquiry, the corpus of works on masculinity has swelled in recent years.[12] As Merry E. Wiesner-Hanks emphasizes, gender is now "an appropriate category of analysis when looking at *all* historical developments … *every* political, intellectual, religious, economic, social, and even military change."[13] Examining these changes through the lens of gender provides a fuller understanding of the lives of both men and women in early modern Europe. Gender relationships were, and remain, at the core of social relationships; an analysis of gender and power provides important insight into the workings of European societies.

Our study is hardly the first to focus on early modern European women who challenged male prerogatives. We hope to build upon the recent research of several scholars. Perhaps the most obvious sphere of activity traditionally seen as a male birthright of the early modern period was to serve in war. A number of writers have complicated the narrative of early modern warfare by examining the roles of women in supporting war efforts. Women were integral, non-combatant members of nearly every war-making party of the era, though they were less frequently decision-making leaders on the battlefield.[14] The political arena offers another venue in which to address women challenging male privilege. The far-reaching *Gender and Political Culture in Early Modern Europe* sheds light upon the various political spaces created by women, but women's leadership in the areas of colonization, piracy, and trade is not among them.[15]

Despite much recent scholarship on travel writing, a genre intricately linked to colonization and exploration, since women were not the principal actors in the theatre of empire in the early modern period, women have not been the sustained focus in these analyses, though discussions of gender and power have formed a significant feature of this scholarship.[16] Exceptions include, however, Susan Bassnett's essay in *The Cambridge Companion to Travel Writing*, which, while concluding that very often men were the ones relating their travel stories, also explores the narratives produced by women, though its focus is on an era slightly later than the one covered in this collection.[17] Similarly, Carolyn James's essay on Isabella d'Este's travel writing of the sixteenth century focuses on the way her correspondence revealed her as a sophisticated cultural tourist in dialogue with her male contemporaries. Though d'Este was not a long-range traveler (compared to the oceanic voyages of the period), her letters show an acute awareness that writing about her experiences offered her a route to social advancement and political prestige.[18] This volume also shows that women not only took part in explorations but that they also played crucial authoritative roles and were, at times, in charge of the decision-making processes that shaped what was to be "discovered" and, just as importantly, who was to participate and benefit. It is important to note, however, that the essays in this volume do not examine travel writing per se, but rather seek to understand its contribution to and role in inspiring European expansion. In other words, the genre provides important perspectives on how trade and piracy were perceived during the early modern period.

Piracy, often intertwined with privateering in this period, was permitted and even encouraged by monarchs and other powerful individuals as a means to weaken enemy states and rivals. Differences between the activities to which these two terms referred can be difficult to distinguish, and which term was used to describe them often depends upon the speaker's perspective. When Elizabeth allowed her "privateer" Francis Drake to attack foreign shipping, his victims and their monarchs perceived him as a "pirate."[19] Claire Jowitt engages with the ways these classifications were contested and finds that "the category of 'pirate' includes a wide variety of figures from all sorts of social, religious, and ethnic backgrounds, who were variously defined in different cultural registers as 'pirates,' 'corsairs,' 'buccaneers,' and 'filibusters'."[20] This collection examines how queens, potential queens, and powerful women participated in these enterprises and how they used violence at sea, and how these activities were represented and discussed by their contemporaries. Our aim is to fill a gap in current scholarship by presenting an alternative view of early modern queenship.

To suggest that early modern women overcame significant barriers in their quests to attain and subsequently maintain power would be an understatement. The father held authority over all household members in patriarchal European societies, and "the state was the household writ large …. It was against nature for women to rule over men."[21] Primogeniture favored males, and sons nearly always inherited the thrones of Europe. Women had to overcome what Cissie Fairchilds calls the "patriarchal paradigm … that women were born inferior to men and therefore destined to live under male guidance and control."[22]

It was especially difficult for women to challenge patriarchy in the public sphere, where the male-dominated patronage system meant roles and privileges were both highly competitive and fiercely guarded.

As the body of scholarship on early modern women and gender studies grows, it becomes ever more important to define precisely what each new study adds to these relatively young subjects of inquiry. This collection presents women as the agents of change: the subjects of the various case studies presented in this volume each, in different and overlapping ways, challenged gender roles of the era, and sought to debate and redefine their boundaries: in certain instances, there were obvious repercussions for their actions.

What makes this edited volume unique and innovative is not only the clear links that it draws between queenship and three emerging preoccupations of early modern Europe, but also the variety and richness of the case studies examined: Whether a queen consort, regent, regnant, governor, or female representative of the crown, each woman wielded power in a distinctive way. Famous queens such as Elizabeth, Mary I, and Catherine de Medici are analyzed alongside less familiar female rulers such as Caterina Cornaro, Isabel Clara Eugenia, and Madame Petit, a representative of the French monarchy in the Mediterranean trade. A similar approach was employed by Anne J. Cruz and Mihoko Suzuki in their recent collection *The Rule of Women in Early Modern Europe*, and this collection likewise provides a "transnational and transcultural perspective on a topic ... largely studied through the lens of a single nation."[23] Each case study offers a compelling story of how women asserted their authority, disputed diplomatic strategies, and were involved with, or represented the exotic and the unknown. Through its examination of colonization, piracy, and trade—activities men traditionally dominated—and foregrounding women's roles within them, this collection challenges orthodox history. Moreover, it highlights specific and significant issues related to the links between female rule and foreign affairs.

Three interrelated though necessarily distinct sections invite the reader to ask important questions about the roles of women in early modern colonization, piracy, and trade. The collection begins with three model case studies that assess how queens imposed their will and authority through trade, espionage, and warfare—spheres that were often entwined with interests in colonizing, invading, and dominating foreign lands. War and colonization were "both strongly gendered masculine,"[24] yet early modern women asserted their authority in both areas. Jonathan Woods examines Anglo-Scottish relations through Mary I's and Mary of Guise's struggle to control Ireland. The so-called Tudor "conquest of Ireland" began in the 1530s with Henry VIII being declared king of Ireland, but the policy of colonization did not gain full momentum until the reigns of his daughters. Land in Ireland held great value to England and Scotland alike in the sixteenth century, and to both, it was seen as conquerable. Indeed, Mary I considered the presence of Scottish soldiers and settlers there a major threat to the full incorporation of Ireland under an English legal and economic system. Thus, Marian policy in Ireland centered on warfare against the Scots not only as a pragmatic necessity for pacifying Gaelic resistance, but also as a means of constructing an overarching Anglo-Irish identity centered on loyalty to the Tudors. In this book's opening chapter, Woods offers a penetrating analysis of the major distinctions between royal rule in England and Scotland, which ultimately led to miscommunication and distrust between Mary I and Mary of Guise, Queen Regent of Scotland, which, in turn, contributed to the outbreak of open war in 1557.

Nate Probasco's case study of Catherine de Medici also deals with the political and military dimensions of colonizing foreign lands. Catherine's plans to relocate French Huguenots to other parts of Europe and the Americas shed light on the complex religio-political motives of her colonial agenda. Probasco stresses Catherine's desire to negotiate peace through colonization, while also demonstrating how she astutely played the Guise family against their Huguenot adversaries. She simultaneously challenged Hapsburg power in the Americas and Europe, while making it appear to King Philip II of Spain that she was an ally. Though never a queen in her own right, she clearly was a skilled and shrewd stateswoman, at home in the cut and thrust of international power politics.

In Chap. 4 of *Colonization, Piracy, and Trade in Early Modern Europe*, Estelle Paranque examines a female ruler's display of power through warfare, trade, and espionage. After the death of Albert VII, Archduke of Austria, Philip IV of Spain appointed Isabel Clara Eugenia to the Governorship of the Spanish Netherlands, a title that was seen as acceptable for a female ruler. Though she was no longer co-monarch due to her husband's recent death, Isabel's change in title should not obscure the fact that she remained very much in charge of the realm until her own death in 1633. Paranque focuses on Isabel's involvement in state and foreign affairs, specifically the way

Isabel became an influential adviser to the Spanish king while simultaneously holding the official role of de facto ruler of the Spanish Netherlands. In this latter role, she engaged in complex trade negotiations with European neighbors and made important decisions during wartime.

Building on the collection's focus in these early chapters on the ways early modern female rulers secured and consolidated their positions through their command of international relations, the second section provides three additional case studies that reveal the range of queens' and powerful women's use of trade and piracy as part of their diplomatic strategy. Lisa Hopkins examines Caterina Cornano's role in colonizing Cyprus as well as how Carlota de Lusignan challenged Cornano for control of the small island. Hopkins explores the ways in which these two women attempted to negotiate queenship through their conduct of trade, and whether Cyprus would be forced into the status of a colony of Venice, or allowed to retain such independence as it had from its Egyptian Mameluke suzerains.

Like Caterina Cornano, Maria Ana—the Spanish Infant—and Henrietta Maria of France were "foreign" princesses and prospective future queens of England. While Hopkins reveals Cornano's key role in the colonization of Cyprus, Valentina Caldari demonstrates that Maria Ana and Henrietta Maria deftly navigated between active and passive subject positions through influencing their respective marriage negotiations rather than simply being manipulated as diplomatic pawns by their ruling families. By examining their marriage treaties, Caldari reveals that the two princesses were able and subtle intermediaries who influenced trade relations between England and their respective countries of origin. She explores how the marriage arrangements for these two queen consorts secured political alliances and created a direct link between themselves and provisions established for trade and piracy.

Junko Takeda's case study diverges from queen consorts and regents to explore the fascinating and adventurous life of an influential bourgeoisie woman who played a pivotal role in the management of foreign affairs for her nation. Her essay highlights the influence of Marie Petit in the earliest official diplomatic exchanges between Bourbon France and Safavid Persia. The owner of a successful gambling house, Petit provided Jean-Baptiste Fabre—a Marseillais wholesale textile trader chosen by Louis XIV to be his first French envoy to Shah Sultan Hosayn—with 12,200 livres to fund his mission to the Safavid court. Madame Petit was no princess or queen, and yet she accompanied Fabre on his mission. When Fabre died *en route* to Isfahan, Petit declared herself his successor and a "representative of the Princesses of France" sent by her king to educate women in the Shah's seraglio. Her story sheds light on the development of French mercantilism and reveals how an extraordinary French woman gained the prominence to represent her monarch to a vital non-European partner.

Takeda describes the emergence of Near Eastern markets and their importance to European commerce, thus providing an effective segue to the final part of the collection that focuses on trade. Carole Levin and Cassandra Auble survey the trade of the highly prized commodity of turquoise during the early modern period in their essay, and they reveal its significance to queens and to early modern culture in general. They also demonstrate how the exchange of this precious stone linked Europe with exotic lands. The trade of turquoise, its origins, its value, and its representation in contemporary literature are all analyzed in order to provide a fuller understanding of its relationship with particular queens and queenship more broadly.

Erzsébet Strobl focuses on representations of such endeavors in contemporary literature and their implication for queens. Utilizing the Latin epic poem *De Navigatione* (c. 1582) by the Hungarian humanist poet and explorer Stephen Parmenius to celebrate Humphrey Gilbert's attempt to colonize the New World, Strobl examines how it depicted Elizabeth I's role in colonization. She is most interested in the poem's central trope, its reference to the Golden Age that signifies, she argues, both the evolutionary state of Native Americans and of the Elizabethan era itself.

The final essay in the collection, by Claire Jowitt, likewise examines early modern cultural depictions, focusing on one of the key themes of the collection, the relationship between gender, politics, and piracy. Her chapter discusses Thomas Middleton's *The Phoenix* (c. 1603–04), a play contemporaneous with the regime change from Elizabeth Tudor to James Stuart that engages with the major alterations in foreign and domestic policies between their reigns. The character of the piratical Captain is, she argues, used to debate the qualities required to steer successfully the ship (or nation) of England to its imperial/colonial destiny. Jowitt explores how the Captain's piracy, misogyny, sexuality, and treatment in the play relate to these larger political changes, to show how this play offers a nuanced and bold discussion of the strengths and weaknesses of the old and new regimes, and of female and male rule.

Although these case studies are diverse and broad ranging in terms of the individual women at their center, and the essays reveal varied perspectives on early modern colonization, piracy, and trade, collectively they reveal what was at stake politically, diplomatically, and culturally in these activities. They also show how queens were intricately involved with, or represented in complex ways in, these traditionally masculine endeavors. In analyzing how female power was constructed through these important aspects of early modern nation building, or how women negotiated peace or trade agreements, this volume sheds new light on the multilayered identity of queenship in general.

NOTES

1. For an authoritative overview on the effects of the Black Death, see Colin Platt, *King Death:* The Black Death and its Aftermath in Late Medieval England (London: University College London Press, 1996).
2. On this topic, see, for instance, Elizabeth L. Eisenstein, *The Printing Revolution in Early Modern Europe*, 2nd, rev. ed. (Cambridge: Cambridge University Press, 2005).
3. See, for example, William E. Burns, *The Scientific Revolution in Global Perspective* (Oxford: Oxford University Press, 2016), and H. Floris Cohen, *The Rise of Modern Science Explained: A Comparative History* (Cambridge: Cambridge University Press, 2015).
4. Scholarship on this topic is immense, but for an overview, see Anthony Pagden, *Lords of all the World: Ideologies of Empire in Spain, Britain and France c. 1500–c. 1800* (New Haven: Yale University Press, 1995).
5. See Daniel Carey and Claire Jowitt, eds., *Richard Hakluyt and Travel Writing in Early Modern Europe* (Ashgate: Farnham, 2012).
6. Among the most recent and comprehensive example is Allyson M. Poska, Jane Couchman, and Katherine A. McIver, eds., *The Ashgate Research Companion to Women and Gender in Early Modern Europe* (Abingdon: Routledge, 2016); See also Susan Broomhall and Jacqueline Van Gent, *Power and Identity in the early modern House of Orange-Nassau* (Aldershot: Ashgate, 2016); Elena Woodacre, ed., *Queenship in the Mediterranean: Negotiating the Role of the Queen in Medieval and Early Modern Eras* (New York: Palgrave Macmillan, 2013); Anne J. Cruz and Mihoko Suzuki, eds., *The Rule of Women in Early Modern Europe* (Champaign: University of Illinois Press, 2009); Carole Levin, Debra Barrett-Graves, and Jo Eldridge Carney, eds., *High and Mighty Queens of Early Modern England: Realities and Representations* (New York: Palgrave Macmillan, 2003).

7. Olivia Weisser, *Ill Composed: Sickness, Gender, and Belief in Early Modern England* (New Haven: Yale University Press, 2015); Allison Levy, ed., *Widowhood and Visual Culture in Early Modern Europe* (Aldershot: Ashgate, 2003); Sandra Cavallo and Lyndan Warner, eds., *Widowhood in Medieval and Early Modern Europe* (Abingdon: Routledge, 1999); Sharon L. Jansen, *Dangerous Talk and Strange Behavior: Women and Popular Resistance to the Reforms of Henry VIII* (New York: St. Martin's Press, 1996); James Daybell and Andrew Gordon, eds., *Women and Epistolary Agency in Early Modern Culture (1450–1690)* (Abingdon: Routledge, 2016).
8. Joan Kelly-Gadol, "Did Women Have a Renaissance?" in *Becoming Visible: Women in European History*, eds. Renata Bridenthal and Claudia Koonz (Boston: Houghton Mifflin, 1977), 137–64.
9. See Susan Ronald, *The Pirate Queen: Queen Elizabeth I, Her Pirate Adventurers, and the Dawn of Empire* (New York: HarperCollins, 2007); Harry Kelsey, *Sir John Hawkins: Queen Elizabeth's Slave Trader* (New York: Yale University Press, 2003).
10. During the Roanoke Voyages, the 1585 colonists (the first voyage) were all men, but the voyage in 1587 (the second voyage) included seventeen women and eleven children. See David Beers Quinn, *Set Fair for Roanoke: Voyages and Colonies 1584–1606* (Chapel Hill and London: University of North Carolina Press, 1985).
11. Recent work has begun to address this imbalance; see, in particular, John C. Appleby, *Women and English Piracy, 1540–1720: Partners and Victims of Crime* (Woodbridge: Boydell and Brewer, 2013).
12. Alexandra Shepard, *Meanings of Manhood in Early Modern England* (Oxford: Oxford University Press, 2006); Elizabeth A. Foyster, *Manhood in Early Modern England* (New York: Routledge, 1999).
13. Merry E. Wiesner-Hanks, *Women and Gender in Early Modern Europe*, 3rd ed. (Cambridge: Cambridge University Press, 2008), 3; See also Wiesner-Hanks, *Gender in History: Global Perspectives*, 2nd ed. (Chichester: Wiley-Blackwell, 2011).
14. John A. Lynn II, *Women, Armies, and Warfare in Early Modern Europe* (Cambridge: Cambridge University Press, 2008); See also Charles J. Esdaile, *Women in the Peninsular War* (Norman: University of Oklahoma Press, 2014); A firsthand account is Rebecca Probert, ed., *Catherine Exley's Diary: The Life and Times of an Army Wife in the Peninsular War* (Kenliworth: Brandram, 2014).
15. James Daybell and Svante Norrhem, eds., *Gender and Political Culture in Early Modern Europe* (Abingdon: Routledge, 2017); See also Elena Woodacre and Carey Fleiner, eds., *Royal Mothers and their Ruling Children: Wielding Political Authority from Antiquity to the Early Modern*

    Era (Houndmills: Palgrave Macmillan, 2015); Sharon L. Jansen, *Debating Women, Politics, and Power and Early Modern Europe* (New York: Palgrave Macmillan, 2008).
16. See Louis Montrose, "The Work of Gender in the Discourse of Discovery," *Representations* 33 (1991): 1–33; Richard Helgerson, *Forms of Nationhood: The Elizabethan Writing of England* (Chicago: The University of Chicago Press, 1992); Andrew Hadfield, *Literature, Travel and Colonial Writing in the English Renaissance 1545–1625* (Oxford: Oxford University Press, 1998); Mary C. Fuller, *Voyages in Print: English Travel to America, 1576–1624* (Cambridge: Cambridge University Press, 1995); Claire Jowitt, *Voyage Drama and Gender Politics: Real and Imagined Worlds* (Manchester: Manchester University Press, 2002).
17. Susan Bassnett, "Travel Writing and Gender," in *The Cambridge Companion to Travel Writing*, eds. Peter Hulme and Tim Young (Cambridge: Cambridge University Press, 2006), 225–41.
18. See Carolyn James, "The Travels of Isabella d'Este, Marchioness of Mantua," *Studies in Travel Writing* 13, 2 (2009): 99–109.
19. See Claire Jowitt, *The Culture of Piracy, 1580–1630: English Literature and Seaborne Crime* (Farnham: Ashgate, 2010), 96; Kenneth R. Andrews, *Elizabethan Privateering: English Privateering during the Spanish War, 1585–1603* (Cambridge: Cambridge University Press, 1964).
20. Jowitt, *Culture of Piracy*, 8.
21. Cissie Fairchilds, *Women in Early Modern Europe, 1500–1700* (Harlow: Longman, 2007), 5.
22. Fairchilds, *Women in Europe*, 7.
23. Cruz and Suzuki, eds., *Rule of Women*, 2.
24. Fairchilds, *Women in Europe*, 5.

Bibliography

Andrews, Kenneth R. *Elizabethan Privateering: English Privateering during the Spanish War, 1585–1603*. Cambridge: Cambridge University Press, 1964.

Appleby, John C. *Women and English Piracy, 1540–1720: Partners and Victims of Crime*. Woodbridge: Boydell and Brewer, 2013.

Bassnett, Susan. "Travel Writing and Gender." In *The Cambridge Companion to Travel Writing*. Edited by Peter Hulme and Tim Youngs, 225–41. Cambridge: Cambridge University Press, 2006.

Beers Quinn, David. *Set Fair for Roanoke: Voyages and Colonies 1584–1606*. Chapel Hill and London: University of North Carolina Press, 1985.

Broomhall, Susan, and Van Gent, Jacqueline. *Power and Identity in the early modern House of Orange-Nassau*. Aldershot: Ashgate, 2016.

Burns, William E. *The Scientific Revolution in Global Perspective.* Oxford: Oxford University Press, 2016.
Carey, Daniel and Jowitt, Claire, eds. *Richard Hakluyt and Travel Writing in Early Modern Europe.* Ashgate: Farnham, 2012.
Cavallo, Sandra and Warner, Lyndan, eds. *Widowhood in Medieval and Early Modern Europe.* Abingdon: Routledge, 1999.
Cruz, Anne J. and Suzuki, Mihoko, eds. *The Rule of Women in Early Modern Europe.* Champaign: University of Illinois Press, 2009.
Daybell, James and Gordon, Andrew, eds. *Women and Epistolary Agency in Early Modern Culture (1450–1690).* Abingdon: Routledge, 2016.
Daybell, James and Norrhem, Svante, eds. *Gender and Political Culture in Early Modern Europe.* Abingdon: Routledge, 2017.
Eisenstein, Elizabeth L. *The Printing Revolution in Early Modern Europe*, 2nd, rev. ed. Cambridge: Cambridge University Press, 2005.
Esdaile, Charles J. *Women in the Peninsular War.* Norman: University of Oklahoma Press, 2014.
Fairchilds, Cissie. *Women in Early Modern Europe, 1500–1700.* Harlow: Longman, 2007.
Floris, Cohen H. *The Rise of Modern Science Explained: A Comparative History.* Cambridge: Cambridge University Press, 2015.
Foyster, Elizabeth A. *Manhood in Early Modern England.* New York: Routledge, 1999.
Fuller, Mary C. *Voyages in Print: English Travel to America, 1576–1624.* Cambridge: Cambridge University Press, 1995.
Hadfield, Andrew. *Literature, Travel and Colonial Writing in the English Renaissance 1545–1625.* Oxford: Oxford University Press, 1998.
Helgerson, Richard. *Forms of Nationhood: The Elizabethan Writing of England.* Chicago: The University of Chicago Press, 1992.
James, Carolyn. "The Travels of Isabella d'Este, Marchioness of Mantua." In *Studies in Travel Writing* 13, 2 (2009): 99–109.
Jansen, Sharon L. *Dangerous Talk and Strange Behavior: Women and Popular Resistance to the Reforms of Henry VIII.* New York: St. Martin's Press, 1996.
Jansen, Sharon L. *Debating Women, Politics, and Power and Early Modern Europe.* New York: Palgrave Macmillan, 2008.
Jowitt, Claire. *Voyage Drama and Gender Politics: Real and Imagined Worlds.* Manchester: Manchester University Press, 2002.
Jowitt, Claire. *The Culture of Piracy, 1580–1630: English Literature and Seaborne Crime.* Farnham: Ashgate, 2010.
Kelly-Gadol, Joan. "Did Women Have a Renaissance?" In *Becoming Visible: Women in European History.* Edited by Renata Bridenthal and Claudia Koonz, 137–64. Boston: Houghton Mifflin, 1977.

Kelsey, Harry. *Sir John Hawkins: Queen Elizabeth's Slave Trader*. New York: Yale University Press, 2003.

Levin, Carole, Barrett-Graves, Debra, and Carney, Jo Eldridge, eds. *High and Mighty Queens of Early Modern England: Realities and Representations*. New York: Palgrave Macmillan, 2003.

Levy, Allison, ed. *Widowhood and Visual Culture in Early Modern Europe*. Aldershot: Ashgate, 2003.

Lynn II, John A. *Women, Armies, and Warfare in Early Modern Europe*. Cambridge: Cambridge University Press, 2008.

Montrose, Louis. "The Work of Gender in the Discourse of Discovery." In *Representations* 33 (1991): 1–33.

Pagden, Anthony. *Lords of all the World: Ideologies of Empire in Spain, Britain and France c. 1500 – c. 1800*. New Haven: Yale University Press, 1995.

Platt, Colin. *King Death: The Black Death and its Aftermath in Late Medieval England*. London: University College London Press, 1996.

Poska, Allyson M., Couchman, Jane, and McIver, Katherine A., eds. *The Ashgate Research Companion to Women and Gender in Early Modern Europe*. Abingdon: Routledge, 2016.

Probert, Rebecca, ed. *Catherine Exley's Diary: The Life and Times of an Army Wife in the Peninsular War*. Kenliworth: Brandram, 2014.

Ronald, Susan. *The Pirate Queen: Queen Elizabeth I, Her Pirate Adventurers, and the Dawn of Empire*. New York: HarperCollins, 2007.

Shepard, Alexandra. *Meanings of Manhood in Early Modern England*. Oxford: Oxford University Press, 2006.

Weisser, Olivia. *Ill Composed: Sickness, Gender, and Belief in Early Modern England*. New Haven: Yale University Press, 2015.

Wiesner-Hanks, Merry E. *Women and Gender in Early Modern Europe*, 3rd ed. Cambridge: Cambridge University Press, 2008.

Wiesner-Hanks, Merry E. *Gender in History: Global Perspectives*, 2nd ed. Chichester: Wiley-Blackwell, 2011.

Woodacre, Elena, ed. *Queenship in the Mediterranean: Negotiating the Role of the Queen in Medieval and Early Modern Eras*. New York: Palgrave Macmillan, 2013.

Woodacre, Elena and Fleiner, Carey, eds. *Royal Mothers and their Ruling Children: Wielding Political Authority from Antiquity to the Early Modern Era*. Houndmills: Palgrave Macmillan, 2015.

PART I

Demonstration of Power

CHAPTER 2

Mary I, Mary of Guise and the Strong Hand of the Scots: Marian Policy in Ulster and Anglo-Scottish Diplomacy, 1553–1558

Jonathan Woods

After her triumphal entry into London as queen regnant in July 1553, Mary I received a letter from her cousin, the Queen of Scots, then residing in France. The Scottish sovereign expressed her desire: "qu'il sera si dieu plaist perpetuelle memoire de deux Roynes auoir esté…en ceste Isle la'ioinctes d'inuiolée amitie (that, if God pleases, there will be a perpetual memory of two Queens in this Isle…having been joined in everlasting friendship)."[1] Despite these sentiments, Anglo-Scottish amity in the 1550s was precarious. In 1555, the north of Ireland was the epicenter of conflict. Increasing migration of Scots from the Western Isles and the expansion of military networks from Scotland into Ireland pitted personal allegiances against political identity, threatening the supremacy claimed by Mary I in Ulster. In February of 1555/6, the Tudor administration complained that Scots "with force and strong hand" were murdering and pillaging to the ruin of the queen's "loving subiects."[2] This chapter explores the development of and context surrounding anti-Scottish language in the letters of Mary I and her Irish governors.

J. Woods (✉)
Fordham University, New York, USA

© The Author(s) 2017
E. Paranque et al. (eds.), *Colonization, Piracy, and Trade in Early Modern Europe*, Queenship and Power, DOI 10.1007/978-3-319-57159-1_2

Scholarly interpretations of Mary I as a strong and effective monarch have grown more common since the 1980s. David Loades, Anna Whitelock, and others have devoted much work to contesting the perception that the mid-Tudor period in general, and Mary I's reign in particular, was a time of crisis and instability.[3] More recently, Jennifer Loach, Judith Richards, and Eamon Duffy have argued that the Marian regime, including its religious policy, was founded on widespread consensus.[4] Much interest in Mary I, England's first sovereign queen, centers on the extent to which she exercised real power. The particular challenge Mary faced was justifying her rule in a society that took for granted that a woman, while the spiritual equal of any man, had a duty to submit to her husband.[5] Mary's marriage to Philip Hapsburg, future king of Spain and son of the Holy Roman Emperor, further occasioned fears that England was to become constitutionally subordinate to Spain through the conjugal relationship. Thus, the question of Mary's authority is closely related to that of the emergence of ethnocentric national identity in England. Recent scholars have argued that, contrary to the crown's push to create a monolithic polity, early modern Britain was a multicultural society.[6] In Ireland, particularly in Ulster, there is little doubt that diversity was a fact of life. The kingdom was shared by Old English, Gaelic Irish, and Scottish populations, well before the New English began to settle in large numbers. Revisions of the mid-Tudor period in Ireland have focused on the debate over the origins of Elizabeth's Irish policy, which sought pacification through military force. Steven Ellis and Ciaran Brady characterized it as the natural consequence of Ireland's status as a kingdom, which necessitated that the Tudors create a monopoly over secular power, while Brendan Bradshaw argued that increased violence stemmed from a deliberate rejection of Mary's liberal reform by the administration of Thomas Radcliffe, baron Fitzwalter and earl of Sussex (from February 1596/7), and lord deputy from 1556 (for ease, called Sussex in this chapter).[7] More recently, attention has centered on the perspective of the Gaelic world, with a number of scholars adopting a Borderlands paradigm to understand why Irish lords vacillated between support for and resistance to the Tudor regime in the sixteenth century.[8] In what follows, this essay considers three phases of Marian policy toward the Scots in Ulster, integration, diplomacy, and expulsion. It argues that though her methodology changed, Mary I's goals in Ireland remained consistent throughout her reign. Politically, she meant to establish a monopoly on secular power and Mary's toleration of the Scots had always been conditional to their obedience. Thus, Sussex's campaign to expel the Ulster Scots did not represent a watershed change in Tudor policy in Ireland, but was the consequence of Mary's claim of full sovereignty.

The Families of Ulster and Early Marian Policy Toward the Scots in Ulster

Mary's goals for Ireland were similar to those for England. Most important was the restoration of the Mass and other sacraments. Secondly, she looked to employ uniform justice and thus "reduce the people to obedience and civile ordre" and bring them to "good civilitie."[9] Mary's sovereignty over Ireland was articulated in terms similar to the kingship established by her father, albeit she did not claim supremacy over the Church, and restored the pope's authority. Nonetheless, all inhabitants were to be incorporated into the Tudor polity by their loyalty to the queen. Civility was defined by obedience to Mary's rule of law. Though she claimed sovereignty, the queen did not yet wield effective power throughout Ireland. In 1553, there was a garrison of three hundred horsemen and two hundred footmen in Ireland, which was hardly enough to establish obedience through force. Furthermore, Mary's reappointment of the moderate Anthony St Leger as lord deputy that year indicated that she meant to continue the process of incorporation through conciliation and consent begun by the practice of surrender and re-grant.[10] The implementation of this policy required the cooperation of the Gaelic nobility.

The entangled fortunes of four families: the O'Donnells of Tyrconnel, the O'Neills of Tyrone, the MacDonalds of Dunyvaig and the Glens, and the Campbells of Argyll dominated the history of Ulster in the mid-sixteenth century. These families occupied lands that straddled the constitutional divide between Scotland and Ireland but which shared a common language, customs, and sense of identity.[11] The O'Donnells and O'Neills were native Irish, but the presence of the Scottish clan Donald in the north of Ireland had its roots in the exchange of military personnel among the Scots and Irish. Scottish migration to Ulster began in earnest in the late fourteenth century when Eoin Mór MacDonald, brother of the lord of the Isles, wed Margaret Brisset of Antrim.[12] The dissolution of the lordship of the Isles in 1493 and the rise of the Campbells of Argyll as the dominant family in the west of Scotland drastically altered the fortunes of the MacDonalds, allowing for the rise of a subordinate branch of the family and shifting their center of gravity toward Ireland.[13] In 1532, Alexander MacDonald of Dunyvaig and the Glens, in the service of the Scottish crown, invaded Ulster with seven thousand men. MacDonald joined his cousins in Antrim, absorbed the rest of the Brisset's land, and began to advance on the O'Neills of Clandeboye and the MacQuillans of the Route. Both families were septs, or dependent kindreds, of the O'Neills of Tyrone, and MacDonald expansion was a threat to O'Neill power in Ulster. By the mid-Tudor period, the O'Donnells, benefiting from three generations of strong lords, had also wrested supremacy in Ulster away from the O'Neills in northern Connacht.

The intricacy of "clan" politics was only exacerbated in the sixteenth century by the recurrence of civil war within the O'Donnell and O'Neill lordships.[14] Manus O'Donnell, for instance, challenged the authority of his father after successfully defending the family's territory against the O'Neills in 1510–1511. In 1547, Manus' son, Calvagh, first defied him, seeking to become lord of Tyrconnell. The rebellion went on intermittently until 1555, when it succeeded thanks to the assistance of the fourth earl of Argyll, Archibald Campbell.[15] Internecine conflict broke out among the O'Neills when the lord of the kindred and first earl of Tyrone, Conn O'Neill, was imprisoned by James Croft, lord deputy, in 1552. Though Croft sought to supplant Conn with his eldest son, Matthew, Baron of Dungannon, Shane O'Neill was able to exploit the chaos and establish military dominance over his brother. While Tudor intervention certainly played a role in internal clan wars, some have argued that the transition from a conciliar lordship, based on legal legitimacy, to coercive lordship, based on the right of conquest, was, in part, begun by the MacDonalds. Gallowglass, men of war often descended of Scottish settlers in Ireland, and seasonal kern, Scottish mercenaries from the Isles, at least increased the presence of military men in Ulster.[16] The MacDonald use of stone keeps to protect land acquisitions changed the landscape of Ireland, though there is disagreement over whether these fortresses were a signal of increasing violence or an indication of stability.[17] In any case, by the mid-sixteenth century, Irish lordship had become more militarized and perhaps more effective at controlling local populations, making it difficult for the English governors to establish Tudor sovereignty.

Recognizing the long history of the MacDonald presence in Ulster, Mary I's administration initially adopted a policy of toleration for the Scots living in Ireland, conditional to the population's submission of Tudor authority: "we will that all scottyshe men, dwelling in the North p*artes* of Irland that haue long contynued & will acknowlege their duties & due obedience vnto vs & o*ur* successors and be sworne to contynue the same & gou*er*ne them self*es* therafter, shalbe suffred to remayne."[18] Thus, the queen recognized that there were entrenched, long-established

Scottish communities in Ulster whose methods of self-governance could provide stability to the territory. The English government expected the Scots in Ireland to become good subjects, defined by their professed and practiced allegiance to the Tudor monarch. They were also expected to facilitate a policy of gradual Anglicization of Gaelic law and land use by contributing to the pacification of internecine clan conflict. However, it is crucial to note that toleration was contingent on obedience to the queen. In light of the potential utility of the Scottish population, Mary also authorized the use of gallowglass, many of whom were of Scottish descent, in the Tudor army in Ireland. Such men were to serve alongside English and Irish soldiers, appointed "amonges the rest continually in our service...for increase of our strength."[19] Private armies would be tolerated so long as they abandoned the practices of Irish lordship: "others that be of the Cuntrey may remayne strong of them selfes, eschuying blak rentes and Coyne and lyveries asmoche as maye be, charging vs with no more then shalbe necessary."[20] Black rent and coign and livery, according to Tudor knowledge of Irish custom, were the means by which Gaelic lords extracted economic and military tribute from the family groups they governed. The abandonment of these practices would lead, presumably, to the disintegration of Gaelic lordship, which was to be replaced with Tudor vassalage and county government. Thus, Mary initially sought to use both the Scottish population and private armies to reinforce her authority.

Within 2 years, the Tudor queen's attitude toward the Scots in Ulster had shifted. Policy in 1555 aimed at gradually eliminating the Scottish population from Ireland: "Touching the north of the Realme, The Scott*es* to be banished thense as the tyme and oportunytie may thereunto best sh*e*ruice and in the meane to be vsed w*ith* discrec*i*on."[21] The policy seemed to have taken the Dublin administration by surprise. St Leger looked to delay the expulsion of Scots by saying they could still be used to the regime's advantage. He also had to defend his appointment of a Scottish man, Coll McOneboye, as the captain of a band of horsemen in December 1555.[22] Considering the deputy was authorized to utilize Scots to the advantage of Tudor aims when possible, it is likely that the objection to McOneboye arose out of his appointment as an officer. It is the first indication that Ulster Scots were deemed to be intrinsically unfit for office in the Tudor state by the Marian regime on the basis of their ethnic origin. St Leger defended his decision by downplaying the extent to which McOneboye ought to be considered Scottish: "tho he be named a Scot, yeat speketh he good englishe and was borne in Irland

and his aunccestors many yeres."²³ He was defined as Scottish, but this was misleading, St Leger argued, and did not adequately represent his English and Irish credentials. St Leger suggested that use of the English language and habitation in Ireland made the man fit for office; thus, he implied that a degree of assimilation to Irish society under Tudor rule was required before men of Gaelic Scottish origin should have been given positions in the government.

In spite of St Leger's defense of McOneboye, perceptions of Scots grew more negative and more categorical in the ensuing months. In February 1555/6, Mary I cited a long list of Scottish crimes in Ulster and ordered her Ambassador in Scotland, Thomas Challoner, to demand the intervention of Mary of Guise, mother of Mary, Queen of Scots and regent of Scotland. Scots in Ulster had burned over sixty square miles of land, kidnapped Manus O'Donnell, the lord of Tyrconnell, and continued to "slaye a great nombre of…loving subiects" and commit various "spoyles, robberies and myrders…within o*ur* realm of Ireland."²⁴ Mary's frustration with the situation in Ulster occasioned a transition in policy and tone to the Scots. Initially, she was open to including them as subjects, so long as they accepted her rule obediently; however, Scottish intervention in Gaelic civil wars necessitated that the queen adopt a policy aimed at their eventual exclusion. It was a tone and attitude that would harden under Sussex, Mary's next lord deputy. However, before embracing Sussex's scheme for the immediate expulsion of the Scots, Mary I attempted to resolve the situation through diplomacy.

Mary of Guise, the Earl of Argyll and Anglo-Scottish Diplomacy

The source of Mary's frustration was the fourth earl of Argyll's intervention in the O'Donnell rebellion on behalf of Calvagh O'Donnell. Argyll accepted Calvagh into his protection via a bond of manrent, or oath of service, on July 13, 1555. Whereas Scottish bonds of manrent, with few exceptions, state explicitly that the Scottish crown superseded the powers of any lord, Calvagh's oath did not recognize either Stuart or Tudor royal authority.²⁵ The bond was silent as to either Argyll's or Calvagh's relationships to monarchy, though it did acknowledge Calvagh as "native l[ord]" of Tyrconnel.²⁶ Argyll, as a maintainer of Calvagh, sought to assume lordship over the O'Donnells. Rather than a recognition of the constitutional distinction between Scotland and Ireland, there was an acknowledgment of Calvagh's native lordship and Argyll's overlordship. The alliance was not only a threat to the peace of Ulster but also challenged Mary's sovereignty. Argyll's continued support was contingent on the successful suppression of Manus O'Donnell, a task for which Argyll furnished Calvagh with men and artillery.[27] The Tudor rebel returned to Ireland with a canon named Gunna-Cam, the crooked gun.[28] Argyll had also lent Highland fighters from the MacCalin kindred to Calvagh, who led them in his personal retinue.[29] The earl sent two more companies to assist Calvagh. One was captained by his heir, Archibald Campbell, the lord of Lorne, and the other by James McDonald of Dunyvaig and the Glens.[30] A letter to Calvagh O'Donnell confirmed James MacDonald's interest in the rebellion in Ulster as early as April 1555.[31]

Mary I instructed Thomas Challoner to remind Mary of Guise that the Stuart government was bound by the treaty of Norham to punish any of its subjects who aided rebels against Tudor authority.[32] Mary I said: "the rebell of the one prince should nether be receaved not any wayes ayded by the Prince or any of their subiects."[33] For Argyll to aid Calvagh was for the Scottish noble to ally himself not only with an enemy of the Tudor state, but also with a traitor, a circumstance that Guise, Mary I argued, was bound to rectify. To preserve amity, Mary I presumed Guise's ignorance of Argyll's intervention in the rebellion, though she demanded that Guise act quickly to reprimand Argyll: "wee have thought meete to gyve o*ur* sayd good sister knowledge of [Argyll and Calvagh's bond], hopynge shee will gyve order for the speedie remeadie of the matter/accordyne to o*ur* expectation."[34] The English and Irish queen made it clear that she desired peace but could not tolerate Argyll's actions. While there is no evidence that Mary of Guise encouraged Argyll to continue his activity in Ulster, neither is there any indication that she ordered him to stop. The earl's letters to Guise from the period did, on the contrary, reveal collaboration between the regent and Argyll. In August 1554, the earl was engaged in a campaign to suppress gangs of bandits in the isles of the Western Highlands.[35] Furthermore, despite the fact that Guise's administration said that the "nator of the pepell" and their "effectione" (kinship ties) caused the "cowmon weill" to "perreche" through vendetta, and a parliamentary act outlawed the practice of swearing manrent in 1554, the regent made no attempts to limit or reform the practice of forming private armies.[36] Rather, she used personal military structures to her political advantage.

Guise exercised regal authority from 1554 onward.[37] As regent for an absentee monarch, she had some notable successes, particularly her negotiation of the crown matrimonial for her son-in-law, Francis Valois, who became king of Scotland with Mary Stuart after their marriage. However, she was met with opposition on more occasions than not. For instance, when she attempted to levy a "perpetuall Tax" in 1556, the nobility would not permit her to make an inventory of their property.[38] During the Anglo-French war of 1557–1558, Guise made every attempt to abide by the norms of Scottish constitutional procedure, summoning a convention of the estates in late February to authorize national mobilization. The parliament agreed to muster for defensive purposes, but refused to attack the English border.[39] She did command a garrison of Valois professional troops in Scotland, which numbered as high as twelve hundred between 1557 and 1559.[40] This force, however, was not strong enough to crush the rebellion against Guise's authority that broke out among Protestants in the summer of 1559. In October of that year, she was deposed as regent. In the decentralized system of Scottish monarchy, Guise had to rely on the participation of her great nobles, among whom was the earl of Argyll, lieutenant of the Isles, to enforce royal authority.[41] Argyll, who could raise an army of five thousand men within a matter of weeks, was the most powerful of her deputies.[42] Furthermore, Guise had alienated the only other man in the kingdom who could challenge Argyll by sheer manpower. This was the earl of Huntly, who retained the title of chancellor, even though Guise had removed the Great Seal from his possession.

Despite not having a substantial standing garrison, Guise did theoretically have her own private army. Between 1540 and 1560, Guise entered into seventeen contracts of manrent or maintenance with eighteen men.[43] This is a remarkably high survival rate for such bonds, suggesting that the dowager formed many more such agreements. Indeed, considering the eventual repudiation of Guise's authority in 1559 by the lords of the congregation, it is surprising that any of her bonds survive. The men bound to Guise were all of high status and included eight nobles, nine members of the gentry, and one burgess. Eight of the bonds were made in 1548–1549, at the height of the Somerset invasions, when Guise championed and helped organize French intervention in Scotland. The dowager continued to use manrent as a means of validating her power after the Rough Wooing, the Anglo-Scottish wars of 1544–1551, ended and even once she became regent.

Guise's status as mother of the sovereign and queen dowager undoubtedly accounts for the abnormality of a woman accepting a large number of men into her military service. Very few women took or accepted oaths of service in the period, and those that did were accompanied by their husbands. In total, nine women besides Guise or Mary, Queen of Scots, appear in bonds of manrent sworn between 1512 and 1568.[44] In most respects, Guise's oaths were typical of other Scottish bonds of manrent and maintenance. For instance, William Sinclare of Roslin promised "all the days of his life to gang and ryde" in the dowager's service in 1546.[45] Bonds of manrent theoretically placed entire private armies at the disposal of a lord. Thus, when Robert, the lord Boyd, and his heir swore their "gude trew and thankfull *ser*vice," they did so for themselves and for "thair kyn freinds assisteris pairttakaris and *ser*vand*is*."[46] Personal obligation to Guise was passed through the proxy of men like Boyd to his social dependents. In theory, the enlargement of Boyd's network of manrent was also a benefit to Guise as an overlord. Several of Guise's bondsmen swore fealty in exchange for pensions and for land. This was an abnormality as most bonds of manrent from the sixteenth century did not involve land exchange or tenure. Guise, however, seems to have used economic incentives as a way of recruiting adherents. For instance, William Sinclare of Roslin was to receive an annual pension of 300 Scottish marks by means of certain rents assigned to him.[47] The earl of Bothwell's pledge was also precipitated by the distribution of a pension of £1000 annually for as long as Guise or Bothwell lived. Likewise, Hector McClane of Duart bound himself with his "air*is* and assignais In manrent and sheruice" to Guise because she had ceded him "hir land*is*…occupiit be me & myne in the Iles."[48] The creation of a network of personal supporters was a testament to Guise's charisma but it did not necessarily translate into political power. Though men promised their allegiance, Guise had no means to enforce such oaths. Around half of those bound to her, or their heirs, forfeited their loyalty during the reformation rebellion of 1559–1560. Only one bondsman, Bothwell, actually fought for her. The dowager's authority was based on the voluntary support of elite landowners, and her regime fell once they withdrew it. It was for this reason that Mary I's demands in 1555 were necessarily ignored.

Anti-Scottish Policy Under Sussex

Sussex became lord deputy in 1556 and with him came a new, more aggressive Tudor policy for the pacification of Ireland. Almost immediately after coming to Dublin, he invaded Ulster and attacked the MacDonalds, spending a month and a half slaughtering Scottish gallowglass in minor skirmishes. By the winter of 1556/7, his efforts at stabilizing Ulster were being frustrated by the MacDonalds. Con Oge O'Neill had broken free from Knockfergus Castle with the aid of James MacDonald of Dunyvaig and the Glens, and the Scots of Antrim. They were able to capture a castle and establish a foothold in Antrim.[49] Furthermore, the development of an alliance between the MacDonalds and Shane O'Neill greatly bolstered opposition to Sussex. The lord deputy simultaneously adopted a harsher policy against the Gaelic lords in western Leinster, where he hoped to begin implementing a plantation strategy in Offaly and Laois. While the MacDonalds were not a direct threat to settlement in the king's and the queen's counties, Sussex argued that they were the main obstacle to a successful implementation of the policy. He claimed that the instability of Ulster was a financial and military burden, which prevented him from suppressing the Leinster clans and focusing on the settlement of Englishmen in Offaly and Laois. If Ulster was lost, Sussex warned, all of Ireland would rebel, and Ulster could not be pacified unless the MacDonalds were expelled. In order to accomplish this goal, he proposed a unification of the Gaelic Irish, Old English, and New English on the basis of anti-Scottish rhetoric.

His priority immediately shifted to preventing any further migration from Scotland to Ulster since: "yt wolbe more hard to expell them… then to keape them owte before they enter."[50] To keep the Scots out, Sussex needed to take English troops from the Pale, Offaly, and Laois and use them to mount a full-scale invasion of Ulster. He noted that he would need £1000 to pay the soldiers, as those stationed in garrisons in Leinster would require a wage increase before they could be sent into danger. Sussex planned "with all the force of the Countrey" to march north and force the Gaelic Irish lords there to "Ioyne toguither against the Scottes."[51] The expulsion of the Scots and the unification of the Irish kindreds were part of the same policy for Sussex, who saw war upon the MacDonalds as an effective tool for unifying the Gaelic Irish under Tudor authority. He argued that a unification of kinship networks would contribute to the stability of Ulster and a monopoly of Tudor justice. He stated that control of Belfast and other strongholds on the border of Antrim and Down, including Knockfergus, would allow the pursuit of a defensive strategy, which forced the MacDonalds to attack his castles. In occupying the fortresses surrounding the Belfast Lough, the lord deputy also hoped to encourage anti-Scottish sentiment among the Gaelic Irish residents of the lands surrounding the Lough. They were to use their own weapons in what Sussex envisioned as a defense of their land from Scottish invaders.

Sussex warned that the crown's policy in Ireland had been unclear, and he called for a more decisive military action to subdue Ulster. He contended that "withowte ordering of that parte of the realme (the north) the rest wyll alwayes be waveryng."[52] He said that in order to subdue the north, all of the English queen's garrisons in Ireland would have to be brought to Ulster, which would leave the rest of the English settlements in Ireland vulnerable to attack from recalcitrant Gaelic lords. To ensure pacification, three hundred soldiers would have to be introduced for the space of a year. Sensitive to the crown's frustration with the cost of pacifying Ireland, Sussex emphasized that this number of soldiers would be temporary and aimed narrowly at the expelling of the Scots, which he believed would allow the English soldiers to fully pacify the north. Sussex guaranteed Mary I that within 2 years, after the Scots were defeated, the same garrisons could be maintained throughout Ireland at a reduced wage. After the expulsion of the Scots was complete, Sussex said that only six hundred men would have to be paid a soldier's wage, while there would be an additional twelve hundred troops, who could man garrisons at a lower wage. Sussex assured the queen that they would have help from mercenary Gaelic soldiers, the gallowglass, who, he argued, had been supplanted by the Scottish redshanks. Apparently, he failed to recognize that many were themselves descended of Scottish origins.

Sussex sought to cultivate hostility for a foreign element in Ulster, while planting new settlers in Offaly and Laois. He argued that northern men and Welsh men were accustomed to farming in harsh climes and to defending their property in areas where royal government was weak. The frontier men of the northern borders of England and Wales would, Sussex argued, be suited to life in Leinster. The pacification of these lands by the English and Welsh frontier men would facilitate trade routes between inland villages and port towns, where the Tudor government could charge tariffs on the exports of Irish hide and tallow. Sussex was concerned primarily with utilizing Ireland's resources for the benefit of the Tudor state, describing eagerly Ireland's deposits of iron ore, timber, peat, gypsum, marble, jasper, and coal. This was a plan for settlement aimed at transforming the land for the best use of the Tudor state and the commonwealth. It was to be accomplished by Tudor frontier men, who were English. He posited this as the most important quality of the future settlers, noting that as long as "they be Inglyshe" it did not matter "of what *con*trey they be."[53] While Sussex recognized the distinctions and advantages of men from the borders and from Wales, he affirmed their status as true Englishmen, who would come to Ireland and establish a civilization built on the Tudor state's supremacy. These men were not invaders, he argued, for they were loyal subjects, albeit from another nation under Mary's authority. This contrasts with Sussex's description of the Scottish MacDonalds, whom he condemns as an "enemy" and a foreign invasion force, though they had deep roots in Ulster.[54]

Sussex also advised Mary I to write to her most powerful nobles in Ireland to rally them to her cause of expelling the Scots. The earls of Kildare, Ormond, and Desmond were descendants of the Norman invaders of the twelfth century, and were members of Ireland's Old English landed elite. The earls of Clanrickard and Tyrone were, by contrast, Gaelic lords incorporated under the Tudor system through surrender and re-grant. Their political distinctions as vassals of the English queen were to trump their ethnic distinctions. Sussex envisioned a multiethnic Irish nobility united by loyalty to the Tudor queen, arguing that Mary ought to command "all…the nobelles of the realme" and the "hole parliament" to band together for the expelling of the Scots; this unity he said will "gyve grete terror to the Scottes."[55] Immediately after informing Mary I about the benefits of uniting the Irish lords against the MacDonalds, Sussex proceeded to explain that the Gaelic Irish lords could not be trusted without "grete force of mere Inglyshe soldyars."[56] The lord deputy said that if her majesty thought she could trust her Gaelic Irish nobles then she had been deceived, and he now increased his financial request to £5000. He again reiterated that if his military requests were executed, the crown could begin its policy of plantation on its own timeline, and that the subsequent facilitation of trade between ports and inland towns would raise tariff revenues for the crown. In other words, a major military investment in Ireland would yield great economic benefit to the Tudor crown in the long run. He also emphasized that beyond the economic benefits, the queen "shalbe knowen and fered as a soverayne" by all her subjects in Ireland and the people "that be savage shall with tyme be browght to more cyvylyte."[57] The lord deputy promised that his goal was only the "advauncement of her [the queen's] honer and royall power the good gouerment of the realme the reducyng of the pepell to obedeyence" and went on to say that "The grete...shall no more be as prynces but shall gladly obbey as subyectes."[58] In other words, the expulsion of the Scots was the first step in the full pacification of Ireland and the final incorporation of the Irish lords into the Tudor state.

Mary I replied to Sussex's advice by penning a letter to the Irish nobility, asking them to cooperate with him and to follow royal policy. She emphasized the need for the nobility to assist "in the maintenance of iustice peax and tranquilite...repressing of suche as shall by any meane attempte to let or breake the same whether by...private misdemeanor and disordre or otherwyse by common assemblie tumulte, or invasion."[59] She also asked for a full participation within the justice system of the Tudor monarchy, from the keeping of her laws to the execution of punishment for those who broke them. Mary I asked her Irish nobles to envision themselves as part of the Tudor polity. She did not mention the Scots by name, nor did she define any specific military policy. Rather, she left this up to Sussex. The English queen told Sussex that she willed him to continue his policies as he saw fit, and to notify the Irish Parliament of her more specific directives at his "discretions."[60] She told Sussex that she trusted his plan better than any she could devise from London. In 1557, the queen sent Sussex the requested £5000. The goal, however, was very clear: The expelling of "the Scottes and other rebelles, who nowe are the troblers of peace and hynderers of good government and pollicie."[61]

Conclusion

Ultimately, Sussex's assaults on the MacDonalds were inconclusive. James MacDonald, and his successor, Sorely Boy MacDonald, continued to interfere in Ulster politics until the 1570s, seeking marriage alliances with the O'Neills of Tyrone, harrying English troops in Ulster, and looking always to establish control over Antrim. While Argyll's men had left Ireland in 1556, the connections between the Campbells and the O'Donnells only grew stronger. The fourth earl of Argyll died in 1558 and his widow, Katherine MacLean, wed Calvagh O'Donnell shortly before both were kidnapped by Shane O'Neill. Through two critical marriages, the MacDonalds regained lost territory in both Kintyre and Antrim and ultimately created the basis for sustained cooperative opposition to Tudor government in Ireland.[62] In 1569, the fifth earl of Argyll arranged a double marriage uniting Agnes Campbell, widow of James MacDonald of Dunyvaig and the Glens and Argyll's aunt, with Turloch O'Neill, heir of Shane O'Neill, and Fionla MacDonald, daughter of Agnes, with Hugh Manus O'Donnell. The cooperation of the MacDonalds, O'Neills, and O'Donnells ensured that resistance to Tudor control of Ulster would be a major problem for Elizabeth I.[63] Ultimately, the permanent presence of the MacDonalds in Ireland was confirmed by the creation of the earldom of Antrim.

Mary I's policy thus failed to establish the sovereignty she claimed and to create a unified identity around her authority. Gaelic resistance continued and eventually led to the usurpation of Gaelic lands by New English settlers. While Mary's policy failed, it is not because of a sudden shift in strategy under Sussex. It is clear that her attitude toward the Scots hardened as a result of Campbell and MacDonald intervention in Ulster and that a strategy of strict expulsion proceeded under Sussex, but the queen implied this would be a consequence of Scottish disobedience as early as 1553. The queen was flexible and pragmatic enough to embrace first integration of the Scots, secondly diplomacy, and thirdly an anti-Scottish policy as the means to achieve her aim, the unification of the peoples of Ireland under her rule. Mary sought to wield full sovereignty, as any king would have, but failed to establish it in Ireland because a monopoly of political power was inconsistent with the decentralized structures of the Gaelic world.

Notes

1. The National Archives (TNA) SP 51/1, f. 14r, Mary, Queen of Scots to Mary I, 1553.
2. TNA SP 51/1, f. 27r, Instructions to Thomas Challoner, February, 1555/6.
3. David Loades, *The Reign of Mary Tudor: Politics Government and Religion, 1553–1558* (New York: St Martin's Press, 1979); Loades, *The Mid-Tudor Crisis, 1545–1565* (New York: St Martin's Press, 1992). Robert Tittler and Jennifer Loach, eds., *The Mid-Tudor Polity c. 1540–1560* (Totowa, NJ: Rowman and Littlefield, 1980). Biographical treatments have also become increasingly sensitive: David Loades, *Mary Tudor: A Life* (New York: Basil Blackwell, 1989); Eric Ives, *Lady Jane Grey: A Tudor Mystery* (Chichester: Blackwell, 2009); Anna Whitelock, *Mary Tudor: England's First Queen* (London: Bloomsbury, 2009), Whitelock, *Mary Tudor: Princess, Bastard, Queen* (London: Bloomsbury, 2009).
4. Jennifer Loach, *Parliament and the Crown in the Reign of Mary Tudor* (New York: Clarendon Press, 1986); Judith Richards, *Mary Tudor* (New

York: Routledge, 2008); Eamon Duffy, *Fires of Faith* (New Haven: Yale University Press, 2009). The revision of the English reformation impacted views on Mary's reign. See Rex Pogson, "Reginald Pole and the Priorities of Government in Mary Tudor's Church," *Historical Journal*, vol. 18, no. 1 (Mar., 1975): 3–20; Susan Brigdan, *London and the Reformation* (Oxford: Oxford University Press, 1989); Eamon Duffy, *Stripping the Altars: Traditional Religion in England, 1400–1580* (New Haven: Yale University Press, 1992); Christopher Haigh, *English Reformations: Religion, Politics and Society Under the Tudors* (Oxford: Oxford University Press, 1993); Thomas Mayer *Reginald Pole: Prince and Prophet* (Cambridge: Cambridge University Press, 2000). For an alternative view of religion in Mary's reign, see Anna Whitelock and Diarmaid MacCulloch, "Princess Mary's Household and the Succession Crisis, July 1553," *Historical Journal*, vol. 50, no. 2, (2007): 265–287.
5. Constance Jordan, "Women's Rule in Sixteenth-Century British Political Thought," *Renaissance Quarterly*, vol. 40, no. 3 (Autumn 1987): 421–451, esp. 427–428; David Loades, "Phillip II and the government of England," *Law and Government Under the Tudors. Essays Presented to Sir Geoffrey Elton*, eds. Claire Cross, David Loades and John J. Scarisbrick (Cambridge: Cambridge University Press, 1988), 177–194; Amanda Shephard, *Gender and Authority in Sixteenth Century England* (Keele: Keele University Press, 1994); Judith Richards, "'To Promote a Woman to Beare Rule': Talking of Queens in Mid-Tudor England," *The Sixteenth Century Journal*, vol. 28, no. 1 (Spring 1997): 101–121; Judith Richards, "Mary Tudor as 'Sole Quene'?: Gendering Tudor Monarchy," *The Historical Journal*, vol. 40, no. 4 (Dec., 1997): 895–924. Alexander Samson, "Changing Places: The Marriage and Royal Entry of Philip, Prince of Austria, and Mary Tudor, July–August 1554," *Sixteenth-Century Journal*, vol. 36, no. 3 (Fall 2005): 61–84.
6. Joseph P. Ward, *Metropolitan Communities: Trade Guilds, Identity and Change in Early Modern London* (Stamford: Stamford University Press, 1997); Scott Oldenburg, "Toward a Multi-Cultural Mid-Tudor England: The Queen's Royal Entry Circa 1553, 'The Interlude of Wealth and Health,' and the Question of Strangers in the Reign of Mary I," *ELH*, vol. 76, no. 1 (Spring 2009): 99–129.
7. See Nicholas Canny, *The Elizabethan Conquest of Ireland, a Pattern Established, 1565–76* (Hassocks: Harvest, 1976). Brendan Bradshaw, *The Irish Constitutional Revolution of the Sixteenth Century* (Cambridge: Cambridge University Press, 1979), esp. 267–275. Steven Ellis, *Tudor Ireland: Crown, Community and the Conflict of Cultures, 1470–1603* (London: Longman, 1985). Ciaran Brady, *The Chief Governors: The Rise and Fall of Reform Government in Tudor Ireland, 1536–1588* (Cambridge: Cambridge University Press, 1994).

8. Steven Ellis, *Tudor Frontiers and Noble Power: The Making of the British State* (Oxford: Oxford University Press, 1995); Jane Dawson, *The Politics of Religion in the Age of Mary, Queen of Scots: The Earl of Argyll and the Struggle for Britain and Ireland* (Cambridge: Cambridge University Press, 2002); Simon Kingston, *Ulster and the Isles in the Fifteenth Century* (Dublin: Four Courts Press, 2004); Christopher Maginn, "Gaelic Ireland's English Frontiers in the late Middle Ages," *Proceedings of the Royal Irish Academy. Section C: Archaeology, Celtic Studies, History, Linguistics, Literature*, vol. 110C (2010): 173–190; Martin MacGregor, "The Campbells: lordship, literature and liminality," *Textual Cultures: Texts, Contexts, Interpretation* 7(1), (2012): 121–157.
9. TNA SP 62/1, f. 5v. Instructions for Ireland, 1553.
10. Bradshaw, *Irish Constitutional Revolution*, 259–260.
11. Maginn, "Gaelic Ireland's English Frontiers," 173–190.
12. Kingston, *Ulster and the Isles*, 15–17. Gerard Hays-McCoy, *Scots Mercenary Forces in Ireland, 1565–1603* (Dublin: Burns Oates and Washbourne, 1937), 13.
13. The rise of the Campbells was achieved by a combination of royal favor and effective lordship. Alison Cathcart, "A Spent Force? The Clan Donald in the Aftermath of 1493," in *The Lordship of the Isles*, ed. Richard D. Oram (Leiden: Brill, 2004), 254–70, at 255–258. See also Alexander Grant, "Scotland's Celtic Fringe in the Late Middle Ages: the MacDonalds Lords of the Isles and the Kingdom of Scotland," in *The British Isles, 1100–1500: Comparisons, Contrasts and Connections*, ed. Robert Rees Davies (Edinburgh: John Donald, 1988), 118–141, esp. 133–134.
14. For a discussion of Irish clans, see Kenneth Nicholls, *Gaelic and Gaelicised Ireland in the Middle Ages* (Dublin: Gill and MacMillan, LTD, 1972), 8.
15. Brendan Bradshaw, "'Manus the Magnificient': O'Donnell as a Renaissance Prince," in *Studies in Irish History Presented to R. Dudley Edwards*, ed. Art Cosgrove and Donald McCartney (Dublin: University College Dublin Press, 1979), 15–37, at 29–36.
16. Kenneth Nicholls, "Scottish Mercenary Kindreds in Ireland 1250–1600," in *The World of the Gallowglass: Kings, Warlords, and Warriors in Ireland and Scotland, 1200–1600*, ed. Sean Duffy (Dublin: Four Courts Press, 2007), 86–105, esp. 86–88.
17. Kingston, *Ulster and the Isles*, 200. T.E. MacNeil, "Organizing a Lordship: the Castle of the MacDonalds of Dunivaig and the Glens," in *The Lordship of the Isles*, ed. R.D. Oram (Leiden: Brill, 2004), 211–226, at 225.
18. TNA SP 62/1, 6v-7r, Instructions for Ireland, October, 1553.
19. TNA SP 62/1, 4v, Instructions for Ireland, October, 1553.

20. TNA SP 62/1, 4v, Instructions for Ireland, October, 1553.
21. TNA SP 62/1, f. 28r, Answers of Sir Anthony St Leger to Objections Surmised against him, December 18, 1555.
22. Accusations of bribery and mismanagement of the Irish treasury had haunted St Leger throughout his long career in Ireland. See Alan Bryson, "St Leger, Sir Anthony (1496–1559)," *Oxford Dictionary of National Biography*, ed. H. C. G. Matthew and Brian Harrison (Oxford: Oxford University Press, 2004); online ed., ed. David Cannadine, January 2008, http://www.oxforddnb.com/view/article/24512 (accessed June 23, 2017).
23. TNA SP 62/1, f. 23v, Answers of Sir Anthony St Leger to Objections Surmised against him, December 18, 1555.
24. TNA SP 51/1, f. 27r, Instructions to Thomas Challoner, February, 1555/6.
25. The only other example can be found among Argyll's bonds and occurred in the summer of 1560, just after the royal administration of Guise had been defeated by the Duke of Norfolk's English army, acting on behalf of the lords of the congregation. See Inveraray Castle (INV) 1083, Bond of Adam Boyd of Pinkill, July 29, 1560.
26. INV 1073, Bond of Calvagh O'Donnell, July 13, 1555.
27. INV 1073, Bond of Calvagh O'Donnell, July 13, 1555; Jenny Wormald, *Lords and Men in Scotland: Bonds of Manrent, 1442–1603* (Edinburgh: John Donald, 1985), 402–412.
28. John O'Donovan, ed. and trans., *Annala rioghachta Eireann/Annals of the Kingdom of Ireland by the Four Masters (AFM)*, 7 vols. (1848–51); 2nd edn (1856), v. 5.1555.
29. The MacCalin family can be linked to Argyll through bonds of manrent. INV 1080, Bond of Alexander Cam McAllen VcRore, August 8, 1519. The individual in this bond is named as chief of Clan Ranald, not Clan MacCalin.
30. The MacDonalds controlled territory in Scotland and Ireland and were important, though not always reliable, deputies to the fourth and fifth earls of Argyll. For instance, INV 1074, Bond of Archibald McConaill of Dunnellaig and the Glens, May 27, 1566.
31. TNA SP 62/1, f. 19r, Agents of James MacDonald to Calvagh O'Donnell, April 24, 1555.
32. April 18, 1550, Acceptation by Mary Queen of Scots in *Calendar of State Paper Related to Mary, Queen of Scots*, ed. Joseph Bain, vol. 1 (Edinburgh: Register House, 1894), 182.
33. TNA SP 51/1, f. 27v, Instructions to Thomas Challoner, February, 1555/6.
34. TNA SP 51/1, f. 27v, Instructions to Thomas Challoner, February, 1555/6.

35. Argyll to the Regent, August 12, 1554, in *The Scottish Correspondence of Mary of Lorraine*, ed. Annie Cameron (Edinburgh: Scottish Historical Society, 1927), 388.
36. Notes of Advice for Punishment of Crime, in *Scott Corr of Mary of Lorraine*, 380. Concerning leagues and bonds, A1555/6/18, in *Records of the Parliament of Scotland to 1707*, ed. Keith M. Brown, Gillian H. MacIntosh, Alastair J. Mann, and Roland J. Tanner, (http://www.rps.ac.uk/) accessed October 28, 1016. Under the governorship of the Duke of Chatelherault, James Hamilton, the Stuart government also sought to incorporate private Scottish armies into the royal state. The primary families of the Borders took an oath at Jedburgh Abbey to forsake any in their service who were condemned by the monarchy. TNA SP 50/5, f. 69r, Copy of Jedburgh Oath, March 24, 1551/2.
37. Mary of Guise has been assessed by Pamela Ritchie, who argued that she was driven not by religion but by dynastic ambition and proved a strong and adept politician. Pamela Ritchie, *Mary of Guise in Scotland, 1548–1560* (East Linton: Tuckwell, 2002). Amy Blakeway's study of regency in Scotland concurs with Ritchie's main thesis regarding dynastic motivations, but is not necessarily willing to admit that Guise was superior to other regents. Blakeway contends there are "hints that Guise struggled financially" and says that her status as the regent for an absentee monarch, as opposed to a minor, likely inhibited her power as the Queen of Scots' consent could be acquired. Amy Blakeway, *Regency in Sixteenth-Century Scotland* (Woodbridge: Boydell, 2015), 45–46, 106.
38. TNA 51/1, f. 28r, Notes on Scottish Parliaments, 1558.
39. A1557/3/41/& 29/1, in *RPS*. TNA SP 51/1, f. 35r, Thomas Martin to the Queen, June 11, 1557.
40. Argyle to Guise, August 12, 1554, in *Scott Corr Mary of Lorraine*, 388–389; Thomas Dickson and James Balfour Paul, eds., *Accounts of the Treasurer of Scotland (TA)*, vol. 10 (Edinburgh: Morrison and Gibb, 1913), 232, 241, 287. For estimations of French company sizes for infantry, see James Wood, *The King's Army: Warfare, Soldiers, and Society During the Wars of Religion in France, 1562–1576* (Cambridge: Cambridge University Press, 1996), 48, 87–89, 92–93. TNA SP 51/1, f. 35r, Thomas Martin to the queen, June 11, 1557.
41. For reports of pensions and salaries for offices, such as wardens, see *TA*, vol. 10, 224, 236, 236, 239, 240, 244, 265, 284, 304, 312, 348; for the wages of gunners, smiths and wrights see 298, 314, 322.
42. Sadler and Croft to Cecil, October 24, 1559, in *Calendar of State Papers, Foreign, Elizabeth I (1559–60)*, ed. Joseph Stevenson (London: Longman, Green, Longman, Roberts and Green, 1865), 54. Armies from the western highlands may have been generally larger. Jacques de

la Brosse said that two unnamed lords of the western isles were able to raise 5000–6000 "hommes sauvaiges" in rebellion against Argyll in 1543. Jacques de la Brosse, "Discours des affaires du Royaume Descosse," in *Two Missions of Jacques de la Brosse*, ed. Galdys Dickinson (Edinburgh: Edinburgh University Press, 1949), 16.

43. National Archives of Scotland (NAS), GD8/159 Bond of Robert, Lord Boyd and his son, November 6, 1557; RH2/2/14 (15) Bond of William Sinclair of Roslin, June 3, 1546; SP13/41, Bond of William, Lord Ruthven, 154-; 42, Bond of Patrick, Lord Bothwell, 1543; 44, Bond of William Cunningham of Glengarnoch, September, 1543; 48, Bond of Hector MacClane of Duart, May 24, 1546; 55, Bond of Alexander Gordon, Postulant of Caithness, January 17, 1547/8; 58, Bond of George Gordon, Earl of Huntly, April 14, 1548; 59, Bond of Robert Ramsay of Kinnard, April 14, 1548; 61, Bond of Sir Walter Scott of Branxholme, August 13, 1548; 63, John, Earl of Sutherland, February 20, 1548/9; 65, Bond of George Meldrum of Fife, March 14, 1548/9; 66, Bond of Sir William Scott of Kirkhurd, June 24, 1549; 68, Bond of John Erskine of Dun, 1548; 74, Bond of James MacGill, February 11, 1551; 78, Bond of James, Earl of Morton, November 15, 1558.
44. NAS GD 112/24/2, ff. 8r, Bond of Marion Keller, October 1, 1550; 8r-v, Bond of David Duncanson in the Caris of Apuadull, July 25, 1552; 18v-19r, Bond of Donald Mackinnocater, October 10, 1560; f. 20v, Bond of Patrick McAllair, May 5, 1561; f. 22v, Bond of John Dow MacGillernan; INV 1080, Bond of Alexander McBrek of Legarclaw, September 17, 1526; INV 1073, Bond of Henry, Lord Methven and Jonet Stewart, April 29, 1552; NAS GD 148/173, Bond by George Houston, March 19, 1549; NAS GD25/2/27, Bond of Elizabeth Colville, July 11, 1514; NAS GD247/182/1, Bond of Gilbert Wauchop and Jonet Her, May 8, 1535; NAS GD25/2/62, Bond of Isabell Ferguson of Kilkarene, May 10, 1540; NAS GD112/24/2, f.18, Bond of Donald McKerlich McConnell and Margaret MacEwen, September 9, 1560.
45. NAS RH2/2/14 (15), Bond of William Sinclair of Roslin, June 3, 1546.
46. NAS GD 8/159, Bond of Robert, Lord Boyd and his Son, November 6, 1557.
47. NAS RH2/2/14 (15), Bond of William Sinclair of Roslin, June 3, 1546.
48. NAS SP 13/48, Bond of Hector MacClane of Duart, May 24, 1546.
49. TNA SP 62/1, f. 69v, Thomas Fitzwalter, Lord Deputy to the Queen, January 2, 1556/7; TNA SP 62/1 93v, Articles Concerning Affairs in Ireland, April 15, 1557.
50. TNA SP 62/1, f. 50r, A Present Remedy for the Reformation of the North and the Rest of Ireland, 1556.

51. TNA SP 62/1, f. 50r, A Present Remedy for the Reformation of the North and the Rest of Ireland, 1556.
52. TNA SP 62/1, 93r, Articles Concerning Affairs in Ireland, April 15, 1557.
53. TNA SP 62/1, f. 73r, Articles Sent by the Queen to Fitzwalter and Answered, February 5, 1556/7.
54. TNA SP 62/1, f. 73r, Articles Sent by the Queen to Fitzwalter and Answered, February 5, 1556/7.
55. TNA SP 62/1, f. 93v, Articles Concerning Affairs in Ireland, April 15, 1557.
56. TNA SP 62/1, f. 93v, Articles Concerning Affairs in Ireland, April 15, 1557.
57. TNA SP 62/1, f. 94r, Articles Concerning Affairs in Ireland, April 15, 1557.
58. TNA SP 62/1, f. 94r, Articles Concerning Affairs in Ireland, April 15, 1557.
59. TNA SP 62/1, f. 107r, King and Queen to the Nobility of Ireland, May, 1557.
60. TNA SP 62/1, ff. 114r–114v, The Queen to the Earl of Sussex, June 1, 1557.
61. TNA SP 62/1, f. 125r, The Queen to the Lord Deputy of Ireland, July, 1557.
62. Dawson, *The Politics of Religion*, 137–144.
63. Cathcart, "A Spent Force?" 270; Hiram Morgan, "The End of Gaelic Ulster: A Thematic Interpretation of Events Between 1534 and 1610," in *Irish Historical Studies* vol. 26, no. 191 (May, 1988): 8–32, esp. 14–20.

Bibliography

Primary Sources

Manuscripts:
The National Archives (Kew):
SP 50, SP 51, SP 62.
National Archives of Scotland (Edinburgh):
GD8, GD112, GD247, GD25, RH2, SP13.
Inveraray Castle (Inveraray):
Bundles 1073–4, 1080, 1083.

Printed sources:
Bain, Joseph ed. *Calendar of State Paper related to Mary, Queen of Scots*. Edinburgh: Register House, 1894.
Brown, Keith M., MacIntosh, Gillian H., Mann, Alastair J., and Tanner, Roland J., eds. *Records of the Parliament of Scotland to 1707* (http://www.rps.ac.uk/).
Cameron, Annie, ed. *The Scottish Correspondence of Mary of Lorraine*. Edinburgh: Scottish Historical Society, 1927.
Dickinson, Gladys, ed. *Two Missions of Jacques de la Brosse*. Edinburgh: Edinburgh University Press, 1949.

Hamilton, Hans Claude, ed. *Calendar of State Papers Relating to Ireland, of the Reigns of Henry VIII, Edward VI, Mary and Elizabeth, 1509–1603*. London: Longman, Green, Longman and Roberts, 1860.
O'Donovan, John, ed. and trans. *Annala rioghachta Eireann/ Annals of the kingdom of Ireland by the four masters (AFM)*, 7 vols. 1848–51, 2nd edn. 1856.
Stevenson, Joseph, ed. *Calendar of State Papers, Foreign, Elizabeth I (1559–60)*. London: Longman, Green, Longman, Roberts and Green, 1865.
Thomas Dickson and James Balfour Paul, eds., *Accounts of the Treasurer of Scotland (TA)*. Edinburgh: Morrison and Gibb, 1913.

Secondary Sources

Blakeway, Amy. *Regency in Sixteenth-Century Scotland*. Woodbridge: Boydell, 2015.
Bradshaw, Brendan. "'Manus the Magnificient': O'Donnell as a Renaissance Prince." In *Studies in Irish History Presented to R. Dudley Edwards*. Edited by Art Cosgrove and Donald McCartney, 15–37. Dublin: University College Dublin Press, 1979.
Bradshaw, Brendan. *The Irish Constitutional Revolution of the Sixteenth Century*. Cambridge: Cambridge University Press, 1979.
Brady, Ciaran. *The Chief Governors: The Rise and Fall of Reform Government in Tudor Ireland, 1536–1588*. Cambridge: Cambridge University Press, 1994.
Brigdan, Susan *London and the Reformation*. Oxford: Oxford University Press, 1989.
Bryson, Alan. "St Leger, Sir Anthony (1496?–1559)." In *Oxford Dictionary of National Biography*. Edited by H. C. G. Matthew and Brian Harrison. Oxford: Oxford University Press, 2004. Online ed., edited by David Cannadine, January 2008. http://www.oxforddnb.com/view/article/24512 (accessed June 23, 2017). online ed. Jan 2008.
Canny, Nicholas. *The Elizabethan Conquest of Ireland, a Pattern Established, 1565–76*. Hassocks: Harvest, 1976.
Cathcart, Alison. "A Spent Force? The Clan Donald in the Aftermath of 1493." In *The Lordship of the Isles*. Edited by Richard D. Oram, 254–270. Leiden: Brill, 2004.
Dawson, Jane. *The Politics of Religion in the Age of Mary, Queen of Scots: The Earl of Argyll and the Struggle for Britain and Ireland*. Cambridge: Cambridge University Press, 2002.
Duffy, Eamon. *Fires of Faith*. New Haven: Yale University Press, 2009.
Duffy, Earmon. *Stripping the Altars: Traditional Religion in England, 1400–1580*. New Haven: Yale University Press, 1992.
Ellis, Steven. *Tudor Frontiers and Noble Power: The Making of the British State*. Oxford: Oxford University Press, 1995.
Ellis, Steven. *Tudor Ireland: Crown, Community and the Conflict of Cultures, 1470–1603*. London: Longman, 1985.

Grant, Alexander. "Scotland's Celtic Fringe in the Late Middle Ages: the MacDonalds Lords of the Isles and the Kingdom of Scotland." In *The British Isles, 1100–1500: Comparisons, Contrasts and Connections*. Edited by Robert Rees Davies, 118–141. Edinburgh: John Donald, 1988.

Haigh, Christopher. *English Reformations: Religion, Politics and Society under the Tudors*. Oxford: Oxford University Press, 1993.

Hays-McCoy, Gerard. *Scots Mercenary Forces in Ireland, 1565–1603*. Dublin: Burns Oates and Washbourne, 1937.

Ives, Eric. *Lady Jane Grey: A Tudor Mystery*. Chichester: Blackwell, 2009.

Jordan, Constance. "Women's Rule in Sixteenth-Century British Political Thought." In *Renaissance Quarterly*, vol. 40, no. 3. (Autumn 1987): 421–451.

Kingston, Simon. *Ulster and the Isles in the Fifteenth Century*. Dublin: Four Courts Press, 2004.

Loach, Jennifer *Parliament and the Crown in the Reign of Mary Tudor*. New York: Clarendon Press, 1986.

Loades, David. "Phillip II and the Government of England." In *Law and Government under the Tudors. Essays Presented to Sir Geoffrey Elton*. Edited by Claire Cross, David Loades and John J. Scarisbrick, 177–194. Cambridge: Cambridge University Press, 1988.

Loades, David. *Mary Tudor: A Life*. New York: Basil Blackwell, 1989.

Loades, David. *The Mid-Tudor Crisis, 1545–1565*. New York: St Martin's Press, 1992.

Loades, David. *The Reign of Mary Tudor: Politics Government and Religion, 1553–8*. New York: St Martin's Press, 1979.

MacGregor, Martin. "The Campbells: Lordship, Literature and Liminality." In *Textual Cultures: Texts, Contexts, Interpretation* 7(1), (2012): 121–157.

Maginn, Christopher. "Gaelic Ireland's English Frontiers in the late Middle Ages." In *Proceedings of the Royal Irish Academy. Section C: Archaeology, Celtic Studies, History, Linguistics, Literature*. Vol. 110C (2010): 173–190.

Maginn, Christopher and Steven Ellis. *The Tudor Discovery of Ireland*. Dublin: Four Courts Press, 2015.

Mayer, Thomas. *Reginald Pole: Prince and Prophet*. Cambridge: Cambridge University Press, 2000.

Morgan, Hiram "The End of Gaelic Ulster: a Thematic Interpretation of Events between 1534 and 1610." In *Irish Historical Studies* vol. 26, no. 191 (May, 1988): 8–32.

Nicholls, Kenneth. *Gaelic and Gaelicised Ireland in the Middle Ages*. Dublin: Gill and MacMillan, LTD, 1972.

Nicholls, Kenneth. "Scottish Mercenary Kindreds in Ireland 1250–1600." In *The World of the Gallowglass: Kings, Warlords, and Warriors in Ireland and*

Scotland, 1200–1600. Edited by Sean Duffy, 86–105. Dublin: Four Courts Press, 2007.

Oldenburg, Scott. "Toward a Multi-Cultural Mid-Tudor England: The Queen's Royal Entry Circa 1553, 'The Interlude of Wealth and Health,' and the Question of Strangers in the Reign of Mary I." In *ELH*, vol. 76, no 1. (Spring 2009): 99–129.

Pogson, Rex. "Reginald Pole and the Priorities of Government in Mary Tudor's Church." In *The Historical Journal*, vol. 18, no. 1. (Mar., 1975): 3–20.

Richards, Judith. "'To Promote a Woman to Beare Rule': Talking of Queens in Mid-Tudor England." In *The Sixteenth Century Journal*, vol. 28, no. 1. (Spring 1997): 101–121.

Richards, Judith. "Mary Tudor as 'Sole Quene'?: Gendering Tudor Monarchy." In *The Historical Journal*, vol. 40, no. 4. (Dec., 1997): 895–924.

Richards, Judith. *Mary Tudor*. New York: Routledge, 2008.

Ritchie, Pamela, *Mary of Guise in Scotland, 1548–1560*. East Linton: Tuckwell, 2002.

Samson, Alexander. "Changing Places: the Marriage and Royal Entry of Philip, Prince of Austria, and Mary Tudor, July-August 1554." In *The Sixteenth-Century Journal*, vol. 36, no. 3. (Fall 2005): 61–84.

Shephard, Amanda. *Gender and Authority in Sixteenth Century England*. Keele: Keele University Press, 1994.

MacNeil, Thomas. "Organizing a Lordship: The Castle of the MacDonalds of Dunivaig and the Glens." In *The Lordship of the Isles*. Edited by R.D. Oram, 211–226. Leiden: Brill, 2004.

Tittler, Robert, and Loach, Jennifer, eds. *The Mid-Tudor Polity c. 1540–1560*. Totowa, NJ: Rowman and Littlefield, 1980.

Ward, Joseph P. *Metropolitan Communities: Trade Guilds, Identity and Change in Early Modern London*. Stamford: Stamford University Press, 1997.

Whitelock, Anna and MacCulloch, Diarmaid. "Princess Mary's Household and the Succession Crisis, July 1553." In *The Historical Journal*. vol. 50, no. 2. (2007): 265–287.

Whitelock, Anna. *Mary Tudor: England's First Queen*. London: Bloomsbury, 2009.

Whitelock, Anna. *Mary Tudor: Princess, Bastard, Queen*. London: Bloomsbury, 2009.

Wood, James. *The King's Army: Warfare, Soldiers, and Society during the Wars of Religion in France, 1562–1576*. Cambridge: Cambridge University Press, 1996.

Wormald, Jenny. *Lords and Men in Scotland: Bonds of Manrent, 1442–1603*. Edinburgh: John Donald, 1985.

CHAPTER 3

Catherine de Medici and Huguenot Colonization, 1560–1567

Nate Probasco

Catherine de Medici, who has been called "King in All but Name" and "unquestionably the most important political actor in France" during her sons' reigns, is a natural choice for a collection on the influence of early modern European women.[1] As the most powerful person in the most populous European state during the "Age of Queens," her impact can scarcely be ignored.[2] Yet, her troubled legacy complicates her story and that of her nation. On the one hand, authors continue to perpetuate the stereotype of Catherine as a Machiavellian schemer. She recently was called a "relentlessly calculating power broker"[3] who "manipulated royal policies and persons as if she had read Machiavelli before she was born,"[4] but on the other hand, scholars like Leonie Frieda and Elaine Kruse have recast her as a realist who managed to keep France from imploding during a volatile time.[5] My interest in Catherine has less to do with her legacy and more to do with her religious policy and, even more specifically, with her willingness to grant sweeping conciliations to the Calvinist Huguenot minority in her realm.

N. Probasco (✉)
Briar Cliff University, Sioux City, IA, USA

© The Author(s) 2017
E. Paranque et al. (eds.), *Colonization, Piracy, and Trade in Early Modern Europe*, Queenship and Power, DOI 10.1007/978-3-319-57159-1_3

Catherine's religious concessions reached their apex during the apogee of her own power: her three-year regency (1560–1563) and the early reign (1563–1567) of her weak-willed son, King Charles IX, when she funded expeditions to transplant Huguenots beyond France's borders. Too often, these relocation plans simply fall under the umbrella of French colonization, which hardly explains their importance. The Huguenot resettlement plans have not been examined in the context of Catherine's foreign and domestic policy. They should not be misconstrued as efforts to simply to be rid of religious non-conformists. Catherine astutely crafted emigration plans to appease Catholic fears and to challenge Spanish domination in the Americas and Europe, all the while remaining disassociated from the schemes. She expertly navigated the thorny geopolitical situation of Western Europe during an era of increasing colonial rivalry in the Americas. By utilizing what John Lewis Gaddis terms "process tracing," I aim to uncover the narrative that led Catherine and her supporters to seek relocation for Huguenots.[6] Because this type of historical inquiry will, in Gaddis' words, "anticipate outcomes," I show that Catherine's decision to legislate in favor of Huguenots and eventually resettle them was the most logical option available to her at the time.

Unlike many of her more uncompromising Valois and Bourbon successors, who clung to the French refrain *"un roi, une loi, une foi"* (one king, one law, one faith), Catherine effectively played the middle ground and for the first time in France's history acknowledged and at times advocated religious pluralism. Partly due to her weak position as a female regent, but also on account of her personal convictions and her intense desire to have her progeny rule, she sought to appease both factions rather than firmly allying with either. Even more so than other early modern *politique* rulers, such as her son King Henry III of France and her contemporary Queen Elizabeth I of England, Catherine enacted religiously liberal legislation. She believed that the state's survival overrode any personal or communal concerns about heresy and orthodoxy, which helped her effectively wield power at a time when women were expected to display deference.

Catherine's Religious Policy During Her Regency (1560–1563)

Following the death of her eldest son King Francis II in December 1560, Catherine became regent for her ten-year-old son Charles and needed to overcome the prejudices facing an Italian Catholic widow ruling in France. Though romantic nationalism would not grip Europe for another two hundred years, xenophobia infected many of her subjects, who found her Florentine, Italian heritage problematic. Frenchmen and foreigners alike questioned her designs, fearing that loyalty to her family and to her homeland took precedence over her allegiance to France.[7] As a middle-aged widow, she did not have the male overseer that early modern Europeans expected. Society feared a woman without a male influence, especially one who ruled over some eighteen million subjects. Catherine also received criticism for hailing from a family of commoners, albeit exceedingly wealthy and influential commoners, because Europeans expected their leaders to come from the noble class.[8] One critic referred to her as "the Florentine grocer's daughter."[9] French Catholics appreciated that she was raised as a Catholic but soon loathed her conciliatory policy toward Protestants. The upstart Huguenot noble class viewed any Catholic compromise as part of a grand intra-European conspiracy to wipe out the new denomination. Such biases limited Catherine and the actions she could take on behalf of her son.

Perhaps, Catherine's greatest challenge was to convince her subjects to support a female sovereign. Of all European nations, France was among the most repressive in its treatment of women due to a long history of misogyny within the government. Historically, France's heteronormative societal structure maintained that men held positions of power and women were relegated to subservient roles. The most notorious of all French anti-female policies was *Lex Salica* dating from the fifth-century reign of Clovis, king of the Salian Franks. It included a clause that prevented women from inheriting land. The clause was nearly forgotten until King Louis X left no male heir when he died in 1316. The Estates General responded by revising Salic Law to exclude women and especially the daughters of French kings, from the royal succession. Ironically, Catherine would not have been regent had the law code not barred Queen Joan II of Navarre and King Edward III of England from inheriting the throne. Instead, the first Valois ruler, Philip VI, became king in 1328.[10] Salic Law was invoked to prevent the candidature for the French throne for the offspring of Catherine's daughter Elisabeth, and by the sixteenth century, France's *Parlements* listed it among the "fundamental laws" of the nation. Not even a king, let alone a queen regent, could question these laws.[11]

For Catherine, Salic Law had one significant consequence: It limited her powers in comparison with Europe's other rulers. Her subjects did not need to give her edicts as much importance as they would have for a king of France. As a regent, she served as a mouthpiece for the boy king, thus lacking the authority she would have commanded as queen regnant. Her detractors further realized that her regency would be short-lived. They only had to wait a few years for Charles to come of age. One of the clearest signs of the constraints on Catherine's power was the activity of the persecuted individuals she sought to protect: the Huguenots. At a time when the principle of *cuius regio, eius religio* (whose realm, his religion) predominated in Western Europe, French Protestants had an obligation to abide by the faith of their sovereign. Catholics in Elizabethan England worshipped in private, as did Protestants in Scotland during the reign of Mary Stewart. French Huguenots generally worshiped at home during the regency of the Catholic queen mother, but they increasingly pushed the limit of acceptable behavior by suggesting and even demanding total religious freedom.[12]

Despite Catherine's circumscribed authority, during the short reign of her eldest son Francis she began to reach out to France's religious minority to counter Catholic power at court. Upon Francis' accession, the Guise faction led by Charles, cardinal of Lorraine and François, Duke of Guise staged a coup and enacted repressive anti-heresy legislation that called for the destruction of Protestant houses of worship and that assigned the death penalty for anyone attending Huguenot meetings.[13] The main Guise adversaries and the rightful regents were the brothers Antoine de Bourbon, king of Navarre and Louis de Bourbon, prince de Condé, as well as the three Châtillon brothers: Gaspard de Coligny, François d'Andelot, and Odet de Châtillon. With rumors of a Huguenot plot against the Guise-controlled government, the king, at the behest of his mother, granted clemency to rebellious Protestants in early March 1560 and gave them the right to petition, much to the dismay of the Guises. Days later, the Huguenot *coup d'état* known as the Amboise Conspiracy went on as planned. It failed miserably and tarnished the Huguenot image. Once considered pious and unduly persecuted victims, they became scheming political dissidents.[14] Yet, 2 months later

Catherine and the moderate chancellor she recently appointed, Michel L'Hospital, brokered the Edict of Romorantin, which was meant to formalize a policy against militant Protestants but also forbid local officials from seeking out heretics.[15]

Following Francis' death, Huguenots gained confidence because Catherine granted them concessions that her husband Henry II would never have considered. To ensure the preservation of France and of her family's power there, she issued several proclamations to protect Huguenots and their right to worship. On December 21, 1560, the Privy Council named Catherine regent and "governor of the kingdom," thereby granting her immense powers. She made appointments for lay and secular offices, dictated foreign and domestic affairs, and chaired the king's council. She approved of letters patent and directed royal dispatches. Her policy of conciliation accelerated as her power grew. Two of her first actions in January 1561 were to discontinue heresy trials and to liberate France's religious prisoners, including the surviving conspirators of Amboise. After the second Calvinist synod petitioned the Estates General to grant more authority to the Huguenot princes of blood, Catherine placed one, the prince of Condé, whom the Guise had sentenced to death for his role at Amboise, on the king's council and promoted the other, Navarre, to the lieutenant-generalship of France, making him second in command of the royal army.[16] Condé, Navarre, Gaspard de Coligny, L'Hospital, and Catherine soon dominated the council, and many prominent Catholic nobles retired to their estates rather than compromise for the regent. The Duke of Guise withdrew from Paris and formed with Marshal Saint-André and Anne de Montmorency "the Triumvirate" to eliminate the Protestant threat. The *parlement* of Paris, the great bastion of Catholic power in France, responded to Catherine's actions by ordering the demolition of all Huguenots places of worship.[17]

Meetings of the Estates General at Orléans in December 1560 and August 1561 did not settle the religious conflict. The Huguenot minority grew bolder following Catherine's initial concessions, and in June 1561, the Reformed churches of France took the unprecedented step of petitioning the new King Charles and his regent mother for freedom of worship and the ability to build houses of worship.[18] Catherine responded with an edict in July that terminated the death penalty for crimes of heresy and granted amnesty to all criminals who agreed to live peacefully as Catholics.[19] More importantly, she personally organized and convened the Colloquy of Poissy from September to October 1561 to reconcile France's Catholics and Protestants. Rather than allowing for an ecumenical council such as the Council of Trent, which sought to reform Catholic dogma while condemning Protestant doctrine, Catherine arranged a state-run religious conference to keep her interests at the forefront. In fact, during his opening statements at the colloquium, Chancellor L'Hospital underscored that it was the monarch's prerogative, rather than the pope's, to provide for the French Church. Pope Pius IV, preoccupied at Trent, dispatched to the conference as papal legate Ippolito d'Este, who was supported by dozens of French cardinals, archbishops, and bishops in attendance. Their opposition included Protestant ministers and noted reformers like Théodore Bèza from Geneva and Peter Martyr Vermigli from Zürich, though John Calvin refused to attend. The Church, for the first time, agreed to pay the French crown a subsidy of 1.6 million livres within six years, and though Catherine was particularly interested in finding a mutually acceptable position on the Eucharist, both factions ultimately rejected the proposed comprise.[20]

Undeterred, Catherine summoned religious leaders for another colloquy in early 1562 at Saint-Germain, but it quickly became evident that the opposition would not reach consensus. The queen regent nonetheless issued the 1562 Edict of Saint-Germain (The Edict of January) resulting from the abortive Colloquy of Poissy. It gave Huguenots in France more freedoms than ever before and represents the first time that a major Western European state formally recognized multiple faiths and granted rights to a religious minority. Huguenots, for the first time, could worship in public, so long as they worshipped unarmed during the day beyond the city walls. It allowed them to worship privately in towns and granted the freedom of conscience to all in France. Huguenots could not build their own churches and were forced to return items taken from Catholic churches.[21]

Unfortunately, legislation and conferences designed to alleviate religious tensions only exacerbated them. The *parlements* of Dijon and Aix would not register the Edict of Saint-Germain, and the Paris *parlement* did not approve of Protestantism and spent weeks debating the edict with Catherine. The magistrates submitted a formal protest directly to Catherine entitled "Every kingdom divided against itself goes to ruin." They suggested that the queen had to follow the religion of her husband—yet another limitation that Catherine faced as a woman in power. She refused to back down, however, and sent the *parlement* two formal letters to force their hand.[22] Before they could register the edict, which they did so only provisionally, the religious tensions that had been building in France for months finally boiled over. In March, the Duke of Guise headed for the French court to meet with Catherine to discuss problems arising from the edict. He and his followers happened upon a large congregation of Huguenots worshipping in a barn and killed dozens of them in the tragedy known as the Massacre at Wassy.[23] Catherine ordered the Duke, his rival Condé, and their supporters to stay out of Paris, but it was too late to prevent retaliation. The Huguenots could not allow such an affront, and in the days that followed the First French War of Religion began.[24]

Following periods of battles and outright massacres, Catherine, who argued that the rebels only covered "themselves in the cloak of religion," mediated a truce in early 1563.[25] Foreign troops, including thousands of German *reiters*, remained on French soil, so she hoped to mend wounds and rally her subjects around a common cause by expelling them. Another 3000 English troops had allied with Condé to conquer the strategic port city Le Havre. The Treaty of Hampton Court signed by Condé and Elizabeth of England created a military and economic alliance between the Huguenot leader and the Protestant queen. Huguenots took the city in May of 1562, and after removing Catholics and destroying their churches, they fortified their location. The English reinforcements that arrived later in the year helped their chances of victory in case of a counterattack by Catholic armies. When the war ended, Elizabeth refused to remove the troops from the Protestant stronghold, holding it as ransom until Catherine agreed to return England's last continental territory, Calais, which had been taken by the French in 1558. Catherine would not negotiate, and in July 1563, she dispatched a mixed army of Huguenot and Catholic forces that easily recaptured the city in three days.[26]

The Edict of Amboise (Edict of Pacification) that Catherine brought to fruition in 1563 to end the war represented another attempt at reconciliation. The edict reaffirmed Huguenot liberties and served as a *modus vivendi* in order to quell dissent. More specific and a bit more restrictive than the 1562 edict, it permitted Huguenots to worship in Protestant garrisoned towns, on the estates of nobles, and in one specified town within each French *baillage* and *sénéchaussée* (district). The freedom of conscience and limited rights to worship that it granted applied to everyone in France, regardless of their beliefs. With it Catherine asked that the previous offenses from the war "should remain extinguished, as if dead and buried and as if they had not happened."[27] Charles even ordered provincial governors, mayors, and town *échevins* to permit Huguenots to sing psalms anywhere and to provide them exemptions from giving alms.[28]

Due to the refusal of some *parlements* to register her earlier edict, Catherine took great lengths to ensure that her magistrates dutifully implemented the Edict of Amboise in the provinces. Yet once again, Bordeaux, Dijon, and Paris initially refused to register it. The Parisians only agreed to register on the condition that a national assembly would revisit the edict upon Charles' coming of age. The criers who broadcast the decision in Paris were pelted with mud by a mob. Catherine shrewdly hastened the king's majority in August 1563 by taking the unprecedented step of using the *lit de justice* (bed of justice) outside of Paris at meeting with the *parlement* of Rouen.[29] Accordingly, Charles became chair of the *parlement* to force the body to register the edict. Catherine recognized that a king regnant wielded much greater power than a queen regent. Charles had little interest in policy anyway, so Catherine retained and in certain respects even enhanced her power.[30]

The Grand Tour of France (1564–1566) that Catherine organized for her son had the ultimate objective of forcing local authorities to ratify the edict. It also introduced the young king to his subjects, and Catherine hoped it would help them attract support in the war-ravaged country. It is no coincidence that the royal retinue of 15,000 courtiers, officials, and soldiers led by the Catholic military commander Montmorency went through the so-called Huguenot crescent in southern and western France, where Catherine could "master Protestant space" and bring rebel towns under control.[31] Even the elaborate entertainments organized by Catherine placed Catholic and Huguenot courtiers side by side to restore amity. Not only would their 2-year progress unite her fractured realm, but it also provided Catherine with an opportunity to observe local officials enforcing the Edict of Amboise. They journeyed to every province and visited each French *parlement* save for Grenoble and Rennes.[32] At Bordeaux, Dijon, Roussillon, and Toulouse, the anointed monarch and her mother forced recalcitrant *parlements* to comply. At Dijon, L'Hospital examined the *parlement's* registers and ensured that the edict was published. Charles replaced the *parlement* of Aix-en-Provence with Parisian *parlementaires* for their refusal to register the edict.[33]

Catherine wished to punish those who disobeyed the ordinances so that "no one may henceforth use pretests for contravening the edicts."[34] Peasants living hundreds of miles from Paris had little reason to obey royal decrees, but local governments held more sway in the countryside.[35] As a final concession to the Huguenots in 1564, the Royal Council, led by L'Hospital and at the urging of Catherine, suppressed the anti-Protestant papal decrees resulting from the Council of Trent. France remained a Catholic nation in allegiance to the papacy, but Rome's hardline stance simply did not correspond with the tolerant religious policies instituted by Catherine.

Remarkably, Catherine kept France at peace until 1567 but not without controversy. Neither the Catholic nor the Huguenot leadership was content with the religious settlement, and signs of discord persisted. The Guise family and their supporters lost their preeminence at court in favor of moderates, who outnumbered Catholics on the king's council.[36] They were dismayed by what they considered undue conciliatory liberties granted to Protestants. Huguenots wanted the complete religious freedom to worship anywhere, and they did not feel that the edicts of toleration sufficiently protected them from Catholic aggression.[37] Though a practicing Catholic herself, Catherine did not account for the extreme religiosity of France's more radical groups. For the population of France, as Mack P. Holt has suggested, the conflict was waged in the name of "a body of believers rather than the more modern definition of a body of beliefs." To them, the struggle was more social and cultural than theological in nature.[38] Doctrine mattered, but for French Catholics the critical element of dispute centered on tradition. Huguenots were not just heretics; they put the nation at risk by challenging centuries of religious unity. In 1562, a French Catholic concisely summarized prevailing belief: "two religions in a single state are as incompatible as light and shadow."[39]

Catherine, however, viewed the conflict through a geopolitical rather than a social or cultural lens. She regularly displayed a willingness to steer the middle course, even if it was unacceptable to many of the religious elite in her realm. The edicts of toleration did not represent a push for religious freedom; they were merely an attempt to keep peace, despite putting France at risk of foreign invasion from Spain. Indeed, Catholics across Europe were shocked by the edicts and would have rejected similar proclamations in their own nations. As a Catholic widow ruling in a foreign land, Catherine made a bold and risky move by granting such sweeping rights to Protestants. Her nearly unprecedented edicts creating a royally sanctioned multi-denominational realm set the stage for further conflict. A taste of toleration led Huguenots to advocate complete religious freedom, but Catholics were unwilling to compromise religious unity by allowing the upstart Protestants to worship as they saw fit.

Huguenot Colonization in *La Florida* (1562–1565)

Near the end of the reign of Catherine's husband, Henry II, the onset of religious violence in France coupled with the nation's dire financial straits had led to the signing of the Treaty of Cateau-Cambrésis (1559) that ended the 60-year conflict known as the Hapsburgs-Valois wars. Despite securing a favorable engagement for their daughter Elisabeth, who married King Philip II of Spain to finalize the armistice, the treaty was not beneficial to France. Henry ceded control of Italy to the Hapsburgs, leaving him with just a few fortified cities on the strategically significant peninsula. The Hapsburgs retained their stranglehold on Western Europe with France surrounded by their territories in Spain, Italy, and the Low Countries. The treaty made possible a tenuous peace in war-torn Western Europe, but it was strangely silent on the pressing issue of American colonization.

Shortly after Christopher Columbus returned to Europe from his first voyage in 1493, Pope Alexander VI issued the Papal Bull of Donation *Inter Caetera* (Among other [works]), which, together with the Treaty of Tordesillas from the following year, granted Spain territorial rights over much of the Americas.[40] The former gave Spain (Castile) all lands lying 100 leagues west and south of the Azores and Cape Verde Islands, while the latter moved the demarcation line another 270 leagues west of the Cape Verdes, thereby granting Portugal everything in the Atlantic east of this meridian. The authors of Cateau-Cambrésis specified that the treaty was not binding to the west of the papal demarcation line, a provision that clearly benefitted France.[41] Yet, none of the documents detailed the specifics of the settlement. Europeans largely agreed that areas settled by Spanish colonists belonged to them, despite the prior claim of millions of Native Americans. The entitlement to areas merely claimed by Philip but not actively settled was more ambiguous. Later, monarchs like King James I of England suggested that Spain did not exhibit possession in practice (*uti possidetis* de facto) everywhere in the Americas, and thus, colonization in unsettled portions was permissible.[42]

Since the definition of "possession" and "settlement" varied from nation to nation, explorers and colonizers from England, France, and the Low Countries openly challenged Spanish authority in the Americas. Moreover, many Europeans were jealous of Spain's wealth and power, and papal bulls carried little weight among Protestant seafarers. Among the first French transatlantic navigators were Basque and Norman fishermen, who frequented the Grand Banks from the 1490s onward, and French pirates preyed upon Spain's treasure fleet beginning in the early 1500s. The first French monarch to show an interest in the Americas was King Francis I, who commissioned the Florentine navigator Giovanni da Verrazzano to search for the Northwest Passage in 1524. He explored the coast of North America from Florida to Newfoundland, and ten years later, Francis spent six thousand livres to send a follow-up mission with the same objective under the leadership of Jacques Cartier. In 1541, Cartier established the short-lived colony Charlesbourg-Royal along the Saint Lawrence River, but few Frenchmen or women followed him to the Americas.[43] For the next two decades, with the nation preoccupied by war and religious strife, French monarchs focused their attention on European affairs.

The uptick in religious dissension had another consequence in France: Huguenots began seeking asylum to profess their beliefs. When Francis I adopted a hardline policy against Protestantism near the end of his reign, persecution of perceived heresies became more common. Henry II tried to eliminate all sedition with the Edicts of Châteaubriant (1551) and Compiègne (1557) that made heresy punishable by death.[44] In spite of such measures, Huguenot numbers continued to grow unabated, and many sought refuge within France's borders. Protestants migrated to walled cities like La Rochelle, from which Condé and Coligny (Admiral of France, Secretary of the Navy, and among the most prominent Huguenots in the realm) dispatched privateers to attack foreign vessels. A relatively large proportion of Huguenots were artisans and nobles, and they clustered in the cities of southern and central France, which, along with Switzerland, was the homeland of Calvinism. Over time they seized and fortified strategic central towns like Angers, Blois, Lyon, Orléans, and Tours. Once entrenched, they erased all instances of iconoclasm. Even though many Huguenots were wealthy urbanites, they were virtually excluded from the French court. This created a tense situation. An affluent and well-armed religious minority yearned for the acceptance and the gifts dispensed only at court. Being barred from a courtly life led to fear and resentment.[45] But Huguenots were not just calling for religious freedom; as both a religious and sociopolitical group, they wanted political change. They had already formed a state within a state in France, and they hoped to create God's kingdom on earth.[46] It became increasingly clear that this was not possible in France. Persecuted and excluded but wealthy and intellectually gifted, Huguenots were the natural choice to lead the charge for colonization.

The first attempt at Huguenot resettlement occurred in 1555, when Coligny sent a colonizing expedition to Brazil, a Portuguese territory that had been visited periodically by French (mainly Norman) merchants since the discovery of brazilwood in the early 1500s. Coligny had an amicable relationship with Catherine, and he convinced Henry II to sponsor the voyage. Under the leadership of the Catholic naval commander Nicolas Durand, Chevalier de Villegagnon, and his assistant, Huguenot Nicolas Barré, an assortment of 600 French Huguenot and Swiss Calvinist soldiers and colonists founded the colony known as France Antarctique at Villegagnon Island across from modern-day Rio de Janeiro. In addition to providing a refuge for the persecuted Europeans, Villegagnon gained access to brazilwood and its precious red dye and, he hoped, an assortment of precious metals. Villegagnon's draconian leadership did not suit Barré and the Huguenots, and eventually infighting broke out over the nature of the Eucharist. After years of disputes, the Portuguese finally destroyed the struggling colony in 1560 and forced the remaining Protestants to convert or face execution.

Coligny remained a vocal advocate of emigration, and in 1562, with Charles and Catherine he organized a second colony led by the Norman Huguenot Jean Ribault, one of the ablest navigators in France. By this point, Coligny was a favorite of the young king, and though a devout Huguenot, he echoed Catherine's sentiments in favoring a strong France above all else. Their project commenced at the perfect time; Philip had just decided to suspend colonization efforts on mainland North America.[47] At age eleven, Charles still had the concerns of a boy, and he simply asked Ribault to explore unknown lands. Catherine had more ambitious objectives. She intended to weaken Spain's remarkably strong position in the Americas in the event that the next Hapsburgs-Valois conflict spilled over to the Americas. Hence, the expedition was heavily armed. The potential to discover precious metals in the largely unexplored North American interior was equally appealing. Catherine financed the expedition with royal funds and provided two royal ships for the voyage.[48] The majority of similar exploratory or colonizing voyages departing from England or Spain were privately funded, putting nearly all of the risk on the shoulders of the explorers themselves. Catherine's benevolence is even more surprising considering the economic situation in France, as the national debt reached more than 43 million livres (4x the national revenue) at the outset of her regency.[49] Catherine gambled by funding Ribault's expedition, due both to France's poor economic state and to the threat of Spanish reprisals.

The organizers of the expedition instructed Ribault to scout for a preferable colony site and to claim the area for France. To that effect, he was entrusted with five marble pillars inscribed with the arms of the king of France to be placed in prominent locations within the new French territory. Coligny chose fellow Huguenots René de Laudonnière and the experienced navigator Barré to assist Ribault as second and third in command. The Villegagnon debacle had made evident the impracticality of a mixed-faith colonizing voyage, so 150 Huguenot soldiers, sailors, and gentlemen accompanied Ribault across the Atlantic. They first made landfall in Florida near present-day Jacksonville, where the colonists memorialized their claim with the first marble pillar. Ribault dubbed the local river the River May (modern-day St. Johns River), having discovered it in that month. The voyagers continued north and eventually settled Parris Island, South Carolina, where the colonists erected another pillar and constructed Charlesfort in honor of the young king. With his claim firmly established, Ribault passed on his command to Captain Albert de la Pierria and then sailed back to Europe for supplies. The few dozen remaining colonists were to hold the fort and await Ribault's reinforcements, at which point they could use their base to attack the Spanish treasure fleets and to search for precious metals. Coligny loathed the Spanish, and the Huguenots had no reservations about attacking the Catholic nation. The treasure ships were easy targets, as they had to sail through the Bahamas Channel to catch favorable currents to bring them to Europe. The potential of finding the Northwest Passage also could jeopardize the Iberian monopoly in Asia.[50]

Ribault returned to France and discovered that war had broken out between Huguenots and Catholics. Many of his fellow colonists expressed their desire to make a speedy return to Charlesfort, but ocean-going ships were needed for the war effort. Even as the fighting intensified in early 1563, the king personally sought out the returned colonists to "be clearly informed on the situation over there" (in Florida),[51] showing his great concern for the endeavor. Meanwhile, Ribault changed his plans and joined the battle alongside his coreligionists at Dieppe, but he fled to England with some Protestant exiles after the city fell to Catholic armies. He had nearly convinced the English to assist him on his return to the colony when Elizabeth detained him as a potential spy.[52] She still held a grudge over the loss of Calais, and England's claim to mainland North America through the 1497 expedition of John Cabot actually predated both the French (1524) and Spanish (1513) claims. Ribault was an interloper in Spanish *and* English eyes. The English planned to take Charlesfort as their own, but when Ribault absconded with a ship for France the project was abandoned.[53] Even without the delay caused by his incarceration, the colonists remaining at Charlesfort probably would not have survived. A fire at the fort burned most of their provisions, and with no sign of reinforcements, the colonists mutinied and killed the domineering Pierria, hastily constructed a boat, and sailed for Europe. A single colonist, Guillaume Rouffin, chose to stay behind and take his chances in the wilderness.

The Massacre at Wassy accelerated calls for emigration among the wealthy Huguenot class, as an already tense situation further deteriorated. When the first war ended in 1563, Ribault remained a prisoner in the Tower of London with little to do but pen his version of the first expedition. Charles, at the behest of Catherine and Coligny, decided to proceed without him. They ordered a relief fleet under the direction Laudonnière, who had returned to France with Ribault several months earlier. They did not realize that the colony had been abandoned and that the surviving colonists had made it to England, where Elizabeth delayed their return to France by questioning them about their intentions.[54] Laudonnière disembarked from Le Havre in 1564 with a diverse group of colonists fleeing religious persecution at home. They included sailors, soldiers, noblemen, and artisans, many of whom were Protestant nobles from France and Germany. Whereas the initial colonists led by Ribault had reconnoitered for a potential colony site in order to claim the territory, these 200 voyagers intended to establish a wholly self-sustainable colony. In the place of so many guns and cannons, they packed livestock, farming implements, and wares to trade with Native Americans. Catherine gave the colonists explicit instructions to leave the Spaniards alone.[55]

Rather than risking the longer voyage to Charlesfort, Laudonnière dropped anchor at Ribault's initial landing site in Florida along the River

May, an area that he believed was better suited to farming and mining. There, on a bluff overlooking the river, the colonists built Fort Caroline, which again had Charles as its namesake.[56] Laudonnière proved himself an effective leader. He explored upriver into the interior and established friendly relations with Timucua and Mocama Indians. Despite the colonists' willingness to farm and trade with their neighbors for food, they quickly ran low on provisions. A dozen men deserted, and seventy more mutinied and arrested Laudonnière. Lured by Spanish gold, they eventually freed their captain and headed for the Caribbean to conduct raids at Cuba and Hispaniola.[57]

Some of the mutineers returned to the colony, but several were captured by Spanish authorities, who had already located and interrogated Rouffin, the only Charlesfort colonist still in the Americas. He and the Fort Caroline mutineers revealed precise details about the location, size, and defenses of the two settlements.[58] King Philip II's agents in either London or Paris even acquired a map of the French colony.[59] His spy in Paris, Dr. Gabriel de Enveja, provided intelligence on a second expedition to be led by Jean Ribault, who had just returned from England. Catherine, Charles, and Coligny were busy preparing an immense expedition to resupply Laudonnière. Enveja informed Philip that the French had assembled no less than 500 arquebusiers, their accoutrements, and several bronze cannons. Due to the magnitude of the venture, Charles had designated Ribault "captain-general and viceroy" of New France.[60]

Philip faced a difficult decision. France and Spain had been at peace for just a few years, and he did not want to provoke a war that would further drain his nation's resources. Furthermore, Philip learned of Ribault's voyage in early 1565, when Catherine and Charles were on their Grand Tour *en route* to a summit meeting at Bayonne in southwestern France. There, they would meet with Philip's representative, the ultra-Catholic Duke of Alva, to resolve various policy disputes between the two nations and to discuss religious matters. Philip refused to attend on account of Catherine's conciliatory policy toward Huguenots, but she was excited to see her daughter (and Philip's wife) Elisabeth for the first time in years.[61] Protestants across Europe feared that this meeting of the world's Catholic powers would result in a pact to eradicate heretics.

At that moment, Philip was more concerned with French treachery that Protestant heresy. He was exceedingly protective over his American possessions, especially Florida, due to its location along the treasure fleet route. Hundreds of French colonists had already reached America without his knowledge, and Ribault's reinforcements might allow the struggling colony to thrive. The Duke of Alva finally convinced Philip to strike. He could not allow France to strengthen or even maintain its foothold on mainland North America. At Bayonne, Alva even offered to give Catherine a document explaining why the French could not legally settle Florida. Instead, Philip wrote to his ambassador in France, telling him to inform the queen that the usurpation of his Florida territory would not be accepted and that the French would be punished for overstepping their bounds. Philip ordered the new Florida *Adelantado* Pedro Menéndez de Avilés to track down Ribault and destroy the French colony.[62]

Menéndez sailed for Florida in June 1565 with 1000 men aboard ten vessels and discovered that Ribault had already arrived at the colony with the 500 soldiers and 300 civilians that Philip had expected. Following a brief skirmish in which the French fled to the sea, Menéndez retreated south and hastily constructed Fort San Augustín on September 8, 1565. Ribault had left the women and children at the fort and attempted to conquer the Spanish settlement, but his ships were scattered in a hurricane. Menéndez wisely headed north by land on September 20 to surprise the French colonists at the weakly defended Fort Caroline. He hanged more than one hundred male colonists "not as Frenchmen but as heretics" and spared the women and children. Meanwhile, Ribault and the others who survived the storm slowly marched north to an inlet along the coast, where Menendez found them and convinced them to surrender. This time he spared some professed Catholics and skilled workers. He killed the rest, including Ribault, which is why the location is now called the *Matanzas* (slaughters) Inlet.

Philip applauded Menéndez when news of his deeds reached Spain in February 1566, and he added to the French humiliation by relegating the captives to a lifetime of service rowing his galleys. He tried to forestall similar incursions into his American territory by constructing twelve ships to patrol the waters from Florida to the Caribbean. Spanish colonists rebuilt Fort Caroline as San Mateo, and Charlesfort was renamed Fort San Felipe. Together with San Augustín and several smaller forts along Florida's coast, they created a formidable barrier to foreign invasions.[63]

Understandably, Catherine had a much different response to the destruction of her colony. When she received word of the massacre at Moulins, the Spanish ambassador reported that "Her Majesty was growling like a lioness."⁶⁴ Laudonnière had managed to escape and return to France in 1566. He offered Catherine, Charles, and Coligny a detailed report of the events.⁶⁵ With Charles ill in bed, his mother responded to Philip through her ambassador that the "unfortunate massacre" caused her "unspeakable sorrow," especially as the colony had been sanctioned by Charles. She called for justice for those slaughtered by Philip's subjects. Catherine feared that her son might "reproach me some day, saying that while he had rested his affairs on me, I had allowed such a stain to be made on his reputation."⁶⁶ Accordingly, she terminated (though later revived) the marriage negotiations between Charles and the Hapsburg Elizabeth of Austria, stating bluntly that "my son is young enough to wait for something better."⁶⁷ She even suggested that he might marry a non-Catholic if brought to extremity, a possibility that would not sit well with Philip. As a final response, during the summer of 1566 she organized a procession of the victim's widows through the streets of Paris, lest the city forgets the Spanish atrocity.⁶⁸

Catherine had good reason to be upset over the attack. She reminded the Spanish king that her son believed "that commerce and navigation are everywhere free to his subjects,"⁶⁹ placing serious doubt on Philip's reasoning for the assault. Catherine suggested that commerce and navigation were permissible in the Atlantic, since the French crown's belief in *mare liberum* meant that sailors from all nations could utilize the open seas. The more conservative *mare clausum* espoused by the Spanish gave them sovereignty in most of the Atlantic on account of the papal bulls of donation. On this point of disagreement, Catherine had the upper hand. The 1538 Treaty of Nice signed by the French and Spanish granted free navigation to both nations. French navigators had a right to sail unmolested in all parts of the Atlantic.

The other point of contention centered on the settlement. Philip disagreed that the French legally could settle lands within his papally endowed jurisdiction, regardless of whether or not Spanish colonists lived in the area. Catherine countered by asserting that North America was French territory, and most Europeans did, in fact, refer to the continent as "*Terre des Bretons*" after the sea-faring region Brittany in northern France. The Spanish ambassador had no suitable response, so he suggested that the presence of Huguenot ministers at the colony prompted the attack. Catherine stressed that the territory was not Philip's to govern, since it belonged to France rather than Spain. She was free to settle it with people of any faith. Catherine's concluding statement sums up her assessment of the colonial project: "I should want all the Huguenots to be in that country." She viewed the 1560s expeditions as part of a larger resettlement scheme to ease religious tensions. Catherine had no qualms about sending large numbers of Huguenots to the Americas.[70]

When Catherine defended her actions to Philip in 1566, she acknowledged that Ribault's successful reconnaissance in 1562 gave her hope that the colony would likewise succeed. In a candid moment between the two most powerful individuals in Western Europe, Catherine informed Philip that she "had indeed intended to send and conquer it" (Florida).[71] In hindsight, her admission makes no sense, because it offered Philip additional fodder to justify his vengeful attack. Catherine had an additional motive: She wanted to make it clear to Philip that he should not trifle with her and her vast nation. France had the manpower and naval expertise to dispatch hundreds if not thousands of emigrants to North America. It was only a matter of time before the Hapsburg-Valois rivalry would reignite with Catherine leading France, and, as the Huguenot colonization expeditions show, she was prepared to take the fight into the Atlantic theater.

Philip's treacherous actions made it unlikely that more Huguenots would be persuaded to emigrate to Florida, but Catherine and Charles refused to allow Philip's affront to pass unanswered. Just as he had embarrassed her and damaged France's reputation, they decided to retaliate by sending a *Catholic* to attack Spain in the Americas. They chose the Gascon gentleman Dominique de Gourgues to lead the expedition. He had been captured by the Spanish as a young soldier and forced to row as a galley slave for several years. Coupled with his experience sailing to Brazil and the West Indies, he was a natural choice for captain. Departing from Bordeaux on August 2, 1567, de Gourgues 200-strong force reached Florida and made contact with Laudonnière's Timucua allies. On Good Friday 1568, the combined force burned San Mateo, the former Fort Caroline, and hanged the defenders "not as ... Spaniards, but as ... liars, thieves, and murderers."[72] Philip called for de Gourgues' head. Catherine said little about the events, though, according to Alva, her countenance "showed her great joy."[73] While she barred de Gourgues from court in order to appease the powerful Spanish king, Coligny stood up for him and ensured that he would be praised rather than punished for his assault. De Gourgues quickly returned to favor and received no punishment for his actions.

Catherine's Overture to the Ottomans (1566)

The Huguenot colonization plans in North America proved fruitless, so during the late 1560s Catherine turned her attention east. Her efforts to use the powerful Ottoman Empire as a counterweight to the equally powerful Spanish Empire was perhaps her boldest foreign policy maneuver. Heads of state across Western Europe considered the Muslim Ottomans the great menace to European hegemony, even if their empire included much of "Europe." Since the fall of Constantinople in 1453, Ottoman armies gradually pushed west, reaching as far as Vienna in 1529. Christian rulers swapped territory often during the Medieval and early modern eras, but not since the conquest of Iberia during the 700s had a Muslim army taken such a large swath of Europe.

Yet, Catherine was just one among many European sovereigns who recognized the significance of an Ottoman alliance in the face of Spain's growing power. Elizabeth of England reached out to Ottoman Sultan Murad III to answer the threat posed by Spain and France. She sent an ambassador to Istanbul in 1578 and 2 years later formed a trade agreement, whereby England supplied the Ottomans with metal from old Catholic church bells to cast weapons to use against Spain. In a letter to Suleiman the Magnificent, Philip's nemesis in the Low Countries, William the Silent, proposed a Dutch-Ottoman alliance to fight their common enemy. The Dutch rebels even adopted the motto *"Liever Turks dan Paaps"* ("Better a Turk than a Papist"). Suleiman responded with a promise of troops for the war in the Low Countries, but William benefitted most from the Ottomans preoccupying Philip's armies in the Mediterranean.[74]

Among all Western European nations, France had the longest standing relationship with the Ottomans due to their mutual rivalry with the Hapsburgs, and Catherine hoped to take advantage of their history. In 1520, King Francis I dispatched an ambassador to Tunis to entice the Ottomans to increase pirate attacks on the Holy Roman Emperor's territory in Naples, offering military equipment and intelligence in return.[75] Two embassies followed in 1533 and 1534, ultimately leading to the Franco-Ottoman alliance forged in 1535–1536 that was arguably the first by a Christian European power with a non-Christian power during the early modern era. The alliance guaranteed trading rights and mutual defense against Spain, while giving extraterritoriality to French Merchants operating in Ottoman lands. During the first Italian War of 1542–1546, Francis and Suleiman united to besiege Nice, the Mediterranean port city whose leaders were allied to the Hapsburgs.[76] During the Italian War of 1551–1559, King Henry II allied with Suleiman to take Corsica, an important way station for ships traveling between Spain and Italy. Europe's other leaders eventually ridiculed the alliance as "the sacrilegious union of the Lily and the Crescent," but French rulers continued to make use of their powerful ally.

Catherine and Charles devised a simple plan that would benefit both France and the Ottoman Empire. They wanted to transplant persecuted Huguenots and Lutherans from France and the Holy Roman Empire to Moldavia in Eastern Europe. The small tributary principality of the Empire on the western coast of the Black Sea had been under Ottoman suzerainty for decades by the 1560s and was ideally situated between the Empire and Spain's allies in central Europe. The well-armed Protestants would help create a formidable buffer state, certainly something the Ottomans would appreciate. In addition to easing tensions at home, Catherine would have loyal French citizens nearer to the lucrative Ottoman trade market, which obtained goods not just from their expansive empire but also from points as far east as China.

The French delegation that departed for Istanbul in 1566 was led by Huguenot Guillaume de Grandchamp de Grantrie, who would serve as French ambassador to the Ottoman Empire from 1566 to 1571. During his meeting with Ottoman officials, he suggested that the French and Ottomans establish a military colony at Moldavia consisting of Huguenots and French and German Lutherans. Grandchamp put himself forward as the potential military leader of the state, and he agreed to marry the sister of the current *voyvoda* (military leader) of Moldavia in order to bring the alliance to fruition. He even offered to become *voyvoda* himself and pay 20,000 ducats annually to the Ottomans.[77]

The negotiations seemed to go well, but the Ottomans had much bigger concerns. In part because the Hapsburg Holy Roman Emperor Maximilian II failed to pay tribute to Suleiman, he marched west during the spring of 1566 to gain retribution. This was his first incursion into the region in more than two decades. The sultan died in September amidst a siege in Hungary.[78] His successor and son, Selim II, was a much less popular and much less effective ruler than the highly regarded Suleiman.[79] Known as "Selim the Sot" or "Selim the Drunkard," the political neophyte lacked the confidence and vision to invite well-armed Christians into his Empire. Suleiman had died fighting against

Maximilian's mixed Catholic and Protestant army, so the new sultan did not want to take the risk. The likelihood of an attack from the Ottoman's Muslim rivals the Safavid Empire only increased following Suleiman's death. Selim was uninterested in military expansion and even left military decisions to his ministers, a first for an Ottoman Sultan. It is no surprise that he shunned the creation of a military colony. Selim's father had ruled during the height of Ottoman power, so he had no reason to seek French assistance at the time. Yet, most scholars agree that 1566 marked a turning point in Ottoman history, as the Empire struggled as a result of poor leadership thereafter. Over the next few decades, the once dominant Ottomans became a second-rate power in Europe.

While the proposal came at a bad time for the Ottomans, it made sense for Catherine to seek a Huguenot haven in Moldavia. The Ottoman Empire was known for its religious toleration, having accepted Protestants starting in the middle sixteenth century. Muslims and Protestants shared a number of religious preferences, such as their rejection of idols, and members of each faith had a common enemy in Spain. Though Selim was not ready for a colony in 1566, 3 years later the French and Ottomans formed a new agreement that allowed French merchants to utilize all Ottoman ports. Within months, the French took command of European trade in the Levant. The mere threat of a French-Ottoman alliance was enough to strike fear in the hearts of the Hapsburg leadership. Huguenots might have had a chance to avoid the religious wars by emigrating to the Empire in 1569, but by that time France's Protestants had lost their good graces with Catherine.

Conclusion (1567, 1572)

The turning point in Catherine's relationship with her Protestant subjects occurred in 1567, following more than four years in which the queen mother had managed to maintain peace in the face of growing tensions. Known as the Surprise of Meaux, Condé and other Huguenot leaders attempted to kidnap Charles and the rest of the royal family. They feared that Charles' Catholic counselors were brainwashing the boy to ally with Philip to eradicate all Protestants. Relaxing at the Montceaux Château, Catherine and Charles heard rumors of a plot and summoned their Swiss mercenaries to the more defensible town of Meaux. They ultimately decided to flee to Paris and barely evaded a contingent of Huguenots pursuing them.⁸⁰ The next day Coligny and Condé blockaded Paris to starve the government into submission. Huguenots performed yet another preemptive strike by massacring Catholic priests at Nîmes and by seizing several fortified towns, including Nîmes, Orléans, and Valence, which brought about the Second War of Religion in October. It was not until 1598 that the Edict of Nantes brought the wars to an end, and sectarian violence continued throughout the seventeenth and eighteenth centuries.

Catherine often forgave betrayals by both Catholic and Protestant factions during the reigns of her sons, but she was personally affected by the Surprise at Meaux, which she decried as "the greatest wickedness in the world."⁸¹ Thereafter, she ceased her attempts to reach out to the Huguenots, even if she continued to issue edicts of toleration in order to attain peace. She demoted L'Hospital and replaced him with the staunch Catholic cardinal of Lorraine, making it clear to all in France that she had chosen a side in the conflict. Worst of all was the conduct of Coligny, who betrayed the woman who had done so much to protect him and his coreligionists. It became clear to Catherine that she could no longer take such drastic steps to help a group who had resorted to violence and kidnapping, regardless of similar atrocities committed by Catholics. She even accepted financial support from Philip II to wage the second religious war against Huguenots.⁸²

Scholars largely agree that Catherine was driven by political expediency rather than religious fervor. Possibly, she hoped, Huguenots would return to the Church if she exhibited a willingness to compromise. Or, even better, they might choose to go away. Having Huguenots thousands of miles away in Florida or Moldavia could have alleviated various problems facing Catherine and her nation. More than anything, she wanted to keep her family in power, and she changed her allegiance from Catholics to Protestants and back again to meet that end. We should think of Catherine less as a power-hungry regent manipulating the leaders of two competing religio-political factions, and more so as a realistic but inexperienced ruler seeking to provide for her family while preventing her subjects or foreigners from destroying France.

Returning to the words of John Lewis Geddis, for Catherine the Surprise at Meaux became a point of no return, "the moment at which an equilibrium that one existed ceased to do so."⁸³ The religious situation had already spun out of control by 1567, but for Catherine the failed plot changed the nature of the conflict and what it meant to her. It ceased to be political. Now, much as the conflict had become for many of the religious fanatics whom she had despised, it became personal. Catherine firmly sided with France's Catholics even as she displayed a willingness to compromise. The days of pitting religious faction against religious faction had ended. The queen mother had made her choice.

The turning point for Huguenots occurred 5 years after the Surprise of Meaux, when France witnessed the greatest sectarian violence of the era, the Saint Bartholomew's Day Massacre.[84] Even though most scholars now doubt the long-held belief that Catherine instigated the event, it convinced Huguenots that she was not looking out for them.[85] The government did little to contain the killings, leading to the death of thousands of Huguenots across France during weeks of mob violence. Just as Catherine experienced in 1567, the middle ground suddenly evaporated for Huguenots. The massacre caused moderate Protestantism to all but disappear in France. Most either radicalized and continued to fight in the prolonged war, or simply converted to the old faith. Others left France altogether. They first emigrated within Europe to England, Switzerland, the Low Countries, the Holy Roman Empire, and other places more accepting of Protestants. By the late 1600s, the Huguenot diaspora stretched to Quebec, Virginia, Nova Scotia, New Amsterdam, and South Africa. At their peak of influence during Catherine's regency, approximately 10% (2 million) of French citizens were Huguenots. After King Louis XIV issued the Edict of Fontainebleau in 1685 that outlawed Protestantism altogether, that figure plummeted to just 0.004%. Only French Protestant pastors were permitted to emigrate, so all other Huguenot exiles had to forfeit their French citizenship.[86] It was not until the French Revolution-era Edict of Toleration (1787) that Huguenots again worshipped freely in France. During an era when religious unity was expected, Catherine's religious policy truly was ahead of its time.

NOTES

1. Kathleen Wellman, *Queens and Mistresses of Renaissance France* (New Haven & London: Yale University Press, 2013), 225–6.
2. Even the European portion of the Ottoman Empire was larger than France, but the population of France was larger.
3. Nancy Goldstone, *The Rival Queens: Catherine de' Medici, Her Daughter Marguerite de Valois, and the Betrayal that Ignited a Kingdom* (New York: Back Bay Books, 2015), 7.

4. Ronald D. Smith, *Fascinating People and Astounding Events from the History of the Western World* (Santa Barbara: ABC-CLIO, 1990), 86–8.
5. See Leonie Frieda, *Catherine de Medici: Renaissance Queen of France* (New York: Fourth Estate, 2003); Elaine Kruse, "The Virgin and the Widow: The Political Finesse of Elizabeth I and Catherine de' Medici," in *Queens & Power in Medieval and Early Modern England*, eds. Carole Levin and Robert Bucholz (Lincoln: University of Nebraska Press, 2009), 126–40; other favorable depictions of Catherine include Denis Crouze, "The Regency of Catherine de Medici: Political Reason during the Wars of Religion," in *Sacred and Secular Agency in Early Modern France: Fragments of Religion*, ed. Sanja Perovic (London: Continuum, 2012), 37–51; Susan Doran, "Elizabeth I and Catherine de Medici," in *"The Contending Kingdoms": England and France, 1420–1700*, ed. Glenn Richardson (Aldershot: Ashgate, 2008): 117–32; Robert J. Knecht, *Catherine de' Medici* (London and New York: Longman, 1998); Susan Broomhall, "'My daughter, my dear': the correspondence of Catherine de Médicis and Elisabeth de Valois," *Women's History Review* 24, 4 (2015): 548–69; for a historiography of Catherine's popular image, see Katherine Crawford, "Constructing Evil Foreign Queens," *Journal of Medieval and Early Modern Studies* 37, 2 (2007): 393–418; "N.M. Sutherland, "Catherine de Medici: The Legend of the Wicked Italian Queen," *Sixteenth Century Journal*, vol. 9, 2 (July, 1978), 45–56.
6. John Lewis Gaddis, *The Landscape of History: How Historians Map the Past* (New York: Oxford University Press, 2002), 65–6.
7. See Henry Heller, *Anti-Italianism in Sixteenth-Century France* (Toronto: University of Toronto Press, 2003), 164–70; Diefendorf, *Beneath the Cross: Catholics and Huguenots in Sixteenth-Century Paris* (New York: Oxford University Press, 1991), 90–1.
8. Anne de Montmorency even called Catherine "a merchant's daughter." See Knecht, *Catherine*, 59.
9. Mark Strage, *Women of Power: The Life and Times of Catherine de' Medici* (New York and London: Harcourt Brace Jovanovich, 1976), 150.
10. Perhaps even more ironically, Salic Law ended the Valois Dynasty. With no male Valois heirs after the death of King Henry III, King Henry IV became the first monarch from the House of Bourbon.
11. Katherine Crawford, "Catherine de Medicis and the Performance of Political Motherhood," *Sixteenth Century Journal* 31, 3 (Autumn, 2000): 645–7.
12. Denice Durkee, "Religion and Power: A Comparison of Queen Elizabeth I and Catherine de Medici" *McNair Scholars Journal* 7, 1 (2003): 65–6; on Catherine's political finesse as a ruler and the limitations that she faced

as a female, see Katherine Crawford, *Perilous Performances: Gender and Regency in Early Modern France* (Cambridge: Harvard University Press), 24–58; Crawford, "Catherine and Political Motherhood," 643–73.
13. Robert J. Knecht, *The French Renaissance Court, 1483–1589* (New Haven: Yale University Press, 2008), 245–6.
14. Geoffrey Treasure, *The Huguenots* (New Haven: Yale University Press, 2013), 136–8; Luc Racaut, "Religious polemic and Huguenot self-perception and identity, 1554–1619," in *Society and Culture in the Huguenot World, 1559–1685*, eds. Raymond A. Mentzer and Andrew Spicer (Cambridge: Cambridge University Press, 2002), 33. Charles even wrote Jean Calvin to complain about his books instigating the tumult. Calvin denied the involvement of himself or his supporters.
15. "Edict of Romorantin, May 1560," in David Potter, ed. and trans., *The French Wars of Religion: Selected Documents* (New York: St. Martin's Press, 1997), 24–5; R.J. Knecht, "Catherine de' Medici and the French Wars of Religion," *Historian* 62 (Summer 1999), 19; Sharon L. Jansen, *The Monstrous Regiment of Women: Female Rulers in Early Modern Europe* (New York: Palgrave Macmillan, 2002), 207; Durkee, "Religion and Power," 65; Treasure, *The Huguenots*, 138–9.
16. Though Condé was a devout Huguenot and leader of their cause, Navarre was less religious but feared by many to be Protestant due to the strong beliefs of his wife, Jeanne III, Queen of Navarre.
17. Stuart Carroll, *Noble Power during the French Wars of Religion: The Guise Affinity and the Catholic Cause in Normandy* (Cambridge: Cambridge University Press, 1998), 107–8; Knecht, *Renaissance Court*, 247–8; Robert J. Knecht, *The French Civil Wars, 1562–1598* (Harlow: Pearson, 2000), 72–4.
18. Penny Roberts, "Huguenot petitioning during the wars of religion," in *Society and Culture*, eds. Mentzer and Spicer (Cambridge: Cambridge University Press, 2002), 63.
19. Knecht, *Renaissance Court*, 248.
20. Treasure, *Huguenots*, 140–3; Knecht, *French Wars*, 78–9.
21. "The Edict of Saint-Germain, 17 January 1562," in Potter, ed., *French Wars*, 31–2.
22. Mack P. Holt, *The French Wars of Religion, 1562–1629*, 2nd ed. (Cambridge: Cambridge University Press, 2005), 47–8.
23. "The Massacre of Vassy, the Protestant view," and "The Massacre of Vassy: the duke of Guise's view," in Potter, ed., *French Wars*, 47–9; See *Jean du Tillet and the French Wars of Religion, Five Tracts, 1562–1569*,

ed. Elizabeth A. R. Brown (Binghamton: Center for Medieval & and Early Renaissance Studies, 1994), 17–18, 30–5.
24. Stuart Carroll, *Martyrs and Murderers: The Guise Family and the Making of Europe* (Oxford: Oxford University Press, 2009), 4–20; Barbara B. Diefendorf, *Beneath the Cross*, 62–3; Crawford, "Catherine and Political Motherhood," 667.
25. "Catherine de Medici and the crisis," in Potter, ed., *French Wars*, 76.
26. Wallace T. MacCaffrey, "The Newhaven expedition, 1562–1563," *Historical Journal* 40 (1997): 1–22; Knecht, *Catherine de' Medici*, 92–3.
27. "The Edict of Amboise, 19 March 1563," in Potter, ed., *French Wars*, 84; See Holt, *French Wars*, 58–60.
28. "Royal attempts to maintain the Edict, 1564," in Potter, ed., *French Wars*, 86.
29. Treasure, *Huguenots*, 159–60; Knecht, *Catherine*, 93–4.
30. "Charles IX's speech on his majority," in Potter, ed., *French Wars*, 89; See Wellman, *Queens and Mistresses*, 244; Knecht, *French Renaissance*, 259; Knecht, *French Wars*, 119–20.
31. Neil Kamil, *Fortress of the Soul: Violence, Metaphysics, and Material Life in the Huguenots' New World, 1517–1751* (Baltimore: Johns Hopkins University Press, 2005), 16; "Blaise de Monluc's analysis, June 1565," in Potter, ed., *French Wars*, 92–3.
32. Charles was crowned at Rouen in 1563 and had already administered the Edict there. Grenoble had been hit by plague, and the party could not reach Rennes due to rebellions.
33. Knecht, *French Renaissance*, 260–3.
34. "Catherine's objectives in the tour of France," in Potter, ed., *French Wars*, 89.
35. "Catherine's objectives in the tour of France," in Potter, ed., *French Wars*, 89–90; see Treasure, *The Huguenots*, 7.
36. Carroll, *Noble Power*, 126–32; Knecht, *Catherine*, 96.
37. Wellman, *Queens and Mistresses*, 246.
38. Holt, *French Wars of Religion*, 2.
39. "Response A lescript du Ministre faict A orleans," in *Jean du Tillet*, ed. Brown, 79.
40. Columbus' voyage breached the 1479 Treaty of Alcáçovas signed by Castile, Aragon, and Portugal, and reiterated the 1481 papal bull *Æterni regis* (Eternal kings). It granted Portugal territorial rights to all lands discovered and undiscovered in the Atlantic south of the Canary Islands, which included Hispaniola, Cuba, and other Caribbean islands. Columbus was convinced that he had reached Asia, however, and with no way to verify the islands' locations, the issue was dropped. The fact that

Pope Alexander hailed from Spain certainly did not help the Portuguese cause.
41. René Laudonnière, *Three Voyages*, trans. Charles E. Bennett (Tuscaloosa: University of Alabama Press, 2001), xv.
42. Europe's rulers did not consider Native American claims to North America, even though tens of millions of them "occupied" the land for thousands of years before Europeans arrived.
43. Margaret F. Pickett and Dwayne W. Pickett, *The European Struggle to Settle North America: Colonizing Attempts by England, France and Spain, 1521–1608* (Jefferson, NC: McFarland, 2011), 47–61.
44. Knecht, *Renaissance Court*, 238–40.
45. "Declaration forbidding the Reformed religion at court, 24 July 1564" in Potter, ed., *French Wars*, 85; Treasure, *The Huguenots*, 20; Knecht, "Medici and Wars of Religion," 10.
46. Mack P. Holt, *The Duke of Anjou and the Politique Struggle during the Wars of Religion* (Cambridge: Cambridge University Press, 2002), 6–7.
47. Pickett and Pickett, *European Struggle*, 68, 82.
48. Laudonnière, *Three Voyages*, 17; Pickett and Pickett, *European Struggle*, 63.
49. "The deficit in the royal budget, 1561," in *French Wars*, ed. Potter, 14; Knecht, *French Wars*, 72.
50. Laudonnière, *Three Voyages*, xiii–xiv.
51. Letter from King Charles IX to Monsieur de Jarnac, January 16, 1563, in *Settlement of Florida*, ed. Charles E. Bennett (Gainesville: University of Florida Press, 1968), 129.
52. While incarcerated Ribault wrote his account of the expedition: *Whole and True Discoverye of New Florida* (1563). The original is at the British Library, Sloane MS 3644, ff. 111–21. Richard Hakluyt published Ribault's work in his *Divers Voyages* (1582) because by that point the 1563 original was impossible to find.
53. Van Ruymbeke, *New Babylon*, 4.
54. Laudonnière, *Three Voyages*, 51.
55. Pickett and Pickett, *European Struggle*, 75.
56. Carolus is the Latin version of Charles.
57. Charles E. Bennett, ed., *Laudonnière & Fort Caroline: History and Documents* (Tuscaloosa: University of Alabama Press, 2001), 12–32; Lyon, "Settlement and Survival," 41–2.
58. Geoffrey Parker, *Imprudent King: A New Life of Philip II* (New Haven & London: Yale University Press, 2014), 153–4; Eugene Lyon, "Settlement and Survival," in *The New History of Florida*, ed. Michael Gannon (Gainesville: University of Florida Press, 1996), 41.

59. Parker, *Imprudent King*, 297.
60. Lyon, "Settlement and Survival," 42.
61. Parker, *Imprudent King*, 144, 154; Goldstone, *Rival Queens*, 91–6.
62. Aleck Loker, *La Florida: Spanish Exploration and Settlement of North America, 1500–1600* (Williamsburg: Solitude, 2010), 195–96.
63. Pickett and Pickett, *European Struggle*, 70–83; Parker, *Imprudent King*, 154; Mary L. Frech, *Chronology and Documentary Handbook of the State of Florida* (Dobbs Ferry, NY: Oceana, 1973), 2; Lyon, "Settlement and Survival," 42–6.
64. Quoted in Freida, *Catherine*, 196.
65. Laudonnière, *Three Voyages*, xix.
66. Letter from Catherine de Medici to Raymond Fourquevaux, French Ambassador to Spain, March 17, 1566, in *Settlement of Florida*, ed. Bennett, 181.
67. Letter from Catherine de Medici to Raymond Fourquevaux, French Ambassador to Spain, March 17, 1566, in *Settlement of Florida*, ed. Bennett, 182.
68. Frieda, *Catherine*, 198.
69. Letter from Catherine de Medici to Raymond Fourquevaux, French Ambassador to Spain, March 17, 1566, in *Settlement of Florida*, ed. Bennett, 178–82.
70. Letter from Catherine de Medici to Raymond Fourquevaux, French Ambassador to Spain, March 17, 1566, in *Settlement of Florida*, ed. Bennett, 178–82.
71. Letter from the Spanish Embassy, April 6, 1566, in *Settlement of Florida*, ed. Bennett, 142.
72. Lyon, "Settlement and Survival," 50; *Settlement of Florida*, ed. Bennett, 204–5.
73. *Settlement of Florida*, ed. Bennett, 188.
74. The threat posed by Spain loomed large in Western Europe. Catherine formed an alliance with Elizabeth I of England against Spain by signing the Treaty of Blois (1572), while England supported the Dutch rebels fighting Spain in the Low Countries.
75. Roger Crowley, *Empires of the Sea: The Siege of Malta, the Battle of Lepanto, and the Contest for the Center of the World* (New York: Random House, 2008), 58.
76. Suraiya Faroqhi, *The Ottoman Empire and the World Around It* (London: I.B. Tauris, 2007), 33–37.
77. Faroqhi, *Ottoman Empire*, 37, 91.
78. Caroline Finkel, *Osman's Dream: The Story of the Ottoman Empire, 1300–1923* (New York: Basic Books, 2006), 151.
79. Crowley, *Empires of the Sea*, 191–2.

80. Claude Haton on the conspiracy of Meaux, 28–9 September 1567, and Condé's justification, October 1567, in Potter, ed., *French Wars*, 102–3; Knecht, "Medici and Wars of Religion," 20; Freida, *Catherine*, 201–3.
81. Quoted in Knecht, *French Renaissance*, 250.
82. Wellman, *Queens and Mistresses*, 243; Goldstone, *Rival Queens*, 107–9.
83. Geddis, *Landscape of History*, 99.
84. *Settlement of Florida*, ed. Bennett, 192–3; for an alternative perspective on the Saint Bartholomew's Day Massacre as a turning point in the Wars of Religion, see Diefendorf, *Beneath the Cross*, 177.
85. See, for example, Holt, *Duke of Anjou*, 19–20; Diefendorf, *Beneath the Cross*, 93–6 doubts her role too.
86. Susanne Lachenicht, "Huguenot Immigrants and the Formation of National Identities, 1548–1787," *The Historical Journal* 50, 2 (2007), 310; Bertrand Van Ruymbeke, "Minority Survival: The Huguenot Paradigm in France and the Diaspora," in *Memory and Identity: The Huguenots in France and the Atlantic Diaspora*, ed. Bertrand Van Ruymbeke and Randy J. Sparks (Columbia: University of South Carolina Press, 2003), 3; Treasure, *Huguenots*, 106; Nigel Aston, *Religion and Revolution in France, 1780–1804* (Washington, D.C.: Catholic University Press of America, 2000), 61–72; Jon Butler, *The Huguenots in America: A Refugee People in New World Society* (Cambridge: Harvard University Press, 1984), 1–15; Knecht, *French Wars*, 59.

Bibliography

Aston, Nigel. *Religion and Revolution in France, 1780–1804.* Washington, D.C.: Catholic University Press of America, 2000.

Bennett, Charles E. ed. *Settlement of Florida*. Gainesville: University of Florida Press, 1968.

Bennett, Charles E. ed. *Laudonnière & Fort Caroline: History and Documents.* Tuscaloosa: University of Alabama Press, 2001.

Broomhall, Susan. "'My daughter, my dear': the correspondence of Catherine de Médicis and Elisabeth de Valois." In *Women's History Review* 24, 4. (2015): 548–69.

Brown, Elizabeth A. R., ed. *Jean du Tillet and the French Wars of Religion, Five Tracts, 1562–1569.* Binghamton: Center for Medieval & and Early Renaissance Studies, 1994.

Butler, Jon. *The Huguenots in America: A Refugee People in New World Society.* Cambridge: Harvard University Press, 1984.

Carroll, Stuart. *Noble Power during the French Wars of Religion: The Guise Affinity and the Catholic Cause in Normandy.* Cambridge: Cambridge University Press, 1998.

Carroll, Stuart. *Martyrs and Murderers: The Guise Family and the Making of Europe.* Oxford: Oxford University Press, 2009.
Crawford, Katherine. "Catherine de Medicis and the Performance of Political Motherhood." *Sixteenth Century Journal* 31, 3. (Autumn, 2000): 643-73.
Crawford, Katherine. "Constructing Evil Foreign Queens." In *Journal of Medieval and Early Modern Studies* 37, 2. (2007): 393-418.
Crawford, Katherine. *Perilous Performances: Gender and Regency in Early Modern France.* Cambridge: Harvard University Press.
Crouze, Denis. "The Regency of Catherine de Medici: Political Reason during the Wars of Religion." In *Sacred and Secular Agency in Early Modern France: Fragments of Religion.* Edited by Sanja Perovic, 37-51. London: Continuum, 2012.
Crowley, Roger. *Empires of the Sea: The Siege of Malta, the Battle of Lepanto, and the Contest for the Center of the World.* New York: Random House, 2008.
Diefendorf, Barbara. *Beneath the Cross: Catholics and Huguenots in Sixteenth-Century Paris.* New York: Oxford University Press, 1991.
Doran, Susan. "Elizabeth I and Catherine de Medici." In *"The Contending Kingdoms": England and France, 1420-1700.* Edited by Glenn Richardson, 115-32. Aldershot: Ashgate, 2008.
Durkee, Denice. "Religion and Power: A Comparison of Queen Elizabeth I and Catherine de Medici." In *McNair Scholars Journal* 7, 1. (2003): 61-9.
Faroqhi, Suraiya. *The Ottoman Empire and the World Around It.* London: I.B. Tauris, 2007.
Finkel, Caroline. *Osman's Dream: The Story of the Ottoman Empire, 1300-1923.* New York: Basic Books, 2006.
Frech, Mary L. *Chronology and Documentary Handbook of the State of Florida.* Dobbs Ferry, NY: Oceana, 1973.
Frieda, Leonie. *Catherine de Medici: Renaissance Queen of France.* New York: Fourth Estate, 2003.
Gaddis, John Lewis. *The Landscape of History: How Historians Map the Past.* New York: Oxford University Press, 2002.
Goldstone, Nancy. *The Rival Queens: Catherine de' Medici, Her Daughter Marguerite de Valois, and the Betrayal that Ignited a Kingdom.* New York: Back Bay Books, 2015.
Heller, Henry. *Anti-Italianism in Sixteenth-Century France.* Toronto: University of Toronto Press, 2003.
Holt, Mack P. *The Duke of Anjou and the Politique Struggle during the Wars of Religion.* Cambridge: Cambridge University Press, 2002.
Holt, Mack P. *The French Wars of Religion, 1562-1629.* 2nd ed. Cambridge: Cambridge University Press, 2005.

Jansen, Sharon L. *The Monstrous Regiment of Women: Female Rulers in Early Modern Europe*. New York: Palgrave Macmillan, 2002.
Kamil, Neil. *Fortress of the Soul: Violence, Metaphysics, and Material Life in the Huguenots' New World, 1517–1751*. Baltimore: Johns Hopkins University Press, 2005.
Knecht, Robert J. *Catherine de' Medici*. London and New York: Longman, 1998.
Knecht, Robert J. "Catherine de' Medici and the French Wars of Religion." In *Historian* 62. (Summer, 1999): 1–39.
Knecht, Robert J. *The French Civil Wars, 1562–1598*. Harlow: Pearson, 2000.
Knecht, Robert J. *The French Renaissance Court, 1483–1589*. New Haven: Yale University Press, 2008.
Kruse, Elaine. "The Virgin and the Widow: The Political Finesse of Elizabeth I and Catherine de' Medici." In *Queens & Power in Medieval and Early Modern England*. Edited by Carole Levin and Robert Bucholz, 126–40. Lincoln: University of Nebraska Press, 2009.
Lachenicht, Susanne. "Huguenot Immigrants and the Formation of National Identities, 1548–1787." In *The Historical Journal* 50, 2. (2007): 309–31.
Laudonnière, René. *Three Voyages*, trans. Charles E. Bennett. Tuscaloosa: University of Alabama Press, 2001.
Loker, Aleck. *La Florida: Spanish Exploration and Settlement of North America, 1500–1600*. Williamsburg: Solitude, 2010.
Lyon, Eugene. "Settlement and Survival." In *The New History of Florida*. Edited by Michael Gannon, 48–58. Gainesville: University of Florida Press, 1996.
MacCaffrey, Wallace T. "The Newhaven expedition, 1562–1563." In *The Historical Journal* 40. (1997): 1–22.
Mentzer, Raymond A., and Andrew Spicer, eds. *Society and Culture in the Huguenot World, 1559–1685*. Cambridge: Cambridge University Press, 2002.
Parker, Geoffrey. *Imprudent King: A New Life of Philip II*. New Haven & London: Yale University Press, 2014.
Pickett, Margaret F., and Dwayne W. Pickett. *The European Struggle to Settle North America: Colonizing Attempts by England, France and Spain, 1521–1608*. Jefferson, NC: McFarland, 2011.
Potter, David, ed. and trans. *The French Wars of Religion: Selected Documents*. New York: St. Martin's Press, 1997.
Roberts, Penny. "Huguenot petitioning during the wars of religion." In *Society and Culture*. Edited by Mentzer and Spicer, 62–77. Cambridge: Cambridge University Press, 2002.

Smith, Ronald D. *Fascinating People and Astounding Events from the History of the Western World*. Santa Barbara: ABC-CLIO, 1990.

Strage, Mark. *Women of Power: The Life and Times of Catherine de' Medici*. New York and London: Harcourt Brace Jovanovich, 1976.

Sutherland, N.M. "Catherine de Medici: The Legend of the Wicked Italian Queen." In *Sixteenth Century Journal* 9, 2. (July, 1978): 45–56.

Treasure, Geoffrey. *The Huguenots*. New Haven: Yale University Press, 2013.

Van Ruymbeke, Bertrand. "Minority Survival: The Huguenot Paradigm in France and the Diaspora." In *Memory and Identity: The Huguenots in France and the Atlantic Diaspora*. Edited by Bertrand Van Ruymbeke and Randy J. Sparks, 1–25. Columbia: University of South Carolina Press, 2003.

Van Ruymbeke, Bertrand. *From New Babylon to Eden: The Huguenots and Their Migration to Colonial South Carolina*. Columbia: University of South Carolina Press, 2006.

Wellman, Kathleen. *Queens and Mistresses of Renaissance France*. New Haven & London: Yale University Press, 2013.

CHAPTER 4

Isabel Clara Eugenia, Governor of the Spanish Netherlands: Trade, Politics, and Warfare, Ruling like a King 1621–1633

Estelle Paranque

Will the Infant have more power than the Governors without any royal blood? It seems that it will be the case, because of her age, of her quality [...] However, her authority has to be limited.[1]

On July 13, 1621, Albert VII, Archduke of Austria and co-sovereign of the Habsburg Netherlands, died. His wife Isabel Clara Eugenia—Infant of Spain and daughter of the late king Philip II of Spain—was appointed by Philip IV of Spain as Governor of the Spanish Netherlands, which was an acceptable title for women at the time.[2] On July 25, 1621, Isabel accepted the governance of the territories, as she had promised to her husband.[3] At that time, the political and military situation in Europe was extremely complicated, as the Thirty Years' War began in 1618 and the Eighty Years' War resumed in 1621, keeping Philip IV and his aunt Isabel greatly preoccupied.

Isabel's involvement in the restoration and defense of the Catholic faith, her representation in literature, and her education have been thoroughly studied. However, her diplomatic skills and her role in the European wars and how that shaped her authority have too often been overlooked.[4] While Manuel Fernandez recognized that Isabel

E. Paranque (✉)
New College of the Humanities, London, UK

© The Author(s) 2017
E. Paranque et al. (eds.), *Colonization, Piracy, and Trade in Early Modern Europe*, Queenship and Power, DOI 10.1007/978-3-319-57159-1_4

demonstrated remarkable political skills as a co-sovereign of the Low Countries with her husband from 1598 to 1621,[5] the focus has remained on her role as a princess or as a wife.[6] As Philip II's eldest daughter, she has drawn lots of attention from scholars and played an important role in dynastic politics. From her first marriage negotiations to her claims to the French throne scene, Cristina Borreguero Beltrán has revealed the importance of Isabel's status on the European political scene.[7] Magdalena S. Sanchez has focused on the significance of Isabel and her husband's fight for their sovereignty and legitimacy.[8] In spite of their limited power imposed by Spain, Isabel and her husband did not compromise their willingness to play an important role in European politics.[9] Sanchez also discusses the change of titles for Isabel before and after her husband's death, and engages with the Infanta's "reaction to her demotion."[10] Despite Sanchez's essay being a much needed initial stepping stone in understanding Isabel's authority and political role in Europe, it fails to engage with her true involvements in crucial events, such as the wars that ravaged Europe during the seventeenth century.

By reviewing the minutes of the letters exchanged between Isabel and Philip IV of Spain from 1621 to 1633, this chapter portrays Isabel as a stateswoman who played a great role in diplomatic relations and was in charge of important decisions regarding trade agreements and warfare.[11] She was more than just a good match for European princes and a devoted wife who let her husband rule more or less on her behalf.[12] Isabel's own influence and authority need to be further considered and analyzed. Beyond the image of her as a chaste widow and pious wife, she also governed the Spanish Netherlands on her own for twelve years and proved to be a skilled councilor to her nephew, the king of Spain, as well as a shrewd politician. This has not been previously acknowledged. Isabel's ability to rule needs to be explored and understood; this essay seeks to determine both the extent to which she was directly involved in establishing commercial relations and her exact role in European politics and warfare.

Isabel's Involvement in Trade

When in 1621 Isabel agreed to become Governor of the Spanish Netherlands, she lost her title of co-sovereign. Yet, the responsibilities that came after her husband's death seemed to have increased. It was no longer her husband or anyone else who was in charge of "day-to-day business of state, meeting with councilors, negotiating issues, and formulating policy."[13] While Albert was alive, he did consult her on some issues, but publicly she had no decision power. After his death, Isabel started to rule on her own—which included making decisions on important aspects of government and dealing with the requests of her nephew Philip IV of Spain and other councilors.

Furthermore, she became Governor at a very difficult time—during the Thirty Years' War that was about to ravage Europe with bloody battles.[14] Securing trade agreements remained a crucial issue. In many instances, Philip IV of Spain gave Isabel direct orders regarding those agreements. This shows that to some extent she could be portrayed as a Spanish puppet who only did what she was told. For instance, on December 3, 1621, Philip wrote to the Infant expressing his desire that she give the order to her ambassador in England to accept the propositions made by English merchants.[15] In that letter, Isabel was not given a choice and could therefore be only perceived as an agent serving the Spanish crown. In another letter sent three years later, Philip's eagerness to remain in charge of the trade agreements between Spain and the Netherlands was clearly stated. In fact, Isabel was ordered to wait for the Spanish ministers and councilors to make a decision on trade agreements with the Netherlands.[16] However, some elements suggest that Isabel was much more involved in trade matters than was believed at first, and that she finally positioned herself as very much in charge in the eyes of not only the Spanish court but also other Europeans countries. Despite playing the role of Spain's puppet, the Governor had her own voice.

Her actual decision power needs to be assessed. Isabel's involvement in trade affairs was twofold: she appointed competent people to secure trade agreements, and made decisions on the specificities of some commercial treaties and how they were pursued. For example, in September 1621, Dutch pirates blocked England's trade with the Spanish Netherlands. The Earl of Gondomar, who was the Spanish ambassador at the English court at that time, was told that he needed to negotiate with the people nominated by Isabel in order to proceed favorably.[17] The fact that the Infant was the one responsible for nominating people who would be in charge of managing the trade affairs of her territory demonstrates her interest and involvement in the matter. In a letter sent to the Spanish king in 1622, Isabel informed him that she examined some measures regarding the commercial relations with Spain in order to protect the profits and to exclude the Dutch.[18] She was well aware of what was at stake, and her role in trade was well established. Other letters showed that she was highly involved in the maintenance thereof. In 1624—without consulting the king of Spain—she ordered the revocation of some of the licenses that enabled English merchants to trade with Holland. Shortly thereafter, the Spanish king wrote a letter saying that he was pleased with her decision, as it partially interrupted the commerce between England and Holland.[19] It shows that Isabel had a good judgment regarding commercial affairs. Furthermore, regarding the trade agreements with Denmark, he again gave her power to make independent decisions, showing his trust in her judgment.[20] In 1631, she informed him of her decision to implement new rules to facilitate the transit of timber through the Meuse and the Rhine.[21] In these letters dealing with trade agreements and commercial relations, we have concrete examples of Isabel's responsibility regarding these matters and how she acted as a ruler in her own right—negotiating with other rulers and defending both Netherlandish and Spanish interests.

On other occasions, Isabel worked closely with Philip in order to reach a compromise and pursue trade agreements with other countries that would be valuable for both of their realms. From the sixteenth century onward, the commerce of salt grew, as did its importance in Europe.[22] In 1630, Isabel shared her concerns with the king of Spain regarding the passports given to the Dutch in order to look for salts in Spanish and Portuguese ports. She suggested that all salt exports should be forbidden without her agreement.[23] Philip seemed to have been reluctant to agree as negotiations between the two continued. In another letter, the Infant expressed distaste for all of the inconvenient solutions that he had suggested on the topic of salt trade, and she offered to refrain from making a decision until further moderated custom rights were implemented for all, except in the case of Holland.[24] The fact that she did not necessarily agree with him and challenged his decisions affirmed her own authority.

Despite Isabel only being the Governor of the Spanish Netherlands, it is clear from these letters that she undertook full responsibility in important aspects of ruling, such as trade agreements and negotiations. While she was working closely with Philip and often receiving orders from him, she did give her opinion as well and showed her willingness to be in charge of commercial relations. Being involved in such a significant part of governing the Spanish Netherlands helped Isabel shape her own authority, demonstrating that her voice mattered on the European scene.

Isabel & European Politics: Representative of Spain, Counsel, and Involvement

In many instances, Isabel was used by the Spanish Court as a representative of the Crown and as such received many orders and requests from Philip. In September 1621, she was commanded to suggest a list of people suitable to be sent to Spain in order to represent the Spanish Netherlands' interests.[25] In other words, she did not have the final word on the appointment but she participated in the process. As a representative of the Spanish Crown, she was asked to maintain "the faith and fidelity" to Spain.[26] Furthermore in 1633, Philip shared his decision with Isabel regarding the truce with Holland because of their demands, such as "the conservation of Pernambuco and the authorization to trade with the Indies."[27] He stipulated that she entrust Pierre Roose—who had been appointed as councilor of state in 1630—with any decisions concerning that matter, which shows the imposed limitations on her role.[28]

At times of crisis, she showed her total obedience and allegiance to her nephew. In 1621, Isabel informed Philip that Van Male, her resident in England, had explained to her that some English merchants requested to serve the Spanish Crown against the Dutch and that she decided to wait for Philip's orders on the subject before acting.[29] In fact, on April 17, 1627, she wrote to him that she would always execute the orders that she received from him.[30] At the death of James I of England on March 27, 1625, Isabel informed Philip that his son Charles I, the new king of England, wrote to her "to let her know his desire to maintain the peace with the king of Spain."[31] In this letter, she appeared as a true mediator between the two monarchs.

Furthermore, it also seemed that she had been implicated in some espionage. Indeed, she was asked to look for information and report back to Philip regarding a Scottish marquess named "Hont" who was secretly "maintaining Catholicism in his country." The Spanish king also requested that she send a religious man to Scotland to assess "the state of Catholicism in this country."[32] Regarding another affair, Isabel disclosed her disappointment with the intelligence services of Emmanuel Sueyro (1587–1629) as there was a lack of results. She therefore decided not to raise his fees, unless Philip decided the contrary.[33] Two years later, the Infant approved a mission given to the Count of Gondomar (1567–1626) regarding some secret services in England and promised to assist him as much as she could.³⁴ To some extent, it could be argued that Isabel was used as a pawn or a mediator in the Spanish politics and that she did not really seem to have greatly participated. However, there were other elements that dominated the letters exchanged between Philip and his aunt that contradicted this view. To some extent, Philip's requests demonstrated that he trusted Isabel's ability to rule the Spanish Netherlands and that he saw in her a skilled councilor.

In many regards, Isabel advised Philip on highly important matters.³⁵ After all, she was defending Spain's interests in the Netherlands and working for the common good of both territories. On September 12, 1624, Isabel gave her honest opinion regarding Holland and the new coming war. She declared that it was "an endless war" and that "all enemies of Spain seek to maintain it, as the best resources of the King will be absorbed." She therefore advised him to put it to an end as soon as possible, as she believed that the war would reach Germany and that both England and France would become involved.³⁶

Four months later, after Isabel's prediction about Germany and England getting involved in the war had come true, she advised her nephew against handing over the Palatinate until the tension in Germany had settled. She did not understand why Holy Roman Emperor Ferdinand II and other Catholic princes were advising Philip otherwise. She warned him that the war would begin again in Germany and that he would regret giving up his control of the Palatinate.³⁷ In these two letters, we have a concrete example of Isabel's power in political matters and how she served Philip not only as a representative of Spain but also as a well-informed councilor. The Infant was determined to give freely her opinion regarding diplomatic alliances. In April 1624, she warned her nephew that the Protestant German princes were about to attack the king of Spain, either in the Spanish Netherlands or in the Palatinate. She also expressed her worries regarding France, predicting that "it is unlikely it will declare war but, that secretly, it will help the enemies."³⁸

Another example of direct counsel can be found in a letter she wrote to Philip in 1630. She boldly advised him on his relations with the Duke of Lorraine. In her mind, it was necessary "to cultivate the friendship" with the Duke as the Spanish king would need him for his affairs with the "Netherlands, Germany, and Italy, and especially against France."³⁹ Isabel proved to be well aware of the political stakes in Europe and how Spain could protect its assets, and she seemed comfortable sharing her views with her nephew. Furthermore, Philip recognized his aunt's ability to advise him well. On December 31, 1625, he sent documents to Isabel regarding the construction of a fort in "Champ-sur-Meuse" and asked for her advice.[40] A month later, he was pleased with Isabel's decision of "incarcerating the Governor of Ysendyck," a Dutch city.[41] He asked her "to discover if there is a secret French intrigue" and disclosed his interest in knowing Isabel's suggestions on the policy to undertake regarding the Dutch.[42] He then congratulated her "for her diligence regarding farms belonging to the Saint-Jean Order in the Palatinate."[43] These examples demonstrated that it was not only Isabel who openly gave her opinion to her nephew, but that he was also interested in having her advise him and was pleased with her political decisions.

On November 7, 1625, Philip informed Isabel regarding the negotiations with the Dutch, and wrote that "the Spanish ministers and councilors have examined the question with great care," yet he requested that she counsel him as he valued her "accustomed prudence"—demonstrating Isabel's significant role and position in Spanish affairs.[44] The term "prudence" is interesting to analyze as women during the early modern period were often seen lacking of it. John Knox (1513–1572), a sixteenth-century Scottish theologian, insisted that women "lack prudence and right reason" and that they were "unconstant, variable, cruelle, and lacking the spirit of counsel."[45] Clearly, in the Spanish king's opinion, Isabel was an exception. Philip also trusted his aunt regarding classified matters. On July 20, 1630, he informed Isabel that his secretary Antonio de Navaz told the Duke of Olivares, one of Philip IV's favorite, that a Scottish priest had Mary Stuart's will that she wrote "the night before her decapitation but only accepts to give it to us upon the conditions that we promise him a canonry or a prebend in the Netherlands and a reward of 1000 ducats."[46] He entrusted Isabel with the mission to assess the authenticity of the will.[47] Unfortunately, I could not find Isabel's reply nor could I find the evidence of what happened to the will but this secret mission implied that Philip undoubtedly trusted Isabel with delicate matters. Furthermore, he also approved of his aunt's domestic political decisions and was pleased to learn that she had dissolved the State Council in Brussels and had decided to replace it.[48] In these letters, we have concrete examples of Philip's appraisal of the Infant's wisdom and the fact that she had a strong voice in European and Spanish politics.

Indeed, at times, the Spanish king delegated tasks to the Infant. In 1621, Isabel was put in charge of ordering Inigo Vélez de Guevara,

7th Count of Onate (1566–1644), and Spanish ambassador to Vienna, to deal with German affairs on behalf of the Governor and the king. In his letter, Philip agreed with Isabel's decision to include the king of England in the negotiations against Holland. He also included a copy of the letter he had sent to the earl of Onate, letting Isabel know his position regarding that political matter.[49] In other cases, Isabel showed her strong desire to have more responsibilities. On July 29, 1624, she was pleased to see that her nephew ordered the earl of Onate to remind Ferdinand II not to hand over the Palatinate "without informing the Infant."[50] Isabel's true authority as Governor of the Spanish Netherlands was demonstrated by this letter in which Philip recognized her as a ruler in her own right. However, she did not need Philip to assert her power and she developed her own policies. A concrete example of her insisting on the importance of her decision-making was when she wrote to the Spanish king and declared that she had started "the negotiations with the Holy Roman ambassadors and the Duke of Bavaria to obtain the closure of the Elbe and of the Weser to the Dutch, the prohibition of the commerce for Germany, and the occupation of one port in the Baltic Sea."[51] She sent him copies of the letters exchanged on that matter, and she informed him that she agreed "with the Venetian ambassador, to demand from the Duke of Bavaria an immediate agreement on these three conditions."[52]

While this chapter has just argued that Isabel could be at times used as a pawn or a mediator in Spanish politics, her direct impact on political and diplomatic issues was indisputable. Indeed, Philip's requests for her advice and his respect for her decisions demonstrated that he trusted Isabel's ability to rule the Spanish Netherlands and that he saw in her a skilled councilor. Yet, with his trust came great responsibility, and Isabel's role in European politics was very much intertwined with the Thirty Years' War—with the fate of the Spanish Netherlands at the heart of the conflict.

Isabel & Warfare I: Finance & Strategy

The war that ravaged Europe during the first period of the seventeenth century forced Isabel to have a bigger hand in European politics. The Thirty Years War devastated Spain's economy, and, as a result, Philip and his aunt discussed at length the state of their realm's finances, which created some tension between them. On January 10, 1622, Isabel explained to her nephew how she had used the money from Naples to buy "three hundred pieces of artillery."[53] A month later, Philip apologized for not sending provisions earlier. He then stated that he had sent her "2,196,000 *écus*, 186,250 for the navy, and the rest for the army." He begged her to ensure that she shared this equally and promised to send the rest of what he owed her shortly.[54] Unfortunately, four months later, Isabel did not receive the funds promised and complained to her nephew that she was waiting with impatience for the rest of the money for this year as well as the special funds for the army in Palatinate, which was absolutely necessary if he wanted to avoid disorder.[55] In July 1622, she insisted again and sent a report showing what her army needed in terms of "artillery, food, recruitment, funding the pensions, ministers' pay, officials' pay, secret expenses (*los gastos secretos*), couriers, etc. Everything is paid on the provisions, as it has always been done, it is why we can only give to the soldiers half of their pay."[56] The Infant showed great care in dealing with expenses and paying her soldiers fairly. A year later, she reminded Philip of the financial situation. She wrote, "I have great sorrow and care, fearing two negative things."[57] She was concerned that the enemy's army might arrive soon and that the lack of funding for the soldiers would lead to some disorder in the king's army.[58] However, Philip's response could not be found.

The tone of Isabel's letters revealed the growing tension between them regarding finance. Twice Philip was displeased with how Isabel spent the money he sent to her. In 1627, the Infant was surprised to receive a letter from her nephew claiming that her soldiers had a "sumptuous life." She insisted that if there were some excess, she would take the necessary measures.[59] Again, in December 1631, the Spanish king showed his discontent with the state of the realms' finances and ordered Isabel to "seek the opinion of the councilors in charge of finances to reduce the expenses."[60] A few weeks later, Philip complained that the Infant did not follow the orders regarding the distributions of the funds. He wanted to make the soldiers' wages a priority, though Isabel protested that she had always acted with their interests in mind.[61] In another letter, it was Isabel's turn to be annoyed with her nephew's financial decisions. She warned him that the imperial armies sent to Westphalia needed funds and that she was surprised to hear that they had not received it yet. She therefore "took the initiative to send the money to the city [Cologne]," as she believed that losing the city would have catastrophic consequences for her realm.[62] However, these disagreements did not prevent Philip and Isabel from working closely together in sharing military strategies from which their realms would greatly benefit.

When Isabel became Governor of the Spanish Netherlands, she could not have imagined that during the next twelve years she would have to develop such strong military skills. On September 22, 1621, in a letter to her nephew, she wrote of her awareness of the army's duties. She explained that Spinola had left on the Wesel River with a great part of the soldiers, that the prince of Orange had met the Dutch army near Rees, and that Count Henri de Berghes had encircled the city of Juliers.[63] Two days later, she insisted on the advantages of having a truce in Palatinate, as it would allow her to send back to the Netherlands part of the army, where soldiers were needed.[64]

Through her involvement, she was able to appear as a strong female Governor and military leader. Beyond her awareness of her army's strategy, Isabel was outspoken about her views on military plans of action. It has been previously argued that Isabel was at times a crucial adviser to Philip IV of Spain. Indeed, not only did she advise him on political matters, but she also contributed greatly to his war strategies. In 1622, Isabel refused to send forces requested by the Archduke Leopold V of Further Austria (1586–1632) to protect Alsace, in case Ernest de Mansfeld would attempt to invade it. For Isabel, "the Spanish army does not have enough soldiers either in the Netherlands, in the duchy of Juliers nor in Palatinate to be able to accept his request."[65] The letters exchanged between the two sovereigns from later that same year reveal the dynamic of Isabel and Philip's relationship. Indeed, "the Infant has examined the question asked by the king if they could bring the new Spanish troops in the Netherlands by land or by sea. The journey by sea would be dangerous, given the naval forces of the enemy."[66] She then suggested that they be sent by land through Italy so that when they arrived in autumn, they could be ready for the next attack.[67] A couple of months later, Philip requested that his aunt examines a number of options for hindering the French with Ambassador Spinola and Ambassador Bermar, as the French were trying to pressure the Spanish forces in Italy.[68]

Three years later, Isabel showed her involvement in further war strategies and wrote that she had examined the document relating the military tactics to use against England.[69] According to this letter, the Governor seemed to have been well aware of the plan and made important suggestions. She stated that it was better to "directly attack England," but she admitted that in order to do so, they would need strong ships.[70] She also pointed out that such an enterprise would raise suspicions from their enemies and that "the English and the Dutch would unite their forces and their squadrons to be equal or superior to the King's."[71] Therefore, she advised to send the troops in merchant ships and to make the journey several times in order to avoid any suspicions of a coming attack. She then raised the issue of Denmark and the fact they needed to be careful if they intended to launch an attack on England as the two crowns were allies.[72] Isabel demonstrated great wisdom by counselling her nephew not to rush into any armed actions as the English had not declared war yet.[73] A year later, after the English had attacked Cadiz, she reiterated her previous declarations and insisted on "preparing the expedition with the greatest care."[74] She was well aware that a victory over the English would put the Dutch at bay and "ruin their commerce."[75] In these letters, Isabel demonstrated her military skills and her ability to plot against her enemy, and she therefore was a direct contributor to Spain's victory.

On February 4, 1627, Isabel wrote to Philip about her discussion with Eugene O'Neill about "a plan to invade Ireland."[76] She suggested that they could use the Irish regiment based in the Netherlands and then find out if the Irish population would be interested in starting a riot. She preferred a secret enterprise so "if it failed, it would not impact the Spanish king's reputation."[77] She warned her nephew not to attack Ireland directly but if he decided to do so, she promised to prepare a dozen ships.[78] Her involvement in military enterprises was a crucial component of her rulership. She was willing to share her ideas and advising her nephew on military matters. In 1629, Philip contemplated the possibility of implementing a truce with the Dutch.[79] Her reply showed that she understood the reasons that forced Philip to seek for peace—notably the state of the finances of their realms. However, she warned him that the Dutch were already taking advantage of Spanish weaknesses and had prepared 84 ships to launch an attack in the Americas. She insisted that the king had to resist the Dutch forces. She saw a great threat in their actions and believed that they were ready to attack at the beginning of April.[80] In all their exchanged letters, Isabel proved to be an important military adviser who was knowledgeable about finances and warfare strategies. The responsibilities she had during the Thirty Years' War helped her develop a strong royal authority and fashion a martial identity that is heavily present in her correspondence.

Isabel & Warfare II: Responsibility, Authority, and Martial Identity

From virtually the moment she was appointed as sole Governor of the Spanish Netherlands in 1621, Isabel became a vital asset for European politics. That same year, the French king Louis XIII sent instructions to his ambassador at her court, M. Vicomte d'Auchy, insisting on maintaining good relations with Spain through Isabel,[81] whose significance to Spain and France lays in her embodiment of "the true union and friendship" between the three courts.[82] As Isabel's responsibilities in the war increased, she began sending reports on the navy and army to Philip. The Infant updated her nephew often about naval enterprises in particular. During the first months of 1622, she informed him that "two ships were sent the day of the Kings, the Saint Alfonse and the Saint Isabel; a third, the Saint Louis, will be sent in two days."[83] In March 1622, she wrote that "the Saint Louis was unfortunately lost in an accident with the goods it had taken" from another ship.[84] Two weeks later, she was pleased to announce that one of her vessels had attacked the Dutch three times.[85] These demonstrations of her being in charge of her navy as well as being very well-aware of where her ships were proved that Isabel was fit to govern like any other male ruler.

In addition, Isabel was also responsible for the nomination of officers in the army. In 1624, "the Infant decided to reinforce the army in Palatinate."[86] She explained that Ambrogio Spinola could not lead the army as he had other commitments in the Spanish Netherlands, and Gonzalès de Cordoba refused, so she named the Count Henri de Berhes head of the army.[87] Three years later, she ordered a raise funds in order to instate eight regiments of infantry in the Spanish Netherlands. She named the Count of Mansfeld to be the head of these forces, as she believed he had great knowledge in building canons, which demonstrates her own understanding of warfare.[88] She also supported Jean de Nassau's application to become "in charge of the artillery, even though it was previously destined to La Motterie."[89] Through these nominations, the Franco-Spanish Governor developed a martial identity.

In delicate and problematic situations, Philip gave special orders to his aunt. In 1626, when Portuguese gentlemen were arrested by the Dutch, he requested that she "must seek, with all means possible, to obtain their release."[90] A year later, the English captured a Spanish vessel sent to the Spanish Netherlands. Isabel was again asked to find a way to free them.[91]

These examples demonstrate that the Infant had concrete responsibilities regarding warfare and was very much trusted by Philip to be involved in fighting for Spain. Her role was key in these difficult times, and Philip IV acknowledged and used her aunt's expertise in martial matters.

Isabel did not shy away from a chance to have her voice heard. In May 1624, she "ordered the construction of eight new vessels."[92] In another letter, she demonstrated her warlike authority over male Governors. She ordered the Governor of Bourgogne to raise funds which would be at the disposition of the Archduke if needed. She ordered the same to the Duke of Lorraine.[93] She gave martial orders to the generals, such as Gonzalès de Cordoba who was requested by Isabel to bring his army near Luxembourg.[94] In 1633, she informed Philip that she had chosen to give the Duke of Lerme the title of Master of the General Military Camp, as it would allow them to have another high-ranking officer to command the soldiers.[95] Later, after hearing that Philip had sent Spanish vessels to attack the Dutch, the Infant sent the navy to support the attack and stated that at that time she had no other order to give but would do so when appropriate.[96] Philip thanked his aunt for her help—demonstrating that he respected her authority in warfare.[97]

Philip also granted her special powers during difficult times, further increasing her authority. In 1629, Philip sought a truce with the Dutch and as a result wrote to Isabel to give her "full power to conclude the truce in the form she judges appropriate." He also informed her that he was giving her "new powers to which he no longer attributes himself, the title of Count of Holland, recommending however to only use it in case of extreme need."[98] Philip clearly trusted her judgment. In 1625, he wrote that she could "accept the proposition that a Dutch pirate had made to come to Spain and serve the king." He asked her to give him a safe-pass. He also trusted her to ensure "the maintenance and expansion of his navy."[99] During the war, Isabel undoubtedly used her growing martial identity to emphasize the importance of her voice and her ability to govern with as much skill as any male leader.

Conclusion

On September 17, 1582, Philip II of Spain, Isabel Clara Eugenia's father, wrote to her: "you say, my oldest daughter, that it has been announced in Madrid the arrival of galleys coming from the Americas:

you have forgotten that they are not galleys, but vessels and very big ones."[100] Philip II wanted his sixteen-year-old daughter to be aware of the greatness of Spain which proved to be useful as she became involved in the wars that had ravaged Europe for decades during the seventeenth century and defended Spanish interests.

Isabel's involvement in trade, diplomatic relations, and warfare has been underestimated to the point that scholars have mostly focused on depicting a devoted wife and a rather discreet co-sovereign. This chapter has taken a new approach and has analyzed how the Governor of the Habsburg Netherlands demonstrated her power on the European political scene. As researchers, we tend to focus on queens' involvement in patronage, literature, and forms of religious devotion. However, this chapter has clearly proved that female rulers were part of masculine activities. From her role as a representative of Spain to a wartime leader, Isabel revealed that her political skills and her ability to govern were comparable to any strong male ruler. She was invested in her governmental duties, as Philip IV recognized in 1629 when he wrote to her that he knew that she "was giving of herself."[101] The Infant herself admitted to being "very affected by the recent defeats."[102] The letters in this chapter show how the fate of Spain and its empire mattered so much to her, which is further proof that Isabel was fit to rule, even without a male co-ruler, and that more work needs to be undertaken to assess her rulership skills. At the death of her husband, Isabel was no longer the discreet wife and Spanish Infant. She had a voice on the European scene, a powerful voice that made her a strong royal authority figure, and she should be remembered as such.

NOTES

1. The Marquis of Bedmar to Philip IV of Spain, July 23, 1621, in *Correspondance de la Cour d'Espagne sur les Affaires des Pays-Bas au XVII siècle, Précis de la Correspondance de Philippe IV d'Espagne avec l'Infante Isabelle*, recueil commencé par Henri Lonchay et continué par Joseph Cuvelier avec la collaboration de Joseph Lefèvre, Tome II (Bruxelles: Librairie Kiessling et Cie, P. Imbreghts, 1927) (later referred only to *Correspondance de la Cour d'Espagne*), 21, "L'Infante aura-t-elle des pouvoirs plus grands que n'eurent les autres gouverneurs de sang royal? il paraît que oui, à cause de son âge, de ses qualités [...]Il faut cependant que son autorité soit limitée."

2. By the death of the Archduke Albert, the region returned to Spain, as proclaimed by the 1598 Act of Cession. See Victor Brants, *Recueil des ordonnances des Pays-Bas, Règne d'Albert et Isabelle, 1597–1621*, vol. 1 (Bruxelles, 1909–1912), 8.
3. Isabel Clara Eugenia to Philip IV of Spain, July 25, 1621, in *Correspondance de la Cour d'Espagne*, 22.
4. In the famous collection on Isabel Clara Eugenia, two chapters are devoted to her Catholic faith and her relations with the Vatican: see René Vermeir, "The Infanta Isabel Clara Eugenia and the Papal Court (1621–33)," 338–357 and Joris Snaet, "Isabel Clara Eugenia and the Capuchin Monastery at Tervuren," 358–381. Another one deals with her representation in literature, Jaime Olmedo Ramos, "Isabel Clara Eugenia and Literature," 226–57 and another focuses on her education, Santiago Martinez Hernandez, "'Enlightened Queen, clear Cynthia, beauteous Moon': The Political and Courtly Apprenticeship of the Infanta Isabel Clara Eugenia," 20–59, in *Isabel Clara Eugenia: Female Sovereignty in the Courts of Madrid and Brussels*, ed. Cordula Van Wyhe (Centro de Estudios Europa Hispanica: Paul Holberton Publishing, 2011).
5. Manuel Fernandez, *Alvarez, Felipe II y su tiempo* (Madrid: Espasa Calpe, 16th edition, 2002), 235.
6. In his fascinating work on Archduke Albert, Luc Duerloo has a chapter where he only mentions Isabel as a wife and political partner. He does not engage with her role as a sovereign. See Luc Duerloo, *Dynasty and Piety: Archduke Albert (1598-1621) and Habsburg Political Culture in an Age of Religious wars* (London: Routledge, 2012), 61–67.
7. Cristina Borreguero Beltran, "Isabel Clara Eugenia: Daughter of the Spanish Empire," in *The Limits of Empire: European Imperial Formations in Early Modern World History: Essays in Honor of Geoffrey Parker*, eds. Tonio Andrade and William Reger (Farnham: Ashgate, 2012), 257–280.
8. Magdalena S. Sanchez, "Sword and Wimple: Isabel Clara Eugenia and Power," in *The Rule of Women in Early Modern Europe*, eds. Anne J. Cruz and Mihoko Suzuki (Urbana and Chicago: University of Illinois Press, 2009), 65.
9. Sanchez, "Sword and Wimple," 66.
10. Sanchez, "Sword and Wimple," 67.
11. The minutes describing the content of the letters were found in *Correspondance de la Cour d'Espagne*.
12. Sanchez, "Sword and Wimple," 71.
13. Sanchez, "Sword and Wimple," 70.

14. See John Theibault, "The Demography of the Thirty Years War Re-visited Günther Franz and his Critics," *German History* 15 (1): 1–21.
15. Philip IV of Spain to Isabel, December 3, 1621, in *Correspondance de la Cour d'Espagne*, 50.
16. Philip IV of Spain to Isabel, April 22, 1624, in *Correspondance de la Cour d'Espagne*, 156.
17. Philip IV of Spain to Isabel, September 4, 1621, in *Correspondance de la Cour d'Espagne*, 30.
18. Isabel to Philip IV of Spain, July 27, 1622, in *Correspondance de la Cour d'Espagne*, 90.
19. Philip IV of Spain to Isabel, April 26, 1624, in *Correspondance de la Cour d'Espagne*, 158.
20. Philip IV of Spain to Isabel, February 24, 1625, in *Correspondance de la Cour d'Espagne*, 203 and Isabel to Philip IV of Spain, February 26, 1625, in *Correspondance de la Cour d'Espagne*, 204.
21. Isabel to Philip IV of Spain, December 3, 1631, in *Correspondance de la Cour d'Espagne*, 593.
22. Guy Saupin, "Le commerce du sel entre Nantes et la côte nord de l'Espagne au XVIIe siècle," in *Le Sel de la Baie: Histoire, Archéologie, Ethnologie des Sels Atlantiques*, eds. Jean-Claude Hocquet and Jean-Luc Sarrazin (Rennes: Presses Universitaires de Rennes, 2006), 259–271; Jan De Vries, *The Economy of Europe in an Age of Crisis, 1600–1750* (Cambridge: Cambridge University Press, 1976).
23. Isabel to Philip IV of Spain, April 6, 1630, in *Correspondance de la Cour d'Espagne*, 526.
24. Isabel to Philip IV of Spain, May 31, 1630, in *Correspondance de la Cour d'Espagne*, 535.
25. Philip IV of Spain to Isabel, September 11, 1621, in *Correspondance de la Cour d'Espagne*, 32.
26. Philip IV of Spain to Isabel, September 11, 1621, 32.
27. Philip IV of spain to Isabel, July 19, 1633, in *Correspondance de la Cour d'Espagne*, 701.
28. Philip IV of spain to Isabel, July 19, 1633, 701.
29. Isabel to Philip IV of Spain, October 28, 1621, in *Correspondance de la Cour d'Espagne*, 46.
30. Isabel to Philip IV of Spain, April 17, 1627, in *Correspondance de la Cour d'Espagne*, 325.
31. Isabel to Philip IV of Spain, April 24, 1625, in *Correspondance de la Cour d'Espagne*, 214.
32. Philip IV of Spain to Isabel, November 27, 1629, in *Correspondance de la Cour d'Espagne*, 499.

33. Isabel to Philip IV of Spain, March 14, 1624, in *Correspondance de la Cour d'Espagne*, 149.
34. Isabel to Philip IV of Spain, February 16, 1626, in *Correspondance de la Cour d'Espagne*, 254.
35. Joanne Paul, Catherine Fletcher and Helen Matheson-Graham are working on an edited collection on *Queenship and Counsel* (New York: Palgrave Macmillan, forthcoming)—shedding light on the importance of women in diplomatic relations and their concrete role in advising others and receiving advice.
36. Isabel to Philip IV of Spain, September 12, 1624, in *Correspondance de la Cour d'Espagne*, 178.
37. Isabel to Philip IV of Spain, January 12, 1625, in *Correspondance de la Cour d'Espagne*, 197.
38. Isabel to Philip IV of Spain, April 19, 1624, in *Correspondance de la Cour d'Espagne*, 155.
39. Isabel to Philip IV of Spain, October 23, 1630, in *Correspondance de la Cour d'Espagne*, 558.
40. Philip IV of Spain to Isabel, December 31, 1625, in *Correspondance de la Cour d'Espagne*, 244.
41. Philip IV of Spain to Isabel, January 4, 1626, in *Correspondance de la Cour d'Espagne*, 246.
42. Philip IV of Spain to Isabel, January 4, 1626, 246.
43. Philip IV of Spain to Isabel, January 4, 1626, 246.
44. Philip IV of Spain to Isabel, November 7, 1625, in *Correspondance de la Cour d'Espagne*, 236.
45. John Knox, *The first blast of the trumpet against the monstruous regiment of women* (Geneva, J. Poullain and A. Rebul, 1558), 24 and 10.
46. Philip IV of Spain to Isabel, July 20, 1630, in *Correspondance de la Cour d'Espagne*, 544.
47. Philip IV of Spain to Isabel, July 20, 1630, 544.
48. Philip IV of Spain to Isabel, July 16, 1632, in *Correspondance de la Cour d'Espagne*, 632.
49. Philip IV of Spain to Isabel, September 11, 1621, in *Correspondance de la Cour d'Espagne*, 33.
50. Isabel to Philip IV of Spain, July 29, 1624, in *Correspondance de la Cour d'Espagne*, 173.
51. Isabel to Philip IV of Spain, July 12, 1626, in *Correspondance de la Cour d'Espagne*, 270.
52. Isabel to Philip IV of Spain, July 12, 1626, 270.
53. Isabel to Philip IV of Spain, January 10, 1622, in *Correspondance de la Cour d'Espagne*, 57.

54. Philip IV of Spain to Isabel, February 4, 1622, in *Correspondance de la Cour d'Espagne*, 59.
55. Isabel to Philip IV of Spain, June 12, 1622, in *Correspondance de la Cour d'Espagne*, 82.
56. Isabel to Philip IV of Spain, July 3, 1622, in *Correspondance de la Cour d'Espagne*, 85.
57. Isabel to Philip IV of Spain, June 2, 1623, in *Correspondance de la Cour d'Espagne*, 127, "Me tiene gran pena y cuidado, temiendo dos malos."
58. Isabel to Philip IV of Spain, June 2, 1623, 127.
59. Isabel to Philip IV of Spain, February 27, 1627, in *Correspondance de la Cour d'Espagne*, 311.
60. Philip IV of Spain to Isabel, December 14, 1631, in *Correspondance de la Cour d'Espagne*, 594.
61. Isabel to Philip IV of Spain, January, 27, 1632, in *Correspondance de la Cour d'Espagne*, 608.
62. Isabel to Philip IV of Spain, August 20, 1633, in *Correspondance de la Cour d'Espagne*, 705.
63. Isabel to Philip IV of Spain, September 22, 1621, in *Correspondance de la Cour d'Espagne*, 37.
64. Isabel to Philip IV of Spain, September 24, 1621, in *Correspondance de la Cour d'Espagne*, 37.
65. Isabel to Philip IV of Spain, January 10, 1622, in *Correspondance de la Cour d'Espagne*, 56.
66. Isabel to Philip IV of Spain, May 23, 1622, in *Correspondance de la Cour d'Espagne*, 78.
67. Isabel to Philip IV of Spain, May 23, 1622, 78.
68. Philip IV of Spain to Isabel, July 28, 1622, in *Correspondance de la Cour d'Espagne*, 92.
69. Isabel to Philip IV of Spain, November 5, 1625, in *Correspondance de la Cour d'Espagne*, 232.
70. Isabel to Philip IV of Spain, November 5, 1625, 232.
71. Isabel to Philip IV of Spain, November 5, 1625, 232.
72. Isabel to Philip IV of Spain, November 5, 1625, 232.
73. Isabel to Philip IV of Spain, May 20, 1624, in *Correspondance de la Cour d'Espagne*, 160.
74. Isabel to Philip IV of Spain, December 5, 1625, in *Correspondance de la Cour d'Espagne*, 241.
75. Isabel to Philip IV of Spain, December 5, 1625, 241.
76. Isabel to Philip IV of Spain, February 4, 1626, in *Correspondance de la Cour d'Espagne*, 307.
77. Isabel to Philip IV of Spain, February 4, 1626, 307.
78. Isabel to Philip IV of Spain, February 4, 1626, 307.

79. Philip IV of Spain to Isabel, February 14, 1629, in *Correspondance de la Cour d'Espagne*, 432.
80. Isabel to Philip IV of Spain, March 3, 1629, in *Correspondance de la Cour d'Espagne*, 434.
81. Louis XIII of France to M. Vicomte d'Auchy, 1621, BNF MS FR 15870, fols. 276–277.
82. Louis XIII of France to M. Vicomte d'Auchy, 1621, fol. 277.
83. Isabel to Philip IV of Spain, January 10, 1622, in *Correspondance de la Cour d'Espagne*, 56.
84. Isabel to Philip IV of Spain, March 21, 1622, in *Correspondance de la Cour d'Espagne*, 66.
85. Isabel to Philip IV of Spain, April 7, 1622, in *Correspondance de la Cour d'Espagne*, 70.
86. Isabel to Philip IV of Spain, July 12, 1624, in *Correspondance de la Cour d'Espagne*, 169.
87. Isabel to Philip IV of Spain, July 12, 1624, 169.
88. Isabel to Philip IV of Spain, February 28, 1627, in *Correspondance de la Cour d'Espagne*, 313.
89. Isabel to Philip IV of Spain, June 19, 1630, in *Correspondance de la Cour d'Espagne*, 537.
90. Philip IV of Spain to Isabel, June 9, 1626, in *Correspondance de la Cour d'Espagne*, 267.
91. Philip IV of Spain to Isabel, March 12, 1627, in *Correspondance de la Cour d'Espagne*, 318.
92. Isabel to Philip IV of Spain, May 20, 1624, in *Correspondance de la Cour d'Espagne*, 160.
93. Isabel to Philip IV of Spain, January 10, 1622, in *Correspondance de la Cour d'Espagne*, 57.
94. Isabel to Philip IV of Spain, August 16, 1622, in *Correspondance de la Cour d'Espagne*, 95.
95. Isabel to Philip IV of Spain, November 12, 1633, in *Correspondance de la Cour d'Espagne*, 724.
96. Isabel to Philip IV of Spain, September 9, 1622, in *Correspondance de la Cour d'Espagne*, 98.
97. Philip IV of Spain to Isabel, September 25, 1622, in *Correspondance de la Cour d'Espagne*, 100.
98. Philip IV of Spain to Isabel, July 26, 1629, in *Correspondance de la Cour d'Espagne*, 466.
99. Philip IV of Spain to Isabel, May 31, 1625, in *Correspondance de la Cour d'Espagne*, 221.
100. Philip II of Spain to the Infantas, September 17, 1582, in *Lettres de Philippe II à ses filles les Infantes Isabelle et Catherine écrite pendant*

son voyage en Portugal (1581–1583) publiées d'après les originaux autographes conservés dans les Archives Royales de Turin, par M. Gachard (Paris: Librarie Plon, 1884), 194.
101. Philip IV of Spain to Isabel, November 27, 1629, in *Correspondance de la Cour d'Espagne*, 498.
102. Isabel to Philip IV of Spain, January 24, 1630, in *Correspondance de la Cour d'Espagne*, 514.

Bibliography

Primary Sources

Manuscripts:
BNF MS FR 15870.

Printed:
Brants, Victor. *Recueil des ordonnances des Pays-Bas, Règne d'Albert et Isabelle, 1597–1621*. Vol. 1. Bruxelles, 1909–1912.
Correspondance de la Cour d'Espagne sur les Affaires des Pays-Bas au XVII siècle, Précis de la Correspondance de Philippe IV d'Espagne avec l'Infante Isabelle. Recueil commencé par Henri Lonchay et continué par Joseph Cuvelier avec la collaboration de Joseph Lefèvre, Tome II. Bruxelles: Librairie Kiessling et Cie, P. Imbreghts, 1927.
Knox, John. *The first blast of the trumpet against the monstruous regiment of women*. J. Poullain Geneva, and A. Rebul, 1558.
Lettres de Philippe II à ses filles les Infantes Isabelle et Catherine écrite pendant son voyage en Portugal (1581–1583) publiées d'après les originaux autographes conservés dans les Archives Royales de Turin. Par M. Gachard. Paris: Librarie Plon, 1884.

Secondary Sources

Borreguero Beltran, Cristina. "Isabel Clara Eugenia: Daughter of the Spanish Empire." In *The Limits of Empire: European Imperial Formations in Early Modern World History: Essays in Honor of Geoffrey Parker*. Edited by Tonio Andrade and William Reger, 257–280. Farnham: Ashgate, 2012.
De Vries, Jan. *The Economy of Europe in an Age of Crisis, 1600–1750*. Cambridge: Cambridge University Press, 1976.
Duerloo, Luc. *Dynasty and Piety: Archduke Albert (1598–1621) and Habsburg Political Culture in an Age of Religious wars*. London: Routledge, 2012.
Fernandez, Manuel. *Alvarez, Felipe II y su tiempo*. Madrid: Espasa Calpe, 16th edition, 2002.

Martinez Hernandez, Santiago. "'Enlightened Queen, clear Cynthia, beauteous Moon': The Political and Courtly Apprenticeship of the Infanta Isabel Clara Eugenia." In *Isabel Clara Eugenia: Female Sovereignty in the Courts of Madrid and Brussels.* Edited by Cordula Van Wyhe, 20–59. Centro de Estudios Europa Hispanica: Paul Holberton Publishing, 2011.

Olmedo Ramos, Jaime. "Isabel Clara Eugenia and Literature." In *Isabel Clara Eugenia: Female Sovereignty in the Courts of Madrid and Brussels.* Edited by Cordula Van Wyhe, 226–57. Centro de Estudios Europa Hispanica: Paul Holberton Publishing, 2011.

Sanchez, Magadalena S. "Sword and Wimple: Isabel Clara Eugenia and Power." In *The Rule of Women in Early Modern Europe.* Edited by Anne J. Cruz, and Mihoko Suzuki, 64–79. Urbana and Chicago: University of Illinois Press, 2009.

Saupin, Guy. "Le commerce du sel entre Nantes et la côte nord de l'Espagne au XVIIe siècle." In *Le Sel de la Baie: Histoire, Archéologie, Ethnologie des Sels Atlantiques.* Edited by Jean-Claude Hocquet, and Jean-Luc Sarrazin, 259–271. Rennes: Presses Universitaires de Rennes, 2006.

Snaet, Joris. "Isabel Clara Eugenia and the Capuchin Monastery at Tervuren." In *Isabel Clara Eugenia: Female Sovereignty in the Courts of Madrid and Brussels.* Edited by Cordula Van Wyhe, 358–381. Centro de Estudios Europa Hispanica: Paul Holberton Publishing, 2011.

Theibault, John. "The Demography of the Thirty Years War Re-visited Günther Franz and his Critics." In *German History* 15 (1): 1–21.

Vermeir, René. "The Infanta Isabel Clara Eugenia and the Papal Court (1621–33)." In *Isabel Clara Eugenia: Female Sovereignty in the Courts of Madrid and Brussels.* Edited by Cordula Van Wyhe, 338–357. Centro de Estudios Europa Hispanica: Paul Holberton Publishing, 2011.

PART II

Diplomatic Strategies

CHAPTER 5

Caterina Cornaro and the Colonization of Cyprus

Lisa Hopkins

Few queens can have had their reigns more closely linked to questions of colonization and trade than Caterina Cornaro, last queen of Cyprus. Married as a teenager to effectively the last of the Lusignan kings, James II (their son James III nominally succeeded his father but died before his first birthday) after having been declared a Daughter of Venice for the occasion, she achieved the surprising feat of translating her initial position of queen consort into that of queen regnant. Although for much of her reign she was in fact little more than a puppet of the Venetian Republic in whose favor she was eventually induced to abdicate, she and her story exercised an extraordinary fascination over both contemporaries and posterity. It is also notable that her principal rival for the crowns of Cyprus, Jerusalem, and Armenia was another potential queen regnant, Carlotta de Lusignan, legitimate sister of the bastard James II; moreover, when a coup was mounted against Caterina in November 1473, its nominal aim was to secure the succession of a third female candidate,[1] James II's illegitimate daughter Charla, even though Charla had two brothers living (though its real beneficiary would have been the

L. Hopkins (✉)
Sheffield Hallam University, Sheffield, UK

husband proposed for Charla, who was the son of Alfonso of Naples).[2] After generations of Lusignan kings, there suddenly appeared to be an appetite for a queen, and a willingness to accept that the queen might be Lusignan either by marriage or by birth. There were some striking similarities between Caterina and Carlotta: Carlotta, like Caterina, had a son who died as a baby and ultimately ceded her rights to her nephew, whom she adopted, as Caterina ceded hers to her "father" and brother and wished to adopt her nephew Giacomo, son of her sister Bianca. This chapter examines the way these two women attempted to negotiate queenship, the conducting of trade, and the vexed question of whether Cyprus would be forced into the status of a colony of Venice or allowed to retain such independence as it had from its Egyptian Mameluke suzerains. I shall suggest that although there were also practical considerations in play, the major difference in the way that Caterina and Carlotta approached the role of queen was that Caterina drew on iconography and symbolism and Carlotta did not.

In 1468, James of Lusignan, by then reigning as James II of Cyprus, married Caterina Cornaro. The Lusignan family had ruled in Cyprus since 1192, when Richard the Lionheart rewarded his ally Guy of Lusignan, already titular king of Jerusalem, with the gift of the island. Until the previous year, Cyprus had been ruled by Isaac Komnenos, a descendant of the Byzantine royal family, but Komnenos was unfortunate enough to refuse water to a ship carrying Richard's bride Berengaria and his sister Joanna when it put in at Limassol and to deal harshly with some of Richard's troops who were shipwrecked on their way to Acre. As a result, Richard expelled him, and for the next 300 years, the island was a Lusignan possession. James's bride was not of the same status, but had attractions of her own. As Liana De Girolami Cheney observes: "the Cornaro family ... had close commercial ties with Cyprus, administering copper and sugar-mills and exporting other Cypriot goods to Venice."[3] They also claimed importance in their own right, since they maintained that they were descended from "the Roman general Scipio Africanus, his daughter Cornelia, and her children, including Gaius and Tiberius Gracchi [sic], from whom the Corner family claimed descent;"[4] Caterina normally included "Cornelii" among her names to signify this supposed link to the *gens Cornelia*. It was a rich irony that Gaius and Tiberius Gracchus derived their fame from the attempt to redistribute land from the wealthy to the poor, whereas the marriage of Caterina was designed to secure yet more land for Venice, but she may have had the precedent of her supposed ancestors in mind when, as queen, she sent shiploads of wheat to the inhabitants of Nicosia and when the epitaph she had erected to James referred to him as "this new Caesar."[5] An extra resonance was added by the fact that Caterina had Hellenic as well as supposedly Roman ancestry: Her mother Fiorenza was the granddaughter of the Emperor of Trebizond and the daughter of the Duke of Naxos, and the Corner family's long history of trade had habituated them to the Hellenic world. From James's perspective, the logic of the marriage was simple: He had no fleet, and Venice could give him one.[6] He was marrying ships, and Caterina was marrying the grain, sugar, salt, and textiles which were vital to the trade interests of her family and city (Cyprus lawn in particular being a commodity that was highly valued, and one with which Caterina was to become associated).

The proxy marriage between Caterina and James took place in the Doge's palace and for the occasion, Caterina was officially adopted as a Daughter of the Republic. Venice presented the adoption as something instigated by James to boost the status of his bride;[7] however, it may also have been important that adoption had a Roman precedent, with a number of emperors having adopted their heirs, given that Caterina's family set considerable store by their supposedly classical antecedents, and given too that Cyprus had also been part of the Roman Empire (it was famously given by Mark Antony to Cleopatra as a love-gift). Her official title was "Daughter of St Mark—an unprecedented honor which caused the Bishop of Turin acidly to observe that he never knew that St Mark had been married and that, even if he had, his wife must surely be a little old to have a child of fourteen."[8] The "adoption" and the grandiose title it brought proved characteristic of the way Caterina's later image was to be constructed in terms of allegory and mythology. Of course, St Mark did not have a wife or a daughter; but then no one seriously supposed it to mean that. St Mark needed to be evoked in connection with the marriage of Caterina because he connoted not only Venice itself but also Alexandria: His body had lain there until the ninth century, when it was said to have been removed by Venetian traders because it would otherwise have been desecrated by hostile Muslims. Alexandria was a hugely important trade center,[9] and the vulnerable geographical position of Cyprus also meant the Egypt had become an increasingly important player in its affairs. The suggestion that the Venetians had bested it by removing an important relic from it offered the chance for valuable political and iconographical capital. For Venice, possession of the body of the saint boosted its own status and presented the city as a bastion of Christendom, implicitly contesting the rival powers of both Ottoman Turkey and Mameluke Egypt.

This did not, however, mask the fact that in the struggle for succession to the Lusignan throne, it was Egypt who was ultimately the power-broker. In the years leading up to the marriage between James II and Caterina, the Sultan helped first James, then his legitimate half-sister Carlotta, after she paid him more, then James again. James told the Sultan (who presumably agreed) that "nature meant royal power for men, not women,"[10] and Carlotta was pushed back to Kyrenia, though the fortress there was so strong that she was able to hold it for the better part of 3 years. Eventually, however, Carlotta's resistance crumbled and she was driven off the island to Rhodes, where her allies the Knights Hospitaller of St John of Jerusalem were willing to receive her. The papacy continued to support her, but when she "tried to persuade a Venetian fleet that 'James, now dead, was a bastard and held the kingdom wrongfully ...,' the commander refused because James was 'the king appointed by the sultan',"[11] a formulation which combined hypocrisy with *realpolitik* in that it acknowledged the unmistakable reality that Egypt was much closer to Cyprus than Venice and much better placed to influence its destiny. It was this political background which conditioned the adoption and the bestowal of the title "Daughter of St Mark," since by invoking St Mark as the authorizing figure for the marriage of James and Caterina, Venice could present itself as having superseded and overreached Egypt by covertly alluding to the way it had outwitted the Egyptians by abstracting the body of the saint from Alexandria and suggest a new future with a different political orientation for Cyprus. In an added iconographical complication, Caterina herself seems not only to have built on the association with Venus brought to her by her marriage, but may also have cultivated an association with her namesake St Catherine of Alexandria, who was reputed to have been born at Famagusta in Cyprus. (Although it is impossible to be certain that the painting often believed to represent her with a Catherine wheel really is of her, the private chapel of her later retreat at Asolo was undoubtedly dedicated to the saint.)

Stressing the link with St Catherine not only boosted Caterina's personal iconography but also increased the sense that what was at stake in her marriage to James was ultimately whether Cyprus would remain part of Christendom. Central to the cultural identity of Lusignan Cyprus was that it was originally a crusader kingdom.[12] Its history was fundamentally bound up with the history of crusade and so too were the histories of both the Cornaro family and of Venice itself: Holly Hurlburt notes that one of Caterina's ancestresses inherited the crusader duchy of Naxos, and Venetian expansion into the eastern Mediterranean was tied to the Fourth Crusade. One of Carlotta's most powerful strategies was to suggest that the Christian status of Cyprus was threatened by her brother's activities: She alleged among other things that her half-brother made gifts of Christian children to the Sultan,[13] and her most faithful allies, the Knights Hospitaller, and successive popes, consistently presented her as the candidate backed by the church. The coup of November 1473, which aimed to have James's bastard daughter Charla and her putative husband Alfonso, son of the king of Naples, named as Caterina's heirs, also drew on the language of religion to oppose Caterina and Venice when the rebel lords bestowed on Alfonso the resonant title of Prince of Galilee.[14] In this climate of competition for religious and iconographic authority, Caterina was wise to stress her own connection to St Catherine.

The marriage between James and Caterina was much more than the union of two individuals: As the declaration that Caterina was a Daughter of St Mark clearly implied, it was an alliance between Venice and Cyprus, in which Venice definitely intended to be the senior partner. The reasons why Venice wanted Cyprus were complicated. Holly Hurlburt notes that "Cyprus, sought after by both the Duchy of Savoy and Naples and nominally claimed by the sultan of Egypt, was a key bulwark in Venetian commerce and defense against the Ottoman Turks;"[15] it is no coincidence that the principal surviving sign of the eventual Venetian occupation of the island is the defensive walls of Nicosia, now the most complete surviving example of a Venetian fortification scheme, but in its day a shocking disruption to the marble and white stucco of the Lusignan city. Cyprus also had material resources to offer as well as the potential for lucrative taxation; Benjamin Arbel notes "the efforts invested by Venice in the financial and economic spheres, aiming at bringing the still formally independent kingdom into total subjection to Venice" and cites a number of records which reveal the conviction of various Venetian officials that somebody somewhere on Cyprus was making money out of the island, but that it was difficult to establish who and how.[16] Yet Antonis Hadjikyriacou has recently argued that when the Turks eventually conquered Cyprus in 1571, they soon found that the island was not particularly useful to them,[17] and for Venice too, it was valuable but not essential in financial terms. Michael Paraskos suggests that in fact Venice's interest in the island was not purely commercial but that it also saw in Cyprus an island of romance and of the imagination, which he sees as influencing the Arcadian and pastoral elements of Venetian art; in particular, he argues that Venice's interest in Cyprus is reflected in a sudden growth of interest in Venus as a subject for paintings, citing, for instance, the *Sleeping Venus* of Giorgione.[18]

In 1473, 5 years after his wedding to Caterina, James II died, possibly poisoned, and a few months afterward the only son whom Caterina had borne him also died. Although James had put his bastards into the line of succession, the legitimate successor was his half-sister Carlotta. According to one English writer, Cyprus did have a precedent of sorts for female rule in the shape of Carlotta's mother, Helena Paleologa:

> Helena the wife of John, king of Cyprus, who perceiving that his husbands weakenesse was a blot whereon the greatest part of his nobility continually plaied, and that the Kingdome was the stake at which they aimed, & which unles hir better skil prevented, they by their false play were like to winne; shee tooke the gouernement into hir owne hands, to the release of the Land, and the reliefe of all his subiects.[19]

Pope Pius II agreed that Helena Paleologa "acted more as king than queen," and Holly Hurlburt notes that the island had also had female regents in the past.[20] As William Monter remarks, several of the Cypriot barons were prepared to see Carlotta crowned,[21] and she also received support from the Knights of St John, who had forty-one estates on Cyprus[22] and who after the fall of Acre had spent nearly 20 years in Limassol before moving to Rhodes.[23] Carlotta was not, however, acceptable to the Venetians, and Caterina was installed instead, reigning at least nominally on her own for 15 years until 1489, when she was effectively forced to abdicate in favor of the Venetian Republic and retire into private life.

Why was Caterina able to see off the challenge of Carlotta, when Carlotta had on her side the advantages of being legitimate, a Lusignan, and someone who had been known since birth to the Cypriot aristocracy? On one level, the answer is both obvious and simple: Caterina, the Daughter of St Mark, had the power of Venice behind her, and the Republic was prepared to back her to the hilt, whereas Carlotta's allies the Knights Hospitaller were prepared to put themselves out for her only in direct proportion to her ability to deliver the sugar concession. The Knights might publicly align themselves with Carlotta's cause, but privately they were prepared to do business with whoever won: Nicholas Coureas notes that although they pleaded with the Sultan on her behalf and supplied reinforcements for her garrison in Kyrenia,

> the Hospitaller desire for an accommodation with James is illustrated by a letter Jacques de Milly sent on 11 October, 1460 to Niccolò de Corogna, the commander of Treviso, and to Jean de Chailly, commander of Auxerre, instructing them to go to Cyprus and have Louis of Savoy [Carlotta's husband] escorted away from Cyprus should he wish, but also to secure his assent for a temporary accommodation with Jacques so that their goods and incomes from Kolossi, under the care of Brother William de Combort, would be secure.[24]

The Knights' support was conditional, and Carlotta ultimately failed to meet the condition.

There is more to it than that, however. Although her own city of Venice grew to distrust her, Caterina seems to have had a hold over the imaginations of the Cypriot citizens, who supported her when some of her late husband's disaffected followers mounted a *coup* in the autumn of 1473. Her appeal may owe something to practical measures such as the shipments of wheat which she sent from Famagusta to Nicosia, or to the fact that she was careful not to outrage Cypriot sensibilities: Gilles Grivaud notes that "Boustronios présente surtout Catherine Cornaro comme une souveraine consciente de l'héritage institutionnel propre à la monarchie des Lusignan" ("Above all [the Cypriot chronicler] Boustronios presents Catherine Cornaro as a sovereign aware of the institutional heritage of the Lusignan monarchy").[25] However, there was also surely an element of simple glamor, as she herself registered when she complained to the Venetian envoy Mocenigo about the fact that the restrictions he had placed on her personal freedom made her unable to show herself to her subjects. Almost the first thing we hear about Caterina is that she was beautiful, and though the one undoubtedly authentic portrait (the Bellini, which was painted c. 1500) shows her when she was older and does little or nothing to capture that legendary beauty, even in it Caterina is deploying her clothes and jewels to very deliberate effect. The pearls and the lawn both connote Cyprus, and both are set off by the background of black which was her favorite color: Black cloth was the most expensive, and black had been the signature color of Philip the Good, Duke of Burgundy, whose court was the richest in Europe, so it spoke of wealth and style. Finally, the mysterious pendant which looks like a shark's tooth may serve to connect her to the sea, evoking her potential identification with Venus and reminding viewers of the fundamentally maritime identities of Venice and Cyprus, both of which Caterina can be seen as emblematizing here. In a sense, it does not even matter that this is the only portrait of her whose status and authenticity is uncontested: The other paintings which may represent her may not be so securely identified, but the fact that they have gravitated into her orbit is in itself testimony to her cultural appeal.

That cultural appeal was to a considerable extent a function of Caterina's gender. James II may have had a point (at least in a fifteenth-century context) when he told the Sultan that Nature intended royal power for men not women, but Art found women a much more fertile ground for mythological inscription. Caterina's body may have limited her potential for wielding political power, but it vastly increased her potential for mythopoeic power. This was something which Elizabeth I of England would also discover in the century which followed, but in a rather different way. In Elizabeth's case, some of her most successful uses of iconography worked by inverting the widespread cultural trope which figured women as land to be colonized, as in the description of Ireland by Luke Gernon:

> This Nymph of Ireland is at all poynts like a yong wenche that hath the greene sicknes for want of occupying. She is very fayre of visage, and hath a smooth skinn of tender grasse …Her breasts are round hillockes of milk-yeelding grasse, and that so fertile, that they content wth the vallyes. And betwixt her leggs (for Ireland is full of havens), she hath an open harbor, but not much frequented…It is nowe since she was drawne out of the wombe of rebellion about sixteen yeares, by'rlady nineteen, and yet she wants a husband, she is not embraced, she is not hedged and ditched, there is noo quicksett putt into her.[26]

Gernon's envisaging of Ireland as a nubile virgin desperate for sex draws on a common Renaissance trope which analogizes land to be conquered to women to be married; Holly Hurlburt neatly notes that "Both before and after Christopher Columbus famously imagined the earth as a woman's breast, [many men] described what Anne McClintock has called 'the porno-tropics'."[27] Elizabeth countered this in images such as the Ditchley Portrait, in which she dominated the land rather than vice versa. However, although Elizabeth used marine imagery, she never went to sea; the closest she came was the legendary speech at Tilbury Docks. Caterina, by contrast, inhabited a watery world. Her youth was spent in Venice, a city configured by its lagoon and canals, and for the duration of her reign, she lived in Cyprus, important above all for its island status and its crucial place on sea routes. In traveling between the two, moreover, she made two long sea journeys. This was of course a practical inevitability, but it also had symbolic and iconographical consequences. On both her arrival in Cyprus and her eventual return to Venice, she came from the sea, as Venus did, and on both occasions, she emitted an almost tangible aura of sexual potential.

Caterina came to Cyprus as a bride, the intended wife of a young king who had conspicuously advertised his virility by already fathering at least four bastards. What one might loosely term the propaganda associated with the marriage repeatedly stressed her beauty and desirability: Bartolomeo Pagello wrote a poem for Caterina's proxy wedding which evokes Venus, goddess of love and beauty, and the obvious intention of the alliance was that she should also prove fertile. The fact that she only ever produced one child and that child died in infancy perhaps blinds us to the importance of her role as prospective breeder, and although once she was widowed, Venice ultimately recalled her, it does not follow that it was always the plan to unseat the Lusignan dynasty and simply annex the island. It is perhaps not beyond the bounds of possibility that James II's death was hastened once Caterina was pregnant, though that would have been a risk, since her child might have been a girl or stillborn; however, it is equally possible (and arguably more probable) that he simply died of natural causes, as Caterina herself always believed. It is even less likely that the death of the small James III was attributable to anything other than natural causes: Small children died at a distressingly high rate, and he seems to have contracted malaria. There is no reason to suppose that a Venetian agent poisoned him, and nothing obvious for Venice to gain by doing so. The Republic's intention was surely that Caterina would produce at least one child (she came from a large family, which might have been thought to bode well for her own fertility) and that child would be allowed to live. This was the promise inherent in her arrival in Cyprus, and it made her a walking emblem of sexuality and fertility. Moreover, one of her favorite political tactics was matchmaking; she proposed marrying James's bastards Janus and Charla to her brother and sister, respectively,[28] strengthening her association with fertility and matrimony.

This association might seem no longer to obtain on her return to Venice. However, Caterina was still a young woman, and she could still have remarried. Again, that she did not ultimately do so may blind us to the fact that she could have, at almost any time after the death of James II. Venice consistently feared this, and it was presumably one reason why the Councilors sent by the Republic to impose order after the failed *coup d'état* kept her from the public view: Having initially (and so recently) marketed her as a paragon of beauty, they now became anxious that beauty should not be seen, since Venice now valued her not for her potential in the marriage market but as their bridge to the island of Cyprus, of which she had in effect become a personification. Throughout the period of her nominal rule, any suggestion of a possible remarriage for her was greeted with alarm and indignation by the Republic, as had happened in the case of other female heiresses to Mediterranean islands such as Caterina's ancestress Fiorenza Sanudo. Certainly, one of their motivations in ultimately recalling her was to close down that possibility, and it is not surprising that the iconography associated with the queen underwent a dramatic shift after her return to Venice and in particular after her move to Asolo, where she was allowed luxury in exchange for a retreat into ethereality and into the rarefied and hence unthreatening values of platonic love and courtly admiration.

In her retreat at Asolo, the chapel of her palace, the *Barco*, was dedicated to Catherine of Alexandria,[29] but in other respects, it was time for a change of iconographical emphasis. Hurlburt notes that:

> according to some interpretations, her chosen lifestyle and sacrifice allowed her to recapture virginal status. In his 1489 oration, Taddeo Bovolini proclaimed,

> you, most illustrious queen, such an inexperienced young woman, in the midst of the realm of Venus, surrounded by so many royal delights, fragile from your feminine sex ... should be praised all the more for your continence, that you remained as if a virgin ... fleeing the marriage knot in order to make an offering of your chastity to God.[30]

When she made a ceremonial entrance into Brescia with her brother, the iconography focused on Diana, goddess of chastity, rather than Venus, goddess of love, and her chariot was drawn by white horses equipped with horns to make them look like unicorns, creatures which according to legend could be tamed only by virgins;[31] later the poet Giambattista Liliani, writing toward the end of Caterina's life, compared her to Dido.[32] The idea of an African queen was not inappropriate given Caterina's supposed descent from Scipio Africanus, but it also chimed with the idea of widowhood. Dido was not a wholly safe example—she had after all fallen in love with Aeneas—but at least she had committed suicide rather than actually marrying him and founding an alternative dynasty. In some ways, indeed, Dido is the ideal analogue for Caterina: A queen who might have been a threat, but was ultimately neutralized. Dido was, moreover, a queen whose kingdom no longer existed, and by recalling Caterina, Venice had effectively ensured that Cyprus, once the seat of nine kingdoms, would no longer be one at all.

Carlotta by contrast wielded none of this soft power. Carlotta was not a self-publicist and seems not to have understood how and why she might become so; there are no known portraits of her mother Helena Paleologa,[33] suggesting that the family lacked an iconographical tradition (at least in respect of its female members), and Carlotta never learned the power of the image. She too was said to be beautiful, but the only known portraits of her are both freschi and hence accessible only to a limited audience. There is a particularly sharp difference between the two women when it comes to coinage.[34] Gilles Grivaud notes that Alice of Jerusalem-Champagne, who in the thirteenth century was regent for her son Henry I, had her image on Cypriot coins; Caterina followed this precedent and had her own image on her coinage. Carlotta by contrast issued coins but does not appear on them; instead, they show the Lusignan arms. After her marriage to Louis of Savoy, her coinage bore his image.[35] As a result of decisions like these, Carlotta never attained the cultural cachet or mythopoeic power of Caterina. Caterina became a figure of myth and legend; Carlotta never captured the imagination in the same way. Carlotta focused on two things in her pursuit of the crown: Right, both in terms of her own legitimate descent and also in the sense that she tried to present the Christian status of Cyprus as contingent on her accession; and trade, in particular the strong investment of the Knights Hospitaller in sugar. These were insufficient either separately or together. Nobody was interested in right (Venice certainly was not), and Carlotta lacked the resources to be able to exploit the potential of the sugar trade with any real degree of effectiveness. At a basic level, it was simply much harder for Carlotta to exert real control over the material resources of Cyprus than it was for Caterina to treat it as an empire of the imagination and to finesse the material into the symbolic. It is also worth thinking for a moment about what Caterina did *not* do: She did not take a lover, unlike that other claimant to the title of Queen of Jerusalem Juana II of Naples, who had been notorious earlier in the century. Nor did she remarry. When Carlotta was left heir to the throne, the Cypriot barons' first move had been to find her a new husband, since her first, John of Portugal, had died after only a year of marriage; the choice fell on Louis, a younger son of the duke of Savoy, whose mother, Anne of Lusignan, was Carlotta's aunt. Caterina by contrast fought it out on her own terms as a woman with some iconographical assistance from a goddess and a female saint, and did even attempt to exercise power independently for a while, partly from Famagusta and partly from her summer palace at Potamia. The other way of putting this is to say that Carlotta tried to be a female king, whereas Caterina acted and presented herself as a queen.

Caterina, in marked contrast with Carlotta, was the subject of a number of important portraits, even though it is not always now possible to be confident about which ones are intended to represent her. The Uffizi's *Portrait of Caterina Cornaro*, for instance, may not only be either by Titian or by Giorgione, but it may not be of Caterina. As Michael Paraskos has recently observed, the title of queen of Cyprus had been charged with new valencies by Boccaccio's resurrection of it as a title for Venus. Hurlburt notes that some visual representations of Caterina effectively cast her personally in the role of accessory to that title: Images "in which the queen hands her crown, the symbol of her authority, to the doge, would be repeated multiple times in prominent private and public spaces across the city in the early modern period."[36] Most notably, Monter notes that "Money was coined and decrees were issued in the name of Catherine of Venice, *Caterina Veneta*"[37] (though it is actually spelt Katerina in deference to the island's Greek culture), so that her personal identity is entirely subsumed into her political one.

Sometimes, however, the queen's own status is boosted. Liana De Girolami Cheney comments on the importance of copper color in her iconography, specifically in the putative Titian painting which may show Caterina as St Catherine, signifying the mineral wealth of Cyprus as well as the etymology of its name.[38] Copper mining was so central to the economy and history of Cyprus that it had even given the island its name, which derives from the Greek word for copper; when Venus was referred to in the classical literature as Cypris, both Cyprus and copper lurked behind the title. To connect Caterina to copper not only identified her with the island but also created powerful allegorical overtones. Pierre de la Primaudaye comments on the labor involved in Renaissance mining, observing that:

> AS God declareth a great and maruellous prouidence in all his creatures (as we haue discoursed in treating vpon them) so also doth he manifest it vnto vs in the creation of mettals, and especially of gold and siluer, which are esteemed for the most precious. For we see how he hath hidden them in the most deepe places of the earth, and hath couered them with great and high mountaines: so that to dig & draw them out of their profound caues, men must therein so trauell, as if they had enterprised to ouerturne and to transport these lofty hils from one place to another, and to search and pierce through the earth from one side to another.[39]

There is a clear sense here that it is not only the miners who are being incommoded and pained, for he speaks of stones and minerals as being conditioned by humors in much the same way as Renaissance medicine supposed the human body to be:

> some precious stones which are white, haue beene generated by an humour hauing the colour of water, which maketh them more cleere and more transparent then others: and so the variety which is in the colours of all stones, bee they greene, blew, red, purple, yealow, or of many mingled colours, one must iudge the humours whereof they did proceede at first to haue beene such: and that other precious stones which are not transparent proceed from troubled, blacke and obscure humours.[40]

De la Primaudaye's implicitly anthropomorphizing image tropes minerals as constituted by much the same processes as were thought to operate in the human body. This symbolic link between woman and the birth of underground materials such as copper makes Caterina doubly an incarnation of the goddess Venus' title of Cypris, as she becomes both personification of Cyprus and goddess of symbolic if not literal motherhood and fertility. Michael Paraskos also notes another potential allusion to Cyprus in the Uffizi painting in the shape of "the fabric falling from the sitter's headdress, which resembles the gauze-like fabric produced in Cyprus at the time."[41] Cyprus lawn was famous for its quality, so it is not surprising that Caterina (if this is indeed a portrait of her) should be wearing it, but it would also further cement the identification with the island and by implication with Venus. Hurlburt notes too that "pearls were a commodity characteristic of Caterina's Cyprus," and that she is shown wearing a large quantity.[42]

This splendor of royal, divine, and hagiological iconography sat uneasily, though, alongside the brutal realities of how circumscribed Caterina's position actually was and how few her options were. A later but equally important (and undoubted) painting of Caterina by Bellini worked in a rather different way from the Uffizi image: De Girolami Cheney notes that "When the Metropolitan Museum restored the painting in 2011, it found an inscription on the back of Bellini's *Caterina Cornaro, Queen of Cyprus*, stating, 'The senate of Venice calles me daughter. Cyprus, seat of nine kingdoms, is subject to me. You see how important I am, yet greater still is the hand of Gentile Bellini, which has captured my image on such a small panel'."[43] Caterina matters, but she matters less than either Venice, which sponsors her, or Bellini, whose art is valorized above her image. Moreover, Caterina's image was also a potential liability to her. Hurlburt observes that "Venice's ethos of individual humility cautioned against lavish personal expenditure, and … the city fathers were especially sensitive to female expenditures, blaming them for the republic's economic woes and misfortunes"; "because Caterina Corner's alleged lavish lifestyle reflected no glory onto a husband, and only simply onto her civic adopted parent, in the eyes of Venice it fulfilled no public function, and was categorized as female vanity."[44] Caterina repeatedly pleaded poverty and was repeatedly accused by Venice of extravagance,[45] and it is certainly true that she did indeed earn some money from the tax on salt. The real point, however, was that as *feme sole*, Caterina was valuable as a potential asset, but also dangerous, particularly if she remarried. It was the same dilemma that Elizabeth I would face in the next century, and like Elizabeth, Caterina was also vulnerable to sexual slander: In the seventeenth century, she was referred to by an Italian writer as "extremely inclined to the burning appetites of the flesh,"[46] and it perhaps did not help that the Lusignan family into which she had married was popularly supposed to descend from the mermaid Melusine, mermaids being notorious as symbols of sexual looseness.

Venice was well aware of the danger of a potential remarriage and treated Caterina from the start as a threat as much as an opportunity. John Julius Norwich notes that after the death of James II, Pietro Mocenigo, Venice's *capitano da mar*, was dispatched to Cyprus; he was "instructed to act through the Queen as far as possible, but was specifically empowered to use force if necessary."[47] Mocenigo did initially try to preserve the fiction that Caterina was ruling independently, but it came to an abrupt end on November 13, 1473 when a group of Cypriots led by the Archbishop of Nicosia invaded the palace at Famagusta, killed Caterina's uncle Andrea Corner and her cousin Marco Bembo, and forced her to agree to betrothing James's bastard daughter Charla to the bastard son of Alfonso of Naples (who was himself shortly to be mooted as a suitor for Caterina). Venice sent first Mocenigo, the *capitano da mar*, and next two Councilors to restore order, making Caterina a puppet; Norwich observes that "At one period she and her father had to complain that her protectors had become more like jailers; she was forbidden to leave the palace, her servants were withdrawn and she was even compelled to take her meals alone, at a little wooden table."[48] By 1475, Caterina was appealing to Mocenigo, now Doge, that her situation had become intolerable and that she herself was invisible,[49] while her father acidly observed that of his five daughters, the one who was nominally a queen was treated much the worst.

Eventually, Caterina gave up the struggle. Her brother Zorzi was sent to Cyprus nominally in order to persuade her to resign the rights to the republic, but in practice to compel her to do so, since it was abundantly clear that she had no choice. Hurlburt attributes Venice's decision to depose her to two things: the threat of the Turks and the fear that she might remarry.[50] They might also have been alarmed at the possibility that the Cornaro family in general, even if not Caterina herself, could try to exercise independent power in Cyprus. Her father Marco at one point proposed sending a hundred elite Venetian families to settle on Cyprus[51]; those families might have stayed loyal to the Serenissima, or they might have drifted away from it. In any case, Venice preferred to found its colonies on its own terms. Benjamin Arbel notes that there were from the outset signs that Venice clearly considered Cyprus "as a subject territory while Queen Caterina Cornaro was still occupying the royal throne" but that those signs strengthened significantly in later years: "towards the end of the protectorate, official Venetian deliberations were less cautious in using colonial terms when referring to Cyprus."[52] Venice needed no help from the Cornaro family in turning the island into a colony.

Caterina sailed from Famagusta on March 1, 1489. Surrender of her crown to Venice brought her political safety and iconographical rehabilitation: As Terence Mullaly has it, "When Caterina again set foot in her native Venice she stepped out of history and into immortality."[53] Her nephew Marco, still only eighteen, became a cardinal; her brother Zorzi, who took to quartering the Lusignan arms with his own, found his fortune made. Hurlburt observes that "Corner's surrender earned her a place in the pantheon of masculine heroism in history, memory, and on the Maggior Consiglio ceiling."[54] Hurlburt notes particularly "The frequent depiction of Corner with a doge" and the careful distinction between what *he* wore and what *she* wore: However, much it might resemble one, the headpiece worn by the doge was not a crown, which is what is worn by both Caterina and the allegorical Venetia as Queen of the Adriatic.[55] In place of Cyprus, the Venetian government supplied Caterina with the small fiefdom of Asolo, where she built a palace named the *Barco*. Insofar as this was a cage, it was an exceptionally gilded one: John Julius Norwich observes that when the Emperor Maximilian invaded Italy, he made Asolo his headquarters,[56] and accommodation that was fit for an emperor was presumably good enough for a queen. Her visitors there included Dürer, who seems to have sketched her, and other artists,[57] a reminder that even after her deposition, her image continued to be important (and was to remain so for a considerable time to come).

In effect, Caterina and Carlotta represented not only competing dynastic claims but also competing ideological positions and contrasting understandings of trade and colonization. Carlotta encapsulated a practical, pragmatic attitude which sought to do business with the Knights of St John over the material resources Cyprus had to offer. Caterina by contrast projected an evocative, romanticized image which disdained the coarse realities of trade and could be used to mystify Venice's acquisition of Cyprus in terms of myth, allegory, and manifest destiny. In the short term, neither won, but in the longer term, while Carlotta has to been virtually forgotten, Caterina has remained a legend in both Venice and Cyprus.

Notes

1. The arrival of Mocenigo on 3 February put an end to the attempted coup, and the citizens of Cyprus appear to have stayed loyal to Caterina throughout.
2. Charla died in Venetian captivity in 1480, at the age of twelve.
3. Liana De Girolami Cheney, "Caterina Cornaro, Queen of Cyprus," in *The Emblematic Queen: Extra-Literary Representations of Early Modern Queenship*, ed. Debra Barrett-Graves (Basingstoke: Palgrave Macmillan, 2013), 11–34, 10.
4. Holly S. Hurlburt, "Body of Empire: Caterina Corner in Venetian History and Iconography," *Early Modern Women* 4 (2009): 61–99, 77.
5. Holly S. Hurlburt, *Daughter of Venice: Caterina Corner, Queen of Cyprus and Woman of the Renaissance* (New Haven: Yale University Press, 2015), 51.
6. William Monter, *The Rise of Female Kings in Europe, 1300–1800* (New Haven: Yale University Press, 2012), 81.
7. Hurlburt, *Daughter of Venice*, 37.
8. John Julius Norwich, *The Middle Sea: A History of the Mediterranean* (London: Vintage, 2007), 251.
9. Hurlburt, *Daughter of Venice*, 112.
10. Hurlburt, *Daughter of Venice*, 22.
11. Monter, *The Rise of Female Kings in Europe*, 82.
12. Hurlburt, *Daughter of Venice*, 4.
13. Hurlburt, *Daughter of Venice*, 22.
14. Hurlburt, *Daughter of Venice*, 61.
15. Hurlburt, "Body of Empire," 66.
16. Benjamin Arbel, "A Fresh Look at the Venetian Protectorate of Cyprus (1475–89)," in *Caterina Cornaro: Last Queen of Cyprus and Daughter of Venice*, eds. Candida Syndikus and Sabine Rogge (Münbster: Waxmann, 2013), 214.
17. Antonis Hadjikyriacou, "The Ottomanisation of Cyprus: towards a spatial imagination beyond the centre-province boundary," *Journal of Mediterranean Studies* 25.1 (2016), 83–98.
18. Michael Paraskos, "Plausible Cypriot Influence on Venetian Art and Society?," unpublished paper.
19. D. T., *Asylum veneria, or A sanctuary for ladies* (Edward Griffin for Laurence L'isle, 1616), 108–9.
20. Hurlburt, *Daughter of Venice*, 19–20.
21. Monter, *The Rise of Female Kings in Europe*, 79–80.
22. Hurlburt, *Daughter of Venice*, 77.

23. Victor Mallia-Milanes, "Introduction to Hospitaller Malta," in *Hospitaller Malta 1530–1798: Studies on Early Modern Malta and the Order of St John of Jerusalem*, ed. Victor Mallia-Milanes (Msida: Moreva, 1993), 2.
24. Nicholas Coureas, "Participants or Mediators? The Hospitallers and Wars Involving 15th Century Lusignan Cypruse," in *Ordines Militaires: Yearbook for the Study of the Military Orders* 28 (2013), 201.
25. Gilles Grivaud, Un règne sans fastes—Catherine Cornaro à travers les sources produites à Chypre, in *Caterina Cornaro: Last Queen of Cyprus and Daughter of Venice*, eds. Candida Syndikus and Sabine Rogge (Münbster: Waxmann, 2013), 242.
26. Andrew Hadfield and Willy Maley, "Introduction: Irish representations and English alternatives," in *Representing Ireland: Literature and the Origins of Conflict, 1534–1660*, eds. Brendan Bradshaw, Andrew Hadfield, and Willy Maley (Cambridge: Cambridge University Press, 2010), 4.
27. Hurlburt, *Daughter of Venice*, 48.
28. Hurlburt, *Daughter of Venice*, 3 and 76.
29. De Girolami Cheney, "Caterina Cornaro," 21.
30. Hurlburt, "Body of Empire," 99.
31. Hurlburt, *Daughter of Venice*, 167.
32. Hurlburt, *Daughter of Venice*, 145.
33. Grivaud, "Un règne sans fastes," 234.
34. Hurlburt, *Daughter of Venice*, 72.
35. Grivaud, "Un règne sans fastes," 232 and 235.
36. Hurlburt, "Body of Empire," 64.
37. Monter, *The Rise of Female Kings in Europe*, 82.
38. De Girolami Cheney, "Caterina Cornaro," 23.
39. Pierre de la Primaudaye, *The French academie Fully discoursed and finished in foure bookes* (1618), 854–855.
40. De la Primaudaye, *The French academie*, 848.
41. Paraskos, "Plausible Cypriot influence on Venetian Art and Society."
42. Hurlburt, *Daughter of Venice*, 207.
43. De Girolami Cheney, "Caterina Cornaro," 25. On what the nine kingdoms were, see Maria Iacovou, "Mapping the Ancient Kingdoms of Cyprus: Cartography and Classical Scholarship during the Enlightenment", in *Eastern Mediterranean Cartographies*, eds. George Tolias and Dimitris Loupis (Athens: Institute for Neohellenic Reseach, 2004), 263–285.
44. Hurlburt, "Body of Empire," 72–73.
45. Hurlburt, *Daughter of Venice*, 87.
46. Hurlburt, *Daughter of Venice*, 48.

47. John Julius Norwich, *The Middle Sea: A History of the Mediterranean* (London: Vintage, 2007), 252.
48. Norwich, *The Middle Sea*, 252–53.
49. Hurlburt, *Daughter of Venice*, 84–85.
50. Hurlburt, *Daughter of Venice*, 102.
51. Hurlburt, *Daughter of Venice*, 88.
52. Arbel, "A Fresh Look at the Venetian Protectorate of Cyprus (1475–89)," 226.
53. Terence Mullaly, "Caterina 'Domina' of Asolo: Lady of the Renaissance," in *Caterina Cornaro, Queen of Cyprus*, eds. David Hunt and Iro Hunt (London: Trigraph, 1989), 147.
54. Hurlburt, "Body of Empire," 73.
55. Hurlburt, "Body of Empire," 83 and 87.
56. Norwich, *The Middle Sea*, 257.
57. De Girolami Cheney, "Caterina Cornaro," 19.

Acknowledgements With thanks to Jim Fitzmaurice, Michael Paraskos, and Nicholas Coureas.

Bibliography

Primary Sources

De la Primaudaye, Pierre. *The French academie Fully discoursed and finished in foure bookes*. 1618.

D. T. *Asylum veneria, or A sanctuary for ladies*. Edward Griffin for Laurence L'isle, 1616.

Secondary Sources

Arbel, Benjamin. "A Fresh Look at the Venetian Protectorate of Cyprus (1475–89)." In *Caterina Cornaro: Last Queen of Cyprus and Daughter of Venice*. Edited by Candida Syndikus and Sabine Rogge, 213–229. Münbster: Waxmann, 2013.

Coureas, Nicholas. "Participants or Mediators? The Hospitallers and Wars Involving 15th Century Lusignan Cypruse." In *Ordines Militaires: Yearbook for the Study of the Military Orders* 28. (2013).

De Girolami Cheney, Liana. "Caterina Cornaro, Queen of Cyprus." In *The Emblematic Queen: Extra-Literary Representations of Early Modern Queenship*. Edited by Debra Barrett-Graves, 11–34. Basingstoke: Palgrave Macmillan, 2013.

Grivaud, Gilles. "Un règne sans fastes - Catherine Cornaro à travers les sources produites à Chypree." In *Caterina Cornaro: Last Queen of Cyprus and*

Daughter of Venice. Edited by Candida Syndikus and Sabine Rogge, 231–254. Münbster: Waxmann, 2013.

Hadfield, Andrew and Maley, Willy. "Introduction: Irish representations and English alternatives." In *Representing Ireland: Literature and the Origins of Conflict, 1534–1660*. Edited by Brendan Bradshaw, Andrew Hadfield, and Willy Maley, 1–23. Cambridge: Cambridge University Press, 2010.

Hadjikyriacou, Antonis. "The Ottomanisation of Cyprus: towards a spatial imagination beyond the centre-province boundary." *Journal of Mediterranean Studies* 25.1 (2016): 83–98.

Hurlburt, Holly S. "Body of Empire: Caterina Corner in Venetian History and Iconography." In *Early Modern Women* 4. (2009): 61–99.

Hurlburt, Holly S. *Daughter of Venice: Caterina Corner, Queen of Cyprus and Woman of the Renaissance*. New Haven: Yale University Press, 2015.

Iacovou, Maria. "Mapping the Ancient Kingdoms of Cyprus: Cartography and Classical Scholarship during the Enlightenment." In *Eastern Mediterranean Cartographies*. Edited by George Tolias and Dimitris Loupis, 263–285. Athens: Institute for Neohellenic Reseach, 2004.

Mallia-Milanes, Victor. "Introduction to Hospitaller Malta." In *Hospitaller Malta 1530–1798: Studies on Early Modern Malta and the Order of St John of Jerusalem*. Edited by Victor Mallia-Milanes. Msida: Moreva, 1993.

Monter, William. *The Rise of Female Kings in Europe, 1300–1800*. New Haven: Yale University Press, 2012.

Mullaly, Terence. "Caterina 'Domina' of Asolo: Lady of the Renaissance." In *Caterina Cornaro, Queen of Cyprus*. Edited by David Hunt and Iro Hunt. London: Trigraph, 1989.

Norwich, John Julius. *The Middle Sea: A History of the Mediterranean*. London: Vintage, 2007.

Paraskos, Michael. Plausible Cypriot Influence on Venetian Art and Society? unpublished paper.

CHAPTER 6

Trade and Piracy: The Role of a Potential Queen Consort in the 1620s

Valentina Caldari

Q.E. *Itwere farre better, that Prince Charles were married to an English Milke-maid, and the Infanta of Spaine mewed up for a nunne in a Cloyster.*[1]

Abbreviations

AGS	Archivo General de Simancas
CD	Commons' Debates
CJ	Commons Journal
BNE	Biblioteca Nacional de España, Madrid
BPR	Biblioteca del Palacio Real, Madrid
DRI	Documentos Remetidos da Índia
EEBO	Early English Books Online
Narrative	Francisco de Jesus, *Narrative of the Spanish Marriage Treaty*, ed. and transl. by Samuel R. Gardiner (Camden Society, 1869)
ODNB	*Oxford Dictionary of National Biography*
SP	State Papers

V. Caldari (✉)
University of Oxford, Oxford, UK

In 1618, when the proposed marriage between Prince Charles and the Infanta María was discussed during a meeting of the Council of State in Madrid, among the many matters considered, there was one deemed particularly important: in England, "queens themselves are subordinate to the laws of the Kingdom just like other subjects."[2] As customary, the Spanish councilors used historical precedent to support their statement and, in this case, they did not have to look too far back. Henry VIII had ignored Pope Clement VII when repudiating Queen Catherine of Aragon, had then executed two of his wives, and sent one, Anne of Cleves, "back to her father's home, as a favor."[3] Subsequently, his daughter Queen Elizabeth I had condemned her fellow queen Mary Stuart, Queen of Scotland, and not many had protested against her execution in 1587. Even the current ruler of England, King James I, was reported to have threatened his queen: According to the Spanish, Anne of Denmark, who "was inclined in favor of the Catholics," was reminded by her husband to think carefully about the way she acted "as the laws of England are little in favor of women."[4] In light of this troubled and violent history, it seems understandable that the Spanish were worried about the dangers faced by the Infanta if she were to marry Charles and become the queen of England. Several among King Philip III and King Philip IV's councilors produced written opinions ("pareceres") cautioning the sovereign on the inadvisability of a union with a heretic. Pedro Mantuano, for instance, wrote on the punishments "which God had sent to those rulers married, or whose sisters were given in marriage to, heretics or pagans."[5] Friar Francisco de Jesús reminded Philip IV that "no convenience for the state was to be gained from this union without first obtaining unity of religion." In this case, worrisome precedents were found in the history of Early Christianity. According to de Jesús, there were not many examples of Catholic women who had managed to convert their husbands. And even in those few cases, the heretics were pagans, not Protestants; the latter being "more dangerous, [...] astute, and difficult to weaken."[6] Indeed, Charles would have prioritized the swift conversion of his bride to his religion knowing that "it is very rare for a wife to resist to such persuasions from her husband."[7]

If at the Spanish court many feared for the Infanta's fate as a queen consort, in London, MPs, pamphleteers, and clergymen were concerned instead that the Infanta would persuade Charles to become a Catholic. Despite James having reassured them that the union with Spain would have been concluded in accordance with the religion and well-being of the Kingdom, MPs remained skeptical when the assembly was summoned in 1621.[8] In John Reynolds's *Vox Coeli*, this religious fear is easily detectable as he is convinced that a Spanish match would inevitably result in England returning to papal obedience.[9] While the pamphlet was only published in 1624, when the project for an Anglo-Spanish match was considered abandoned by the majority of the Protestant political nation, Reynolds' description of a meeting in heaven among past English sovereigns, such as Henry VIII, and his daughters, Mary I and Elizabeth, offered a powerful warning against the risks of a union with the Catholic monarchy. According to the author of *Vox Coeli*, Spain's "boundlesse ambition" sought to increase Rome's spiritual power and the Infanta would have soon been able to "introduce the Masse, and usher in the Pope."[10] Reynolds's work needs to be read and understood in light of the English parliaments of the early 1620s. During the Parliaments of 1621 and 1624, the dynastic alliance with Spain was put under severe scrutiny, not only for the dangers that a Spanish bride could bring at home,[11] but also for the global consequences that a closer alliance with the Habsburgs would produce on trade in the East and newly created English settlements in the Americas. Already in the 1580s, the promoter of English expansionism in trade and territory Richard Hakluyt had recognized the king of Spain's economic and political dependence on the Indies. Attacking his overseas possessions—stated Hakluyt—meant to "touch the apple of his eye, for you take away his treasure which is *nervus belli*," suggesting that their decay would be highly advantageous to the English, since Spain's wars in Europe were financed by the wealth of the Indies.[12] During the 1624 Parliament, an analogous reasoning was behind the idea of waging a war of diversion against Spain in the Indies rather than on European soil.[13]

In addressing Spain's and England's diverging positions concerning the Infanta's political and religious roles and influence on her prospective husband, this chapter's focus is not religious dichotomies but instead those aspects of marriage treaties' negotiations, such as trade agreements and provisions against piracy, where the role of the bride as (potential) queen consort is often overlooked. Indeed, when using marriage treaties between European ruling houses as historical sources to discuss wider political and religious issues, historians of the early modern period rarely focus on the role that queen consorts were to play *beyond* the religious sphere and the education of their children. I discuss this neglected aspect by focusing on the treaty for a union between Charles, son and heir of King James I of England, and María, daughter of Philip III of Spain and sister of Philip IV.[14] In doing so, I consider the context in which an Anglo-Spanish marriage agreement was first considered between Henry, James's eldest son, and the Infanta Ana, between 1603 and 1604, and briefly address that which was perceived as a potential precedent: Queen Mary's marriage to Philip II. Rather than providing firm conclusions on the specific role of the Infanta María in influencing trade relations between England and Spain (which would, of course, be extremely difficult to achieve given that the union never reached a successful conclusion), this essay assesses the political and diplomatic discussions surrounding the perceived agency of the prospective bride.

JAMES I'S DYNASTIC POLICIES IN ENGLAND AND SPAIN

When James VI of Scotland ascended to the English throne as James I in 1603, he did so as a foreigner. Many of the king's new English subjects were prone to judge him against the legacy of the late Queen Elizabeth, a monarch who was often portrayed as a symbol of Protestantism and Englishness. Following his accession, James continued to legitimize his rule by citing his position as the successor of a prestigious earlier dynasty.[15] However, King James's dedication to pursuing an alliance through marriage with Habsburg Spain meant that his religious commitment toward Protestantism was questioned, especially following the outbreak of the Thirty Years War.[16] Doubts concerning his loyalty to the Protestant cause had various origins. Already before his accession to the English throne, a Scottish observer wrote to Spain stating that "he promises to become a Catholic."[17] Moreover, the king's wife, Anne, was considered to be strongly pro-Spanish and "desiring much a union between the Infanta and her son."[18] Consequently, during the lengthy negotiations for an Habsburg-Stuart union, the religious convictions of the first Stuart king of England were under scrutiny at home, by those who believed him to be *less* Protestant than Elizabeth I and less willing to answer the call for a pan-Protestant movement.[19]

James's reign has been more recently reassessed by several scholars, *inter alia* Pauline Croft, W.B. Patterson, and the late Jenny Wormald. These scholars have argued that he was a perspicacious ruler who consistently pursued a sophisticated irenic policy, to be achieved via dynastic unions for his children.[20] Marrying "into a specific set of other families" was one of the most effective ways to legitimize a new dynasty on the throne as well as maintaining and reinforcing trading links in an increasingly connected early modern world.[21] Thanks to his daughter Elizabeth's marriage to the Protestant Frederick V, Elector Palatine and, as Frederick I, king of Bohemia, and the hope of a union between his son, Henry and, after Henry's death in 1612, Charles with a Spanish Infanta, James aspired to maintain peace by counterbalancing opposing powers in Europe. However, while James was proud of keeping his kingdom at peace, English observers attributed his foreign policy to cowardice and regarded his pacific inclinations, especially toward Spain, as testament to a weak character and general failure to realize that Spain was the *natural* enemy, as it aimed to establish a universal monarchy.[22] As recognised by John Cramsie, there is no doubt that the potential match between the Prince of Wales and the Spanish Infant was the most controversial diplomatic issue in James's reign. If successful, the Anglo-Spanish match would have had dramatic consequences not only on the European scene but also on the increasingly problematic balance of power in the West and East Indies. The complexity of overseas relations between England and the Iberian Peninsula had worsened after the Union of the Crowns in 1580. Once the Habsburgs were ruling over both Spain and Portugal, England considered Portuguese territories in the East as a justified target, Portugal was concerned of the many enemies they had gained because of Philip II's conflicts, and Spain still wanted its privileges in the New World to be recognized.[23]

After a period of stalemate, the marriage negotiations were revived in 1616–1617 when James sent John Digby as his ambassador to Spain to conclude the union. The Spanish now questioned the reasons why James wanted his son to marry a Catholic princess as much as the English did. Of the potential reasons behind the king of England's intentions, religion was not considered realistic as no one was "more passionate against the Catholic faith" than the Stuart sovereign. Therefore, either James must have had an agenda against the king of Spain as a pillar of Catholicism or he may have been interested in something other than religion, such as "wealth" or "the security of his person and his kingdom."[24] On the one hand, it was not difficult for the Spanish to imagine that, given that the Protestant king was to benefit greatly from the large dowry, the pursuit of "wealth" could have been a significant attraction. On the other hand, great attention was given in the account to James's need for physical, as well as dynastic, security.[25] Spanish help in protecting English trading routes from competitors and coasts from pirates was deemed a crucial advantage, in exchange for which the king of Spain aimed to ensure that the necessary articles and laws were in place to help and protect the Infanta while she was surrounded by "heretics."[26] While the Spanish were preoccupied for the religion of the Infanta and any future progeny, the English were absorbed by economic considerations. They were aware of the need for an ally to preserve the "honor, safety, and profit of the King and Kingdom" given the decay of trade, "the boldness of the Hollanders," and the treasury being nearly empty.[27] An alliance, to stimulate trade and implement a shared commitment against piracy in exchange for religious concessions to the Infanta and her household, appeared a seemingly straightforward quid pro quo.

The Treaty of London

On August 16, 1604, a peace agreement between England and the Iberian monarchy was signed in London by representatives of James I and Philip III following eighteen conference sessions. English, Spanish, and Flemish delegates met around the carpeted table famously portrayed in the Somerset House painting, thus linking two of the major European powers in a multifaceted set of binding political and economic relationships. As much as the 1604 Treaty of London, the lengthy marriage negotiations that followed for a union between the Prince of Wales and the Spanish Infanta transcended national boundaries. Indeed, the relations among countries directly or indirectly interested in the outcome of the dynastic diplomacy were intertwined with concerns overseas as well as in Europe.

When James I and Philip III signed the peace treaty so early on in their respective reigns, several among their subjects were convinced that conflict between the Protestant country and the Catholic monarchy was not necessary.[28] Some commentators believed that the tensions must have resulted from the actions of the previous sovereigns[29] and hoped that the alliance between the English and the Spanish crowns would strengthen trading relations between the two countries.[30] Not all agreed. On the contrary, Sir Walter Raleigh argued that the negative consequences of an agreement with Spain were "many and most weighty."[31]

The conflicting opinions originating from the signing of the peace treaty should not make us overlook the fact that commerce between England and the Iberian Peninsula had always been crucially beneficial to both powers and commercial links had not stopped completely even during the war.[32] According to Article IX of the 1604 Treaty of London, free commerce was to be established and maintained between the king of Spain and the king of England "as well by Land as by Sea and fresh Water, in all and singular the Kingdoms, Dominions and Islands." The kingdoms and dominions mentioned in the treaty, however, were by no means *all* the territories belonging to Spain but only those "in which commerce was held before the breaking out of the War."[33] The Spanish believed that while the peace treaty was necessary for the safety of the overseas possessions of the Iberian monarchy,[34] it was nevertheless imperative for the freedom of trade only to be granted to territories that had previously traded in this way. Spanish settlements in the New World could not be touched,[35] and the East Indies ought to remain excluded from the free trade "as they always have been."[36]

Given the criticism that accompanied the signing of the Treaty in 1604, predictably the first articles to be disregarded were those concerning trade in the East Indies. At the beginning of the seventeenth century, the English did not agree with the Iberian powers forbidding their commerce in the East: contemporary commentators criticized Philip III and his ministers for restricting trade despite the treaty concluded with James I, and English merchants often complained of the treatment the Spanish subjected them to. Spanish traders were accused of treating the English "whose hands are bound [by the 1604 Anglo-Spanish peace] with any contumely and treachery."[37] Indeed, not only were pirates involved in actions potentially disruptive to the peace agreement of 1604 and the ongoing marriage negotiations,[38] but also chartered companies and individuals carrying patents granted by the sovereign himself, as in the case of Raleigh. He was granted a royal patent to travel to the New World with the assurance that he "would not commit any offence" against the king of Spain.[39] However, having attacked a Spanish settlement in San Thomé in 1617, he was executed shortly after his return to England. In 1622, the English East India Company allied with the Safavid Shah and conquered Hormuz, a strategic Portuguese fortress in the Persian Gulf.[40] This produced numerous requests for reparation and endangered the ongoing marriage diplomacy.

In order to make the peace binding and to reduce rivalry overseas, the possibility of a marriage agreement between Prince Henry and the Infanta Ana was considered even before the treaty was concluded in 1604. James hoped that a dynastic union between the Stuarts and the

Habsburgs would maintain peace in Europe. In turn, the Spanish considered the marriage as an effective means of strengthening the peace, but they agreed during a meeting of the Council of State in March 1604 that any potential dynastic union had to be discussed only *after* the peace agreement was ratified "according to the order that has always been followed in matters of this kind."[41] Since the beginning of the discussion for a Habsburg-Stuart union, the Spanish linked the possibility of a marriage to an increased toleration for Catholics in England. They also suggested that the Prince of Wales would be raised at the Spanish court,[42] as they could not believe that the king of England was "so foolish (*desatinado*) to think that he can obtain this without becoming a Catholic."[43] As much as England, Spain was also concerned about the increasingly strong links between European diplomacy and overseas dominions.[44] Indeed, already in 1604, the Council of State had agreed that the maintenance of peace with England was "the only possibility for the security of the Indies."[45]

Before the 1620s, when Spanish demands appeared excessive regarding religion, the king of England had considered a dynastic union with France, rather than Spain, for his son.[46] Spain regarded the possibility of an Anglo-French union as alarming because of "the concerns and dangerous designs that can follow from the alliance between the two crowns."[47] In 1606, James I and Henry IV had already signed an agreement that allowed their merchants to "traffick safely and freely with one another."[48] Preventing such trade alliances among rivals was critical if the Iberian crown hoped to maintain its monopoly in the Indies as well as favorable bilateral agreements with other powers in Europe. The Catholic monarchy was already aware of the special relation between the Dutch and the English as confirmed by treaties signed in 1608 and 1619.[49] Spain, therefore, could not allow a potential dynastic union between England and France to threaten its position further.

Mary I and Philip of Spain

The ways in which the public sphere discussed royal marriage in the 1620s were strongly influenced by the earlier reigns of Mary and Elizabeth. English concern about the role of the Spanish Infanta was heightened due to the nation's history of fifty years of female rule.[50] Having experienced how quickly religious debate could lead to reformation and counter-reformation, in the 1620s the political nation feared that the Protestant commonwealth could fall apart if Charles was to be converted by his prospective Catholic bride. Mary's decision to marry Philip of Spain as soon as she ascended to the throne and Elizabeth's refusal to share her choices with parliament in terms of a possible husband created concern through the political classes that important decisions on dynastic unions would be taken without the assembly's advice.[51] The situation in the 1620s was reversed with respect to the reigns of two Tudor queens. If in the second half of the sixteenth century the concern was what role would the king consort play in England, in the 1620s the political nation was concerned that the marriage treaty had to impose sufficient restrictions on the role that the Infanta was to play if she was going to marry Charles. As the traditional assumption was that the bride would convert to her husband's religion rather than vice versa, the skepticism surrounding the Prince of Wales's marriage seems to originate, at least partly, from the inherent ineptitude that contemporaries ascribed to the Stuarts. Especially when compared to their Tudor predecessors or the rulers of continental Europe, the early Stuarts appeared indecisive and weak to both modern historians[52] and contemporaries, continuously attempting to either "satisfy Spain"[53] or "the Puritan faction."[54]

When debating Charles's Spanish match and the role that a consort would play in England, Queen Mary's marriage to Philip II was the closest precedent, chronologically, to which the political nation could appeal. Nevertheless, as noted by Sir Robert Phelips in 1621, there were no suitable English precedents for the marriage between Charles and the Infanta as, unlike Charles, Mary Tudor was a Catholic and she wanted to marry a co-religionist.[55] Another possible precedent, that of Henry VIII who had married Catherine of Aragon, was hardly applicable to Prince Charles's situation. In 1509, when Henry and Catherine were married, the king was still a "papist" himself since the break from Rome had not yet occurred. In short, both Henry VIII and Mary married someone who shared their own religious beliefs. In contrast, Charles's union with the Infanta in the 1620s would have meant the union of individuals of two different faiths and, while there were continental models for this, there was no precedent to look at in England for such an eventuality.

In the 1550s, it was feared that if Mary married a foreign sovereign, England would lose its autonomy.[56] Similarly, in the 1620s, the political nation feared that England would have become a "province" of Spain if Charles married a Spanish Catholic bride. Despite the circulation of prescriptive marriage articles, Mary's Spanish marriage was extremely unpopular because the political nation feared that England would be subject to Spain in political and religious terms.[57] In the 1620s behind the debates on Charles's dynastic union, there were the same fears of subjection to Spain, despite James's reassurance that he would "never conclude a match that shall not be for the glory of God and furtherance of religion."[58] Mary's promise not to conclude her marriage in 1554 without the agreement of parliament had, in the eyes of members of the House of 1621, the same value as James's promise.[59] In fact, albeit for different reasons, Mary's and Charles's Spanish matches involved the same contradiction: that of England's political relationship with the sovereign consort's nation of origin, Spain. Yet it was a Spanish wife in the case of Charles; therefore, the fears of the political nation seem disproportionate, since according to the Scriptures, "the husband is the head of the wife."[60]

Two main reasons made the fears of the 1620s similar to the fears of the 1550s, although the gender power dynamic was reversed. First, the opinion that the Stuarts were incompetent, unable to handle matters of state as effectively as the Tudors had, was widespread and persistent among contemporaries. The second reason concerned the actual value of a marriage treaty. Although the treaty imposed prescriptive clauses to Prince Philip, and he was never crowned king of England for fear that he would have claimed the kingdom in his own right, he enjoyed extensive powers.[61] In addition to involving England in his war against France, Philip regularly attended the Privy Council and all the acts passed between 1554 and 1558 were recorded under the name "Philippi et Mariae Regis et Regine."[62] The concerns and the doubts of the political nation in the 1620s, however, were more subtle and deep-seated than the memory of Mary's unpopular marriage. Pamphlets used Mary's precedent to highlight the dilemma of whether or not a prince or a king was bound by a marriage treaty, and to what extent a prince was bound by law. According to King James's own words in his *Trew Law of Free Monarchies*: "A good king will frame all his actions to be according to the law; yet is hee not bound thereto but of his good will, and for good example-giuing to his subiects."[63] In the 1620s, the political nation wondered whether a prescriptive marriage treaty would be a sufficient guarantee for Prince Charles's Spanish match, or if the Infanta could simply ignore it, in whole or in part, as Philip had done.

Turks and Pirates

When the rulers discuss the match in heaven in *Vox Coeli*, Queen Mary states that the main reason why King James likes the idea of a union with Spain for his son is that "his Exchequer is poore, and King Philips Indies rich."[64] A large dowry, promised by Spain since the beginning of the negotiations in 1604, and increased trading links were priorities that King James was not ready to abandon. Several times the two parties had attempted to conclude binding agreements on trade, especially in light of an increasingly strong Dutch presence in the East Indies, and in order to join forces against piracy in the Mediterranean. Ambassador Gondomar and Mendo da Mota, the latter one of the most prominent members of the Council of State, had suggested that the Iberian powers should make a league with England against the Dutch.[65] The Spanish were worried that the king of England would ally with Protestant powers and "the sea would be covered with ships if he [i.e. King James] gave them leave to form fleets and to practice piracy against Spain."[66] This was considered a likely possibility given that even Queen Elizabeth "who being a woman [was] less powerful than he is" had managed to sustain a profitable war against the Catholic monarchy during her reign.[67]

In 1604, in spite of the peace agreement between Philip III and James I, Spain continued to refuse the English a presence in the East and in the New World.[68] The peace between the two powers was therefore vulnerable. After a first failed attempt in 1603–1604, James's proposal for a dynastic marriage that would have made, in his mind, the treaty fully binding was unanswered until at least 1612–1613,[69] despite "continuance of trade" being identified by both parties as one of the key advantages of the union.[70] At the same time as the marriage between the prince and the Infanta was negotiated, however, the East India Company had organized an anti-Iberian alliance with the Dutch VOC in the East Indies. The agreement, signed in 1619, was intended to last 20 years and aimed to counterbalance the power of the Iberian monarchy in the spice trade.[71] Concerns were expressed by the Council of State in Madrid regarding the alliance between the two trading companies, especially given the numerous letters received weekly in the Spanish capital concerning rivalries between the English and the Portuguese, and the difficulties in reaching any compromise between the English company and the Council of Portugal.[72] A match between England and Spain would have brought trading advantages outside Europe where the Iberian Empire had begun to falter due to the competition for dominance with the Dutch and the English.[73] An Habsburg-Stuart union would avoid a marriage between England and France, that the Spanish ambassador thought was still being discussed at court, and also prevent James from providing help to the Dutch rebels.[74] Another Infanta, the Archduchess Isabel, repeatedly complained to the English about trade as nothing positive, she argued, could result from maintaining an adversarial attitude toward the Spanish Netherlands.[75] In the 1620s, the Netherlands wanted the Infanta María to marry Charles in order to benefit from the closer relationship between Spain and the king of England.

A formal agreement with the English regarding trade in the East was considered necessary, as it appeared to the Council of Portugal that the long-running dynastic negotiations between King James and Spain were not enough to deter the English from attacking Portuguese possessions.[76] In Portuguese Asia, the viceroy's assumption was indeed that foreign attacks on Portuguese ports and trade routes would decrease as a result of the dynastic union between England and Spain.[77] Since the beginning of Philip IV's reign in 1621, and especially following the capture of Hormuz in 1622, several influential figures in the Council of State, and especially da Mota and Gondomar, were convinced that the only way to save what was left of the Portuguese possessions in Asia was through an alliance with the English East India Company in order to share the trade in the Indies.[78]

When attempts to reach agreements to share trade failed, both England and Spain resorted to discussing the possibility of joining forces against piracy. In London, James was aware that piracy, especially on the coasts of Africa, was a recurrent concern of the Catholic king.[79] In Madrid, the idea that the Infanta's presence in England would have made it easier for the two countries to fight together against "Turcos y corsarios" was often mentioned in meetings of the Council of State, and became a common feature of any discussions post-1617, when Raleigh's expedition (and subsequent execution) had alerted the Spanish of the importance of convincing the English that pirates were the common enemy.[80] In the case of the attack on Hormuz by the English East India Company, Spain decided instead to renegotiate the amount of the Infanta's dowry. Pedro de Toledo acknowledged that if Spain were to grant a two-million ducat dowry to England to be delivered with the Infanta, "India would cease to be in our power."[81] This prominent member of the Council of State considered how, by granting such a large sum, the already precarious financial situation of the Iberian Crown would worsen to the point of no return and subsequently it would prove impossible to protect the Indies.

As the Prince was in Madrid in 1623, the Spanish thought that his closeness in space to the Infanta may facilitate discussions on the dowry: this is crucial in understanding the *soft power* ascribed to the Spanish princess. While it would be easy to dismiss any discussions concerning the dowry as secondary "mundane considerations,"[82] this is instead the moment when concerns for trade and colonization come together in what is the most traditional contribution by the bride to the husband's family. And it had little to do with money, and much to do with the extent to which the Infanta could influence Prince Charles through her proximity to him. When the prospect of a successful conclusion for the dynastic union faded in 1624, Chamberlain reported to Ambassador Carleton that envoys had "brought back the Princes letter to the Infanta unopened."[83] Cooling diplomatic relations between England and the Catholic monarchy, as testified by the Spanish princess's refusal to answer, or even open, Charles's missive, persuaded Chamberlain to report that "our merchants are cautioned against trading with Spain."[84]

Conclusion

One of the recurrent points in both the 1604 peace treaty and the marriage negotiations that followed was trade and the right of merchants to sell and buy products in each other's ports. Moreover, the agreements discussed security against pirates at sea and the relationship between European commercial companies and local powers.[85] The role that potential queen consorts were asked to play by their country of origin was often implicit, and secondary to the more traditional responsibilities for religious conversion and care for children produced by the union.[86] However, the thought that, once married, the Infanta María could exert influence on Charles regarding shared trading routes and a joint fleet against piracy was more than an exercise in wishful thinking.

If we fail to read between the lines of marriage treaties in the context of the diplomatic, political, and commercial relations of the countries involved, we leave something unopened, like Charles's letter to the Spanish princess. Indeed, the tendency to concentrate on religion has often gone beyond European boundaries in an attempt to explain European relations with the rest of the world through confessional divisions. Not taking into account the role of queen consorts within the global connectedness of the early seventeenth century creates weak foundations for our understanding of the negotiation of subsequent alliances, such as when Tangier and the Islands of Bombay formed part of Catherine of Braganza's dowry to secure her marriage with Charles II in 1661. Then, overseas possessions were exchanged at a moment when the role of the queen consort was crucial in legitimizing the rule of Catherine's father, considered by the Spanish as the "tyrant" of Portugal, following the end of the Union of the Crowns.[87] This essay has discussed a precursor to this episode, as the protracted negotiations for a union between Charles and the Infanta María are one of the first instances in which attacks to overseas possessions were quantified in terms of a diminished dowry to be given to the prospective bride to take to her husband's country. Even when religious articles were agreed upon, the extent to which the dowry, and the departure of the Infanta to England were to be affected by discussions on trading rights, commercial companies, and joint expeditions against pirates, delayed the negotiations. Since early modern contemporaries were so concerned with the role of the queen-to-be when drafting marriage articles, discussing trade agreements, and provisions against piracy, we should be too.

Notes

1. John Reynolds, *Vox Coeli* (London, 1624), 46. "Q.E." refers to Queen Elizabeth as the pamphlet is structured in the form of a dialogue among former rulers of England.
2. AGS, Libro 369, f. 56r.
3. AGS, Libro 369, f. 56r. Anna of Cleves is mistakenly listed as Henry VIII's third wife rather than his fourth.
4. AGS, Libro 369, f. 56r.
5. BNE, Mss/10794, fols. 201–12, Opinion of Pedro Mantuano. See also, for example, RAH, L-24, fols. 535r–562r, Opinion of Doctor Roco Campofrío; fols. 606r–624r, Opinion of Friar Antonio Perez; fols. 626r–645r Opinion of Doctor Juan Miguel; fols. 663r–678r, Opinion of the Jesuit Father Ivan de Montemayor.
6. Henar Pizarro Llorente, Pablo María Garrido (eds.), *Fray Francisco de Jesús Jódar. Papeles sobre el Tratado de Matrimonio entre el Príncipe de Gales y la Infanta María de Austria (1623)* (Madrid: Ediciones Carmelitanas, 2009), 148 and 143.
7. Pizarro Llorente, *Fray Francisco*, 143.

8. *CD 1621*, vol. IV, pp. 3–4; *CD 1621*, vol. II, p. 7. For instances of criticism from the pulpit, see Jeanne Shami, *John Donne and Conformity in Crisis in the Late Jacobean Pulpit* (Cambridge, 2003), 42–45.
9. Reynolds, *Vox Coeli*.
10. Reynolds, *Vox Coeli*, 39.
11. On the hopes that English Catholics linked to a successful conclusion of the Anglo-Spanish union, see Michael Questier (ed.), *Stuart Dynastic Policy and Religious Politics, 1621–1625* (Camden Fifth Series, vol. 34, Cambridge University Press, 2009), 131–379.
12. Richard Hakluyt, *A particular discourse concerning the great necessity and manifold commodities that are like to grow to this Realm of England by the Western discoveries lately attempted* (London, 1584).
13. *CJ*, PA, HC/CL/JO/1/12, see speeches by Sir Robert Phelips and Sir Miles Fleetwood, 1 March 1624. On the war of diversion called for already during the 1621 Parliament, see also Glyn Redworth, *The Prince and the Infanta. The Cultural Politics of the Spanish Match* (New Haven and London: Yale University Press, 2003), 30–32.
14. For a discussion of the Anglo-Spanish match negotiations, see Thomas Cogswell, *The Blessed Revolution. English Politics and the coming of war 1621–1624* (Cambridge: Cambridge University Press, 1989); Brennan Pursell, "The End of the Spanish Match," *Historical Journal*, 45 (2002): 699–726; Redworth, *The Prince and the Infanta*. Alexander Samson (ed.), *The Spanish Match. Prince Charles's Journey to Madrid, 1623* (Aldershot: Ashgate, 2006).
15. For an analysis of the means by which successors would maintain ties with the earlier ruling house, see Jeroen Duindam, "Dynasties," *Medieval Worlds*, 2 (2015): 59–78 (67–68). See also Liesbeth Geevers and Mirella Marini (eds.), *Aristocracy, Dynasty and Identity in Early Modern Europe, 1520–1700* (Aldershot: Ashgate, 2016).
16. For a discussion of James's lukewarm support to his son-in-law, Frederick V, and to the Elector Palatine's hope for a pan-Protestant anti-Habsburgs league, see Glyn Redworth, "Of Pimps and Princes: Three Unpublished Letters from James I and the Prince of Wales relating to the Spanish Match," *Historical Journal*, 37 (1994), 401.
17. Quoted in Albert J. Loomie, "Philip III and the Stuart Succession in England, 1600–1603," *Revue belge de Philologie et d'Histoire*, 43 (1965), 497.
18. AGS, E., Leg. 2557, doc. 8 and 12 and AGS, E., Leg. 2514, doc. 73. See also, Garrett Mattingly, *Renaissance Diplomacy* (New York: Cosimo Classics, repr. 2008), 260; Redworth, *The Prince and the Infanta*, 12; and Glyn Redworth, "Sarmiento de Acuña, Diego, count of Gondomar in the Spanish nobility (1567–1626)," *ODNB*.

19. See, for example, "Negotiations with Catholic Powers before James' accession to the English throne," in Robert Ashton (ed.), *James I by his contemporaries* (Hutchinson, 1969), 188–191; Reynolds. In contrast to my reading of events, Sharpe stated that despite James's desire for a Spanish marriage, few doubted the King's Protestantism. See Kevin Sharpe, "Parliamentary History 1603–1629: In or out of Perspective?," in Sharpe (ed.), *Faction and Parliament. Essays on Early Stuart History* (London and New York: Clarendon Press, 1978), 22.
20. Pauline Croft, *King James* (Basingstoke: Palgrave Macmillan, 2003); Jenny Wormald, "James VI and I: two Kings or one?," *History*, 68 (1983), 187–209; Jenny Wormald, "James VI and I (1566–1625), king of Scotland, England, and Ireland," *ODNB*; Patterson, *The Reunion of Christendom*.
21. Geevers and Marini (eds.), *Aristocracy, Dynasty and Identity*, 9.
22. Thomas Cogswell & Alastair Bellany, *The Murder of King James I* (New Haven: Yale University Press, 2015), 2.
23. Anthony Disney, *A History of Portugal and the Portuguese Empire* (Cambridge: Cambridge University Press, 2009), vol. I, 210–11; Dejanira Couto and Rui Loureiro, *Ormuz 1507 e 1622 Conquista e Perda* (Tribuna de História, 2007), 66; BL, Eg. ms. 1131, f. 103v.
24. AGS, Libro 369, f. 56v.
25. AGS, Libro 369, fols. 57–58.
26. See, for example, RAH, Z-8, f. 53v.
27. TNA, SP 14/120, f. 182, Notes by Sir Robert Heath, April 1621.
28. On the 1604 Anglo-Spanish peace and the importance of James I's initiative in the conclusion of the treaty, see Robert Cross, "To Counterbalance the World: England, Spain, and Peace in the early seventeenth century" (Princeton University, unpublished PhD thesis, 2012), 33–70.
29. RAH, Z-8, Anthony Sherley, *Discurso excelentisimo de la conueniencia de Los Casamientos del Principe de Inglaterra con la serenissima Infanta de Hespaña*, f. 9v: "Esta guerra que nació entre España y Inglaterra tuvo su principio mas de lo imaginado que de lo esencial, y se apago luego con la mudanza de los Reyes que la encendieron, como cossa que Realmente nacio de la opinion dellos." Another copy of Sherley's text can be found at BNE, Mss/10794, fols. 151r–200v.
30. BL, Stowe, ms 164, f. 86r. On Anglo-Habsburg trade relations being intertwined with politics, see Alexander Samson, "The Marriage of Philip of Habsburg and Mary Tudor and Anti-Spanish Sentiment in England: Political Economies and Culture, 1553–1557" (Queen Mary and Westfield College, unplished PhD thesis, 1999), 22.
31. Walter Raleigh, "A Discourse Touching a War with Spain, and of the Protecting of the Netherlands," in *The Works of Sir Walter Ralegh*, eds. William Oldys and Thomas Birch (Oxford, 1829), vol. 8, 314.

32. Pauline Croft, "Trading with the Enemy 1585–1604," *Historical Journal*, 32 (1989): 281–302. See also Richard Stone, "The Overseas Trade of Bristol before the Civil War," *International Journal of Maritime History*, 23 (2011): 211–39.
33. "A Treaty of Perpetual Peace and Alliance between Philip III, king of Spain, and the Archduke and Archduchess Albert and Isabella on the one side, and James I of England on the other side, 1604," in *Treaties*, 137.
34. AGS, E., Leg., 2557, doc. 22, Meeting of the Council of State, Madrid, April 14, 1604.
35. Raleigh was executed in 1618 after being accused of attacking a Spanish settlement in San Thomé. On this, see V.T. Harlow, *Raleigh's Last Voyage. Being an account drawn out of contemporary letters and relations both Spanish and English* (London, 1932).
36. AGS, E., Leg. 2557, doc. 12, Meeting of the Council of State, Madrid, March 25 1604: "El comercio entre sus Reynos sea abierto comun y libre y asegurado en las partes donde por lo pasado lo a sido, fuera de las Indias [...] que deven quedar excluydas dellas como siempre lo han sido."
37. Thomas Roe to the Earl of Salisbury, February 28, 1611, quot. in *Raleigh's Last Voyage*, 104.
38. On piracy being condemned more during James's reign than it had been under Queen Elizabeth, see Claire Jowitt, *The Culture of Piracy, 1580–1630: English Literature and Seaborne Crime* (Farnham: Ashgate, 2010), 137.
39. AGS, E., Leg. 2515, doc. 7: "[...] asegurando que no haría offensa ninguna; y si la hiziesse se daría entera satisfación."
40. Couto and Loureiro, *Ormuz 1507 e 1622*; Sanjay Subrahmanyam, *The Portuguese empire in Asia 1500–1700: A political and economic history* (London and New York: Longman, 1993); Rudi Matthee and Jorge Flores, *Portugal, the Persian Gulf and Safavid Persia*, Acta Iranica, 52 (Leuven: Peeters, 2011).
41. AGS, E., Leg. 2557, doc. 12, Meeting of the Council of State, March 25, 1604: "in order to discuss this [marriage between Prince Henry and the Infanta Ana] it is convenient that the Prince becomes Catholic and so does his Kingdom."
42. See Robert Cross, "Closer Together and Further Apart. Religious Politics and Political Culture in the British-Spanish Match, 1596–1625," in *Stuart Marriage Diplomacy. Dynastic Politics in their European Context, 1604–1630*, eds. Valentina Caldari and Sara Wolfson (Boydell and Brewer, forthcoming 2017).
43. AGS, E., Leg. 2557, doc. 12. On the importance of Prince Henry's conversion given that the Infanta Ana was then Philip III's heiress presumptive as the Spanish king had not yet fathered a son, see Redworth, *The Prince and the Infanta*, 8–9.

44. This is a recurring *topos* also in Protestant propaganda against Spain. In the early 1620s, Thomas Scott commented that the Spanish boundless ambition was not extinguished "with the Conquest of all the New World discovered by them, nor with so great a part which they possesse in the old." See [Thomas Scott] (transl.), *News from Pernassvs* (1622), 46.
45. AGS, E., Leg. 2557, doc. 22.
46. Andrew Thrush, "The French marriage and the Origins of the 1614 Parliament." in *The Crisis of 1614 and the Addled Parliament: Literary and Historical Perspectives*, eds. Stephen Clucas and Rosalind Davies (Ashgate, 2003), 25–36.
47. AGS, E., Leg. 2514, doc. 10.
48. "A Treaty between Henry IVth, king of France, and James the Ist, king of England, for the Security and Freedom of Commerce between their Subjects," Paris, 1606, in *Treaties*, 148.
49. "A Treaty of Guaranty by James I for the Treaty between the Archduke and Archduchess Albert and Isabella, and the States General of the United Provinces," The Hague, 26 June 1608, in *Treaties*, 157–61. According to this treaty, the help to the United Provinces and any other agreement ratified by Elizabeth I was going to remain in place during James's reign. See also, "A Treaty between the English and Dutch East India Companies," London, June 2 1619, in *Treaties*, 188–202.
50. For a discussion of the importance of considering the legacy of fifty years of female rule, see Susan Doran and Paulina Kewes, eds., *Doubtful and Dangerous. The question of succession in late Elizabethan England* (Manchester: Manchester University Press, 2014). Susan Doran and Thomas S. Freeman, *Mary Tudor. Old and New Perspectives* (London: Macmillan, 2011); Anna Whitelock and Alice Hunt, eds., *Tudor Queenship: the Reigns of Mary and Elizabeth* (Basingstoke: Palgrave Macmillan, 2010).
51. Reynolds, *Vox Coeli*, 39–40: H.8. Who made and concluded the match with King Philip?/Q.M. My Selfe and the Parliament/Q.E. Nay Sister, put in Woolsey and Gardyner, and leave out the Parliament; for you only proposed it them but for forme, and had secretly concluded it before hand yourselfe./Q.M. Suppose I did, I might doe it of mine owne authority, and prerogative Royall./Q.E. But you offered no faire play to the Parliament though, in asking their advise when the Contracts were ready to be sealed./Q.M. But I had reason to follow mine owne iudgement, not their Passions.
52. Guizot, *Un projet de mariage*, 13: "Guillame d'Orange, Philippe II et Élisabeth étaient morts; à leur place, l'Espagne n'avait plus que l'apathique Philippe III, l'Angleterre que le pusillanime Jacques Ier."
53. Letter from an English minister of State to Francis Cottington, English agent in Spain, 1618, in Ashton, 213–15.

54. AGS, E., Leg. 2559, doc. 33 Opinion Pedro de Toledo.
55. Sir Robert Phelips, Dec. 3, 1621, "The Notes by Sir Thomas Barrington of the House of Commons in 1621," in *CD in 1621*, Vol. III, 493: "For matters of precedents, there is no need of precedents in this case for there was never this case before, all in those times being papists; but in a thing of so high a nature we may make a precedent but in the reason of state which is most proper for this House."
56. On a nuanced view of the Anglo-Spanish court of Philip when king consort of England, see Sarah Duncan, "He to be intituled Kinge. King Philip of England and the Anglo-Spanish court," in *The Man Behind the Queen. Male Consorts in History*, eds. Charles Beem and Miles Taylor (Palgrave Macmillan, 2014), 55–80.
57. On the protests during Mary's reign, see Conrad Russell, "The Reign of Mary I, 1553–1558," in *The Crisis of Parliaments. English History 1509–1660* (Oxford: Oxford University Press, 1971), 133–45 and Corinna Streckfuss, "Spes Maxima Nostra: European Propaganda and the Spanish Match," in Whitelock and Hunt, 145.
58. "King James's Opening Speech," Jan. 30, 1621, in *CD in 1621*, Vol. II, 8. On the use of Mary's precedent concerning her concessions to English Catholics, see "Charles and Buckingham to James I, Madrid, 29 June 1623," in *The Letters, Speeches and Proclamations of King Charles I*, ed. by Charles Petrie (London: Cassell, 1968), 21.
59. See, for example, "Edward Gyles speech in November 1621, *CJ*, 26 November 1621," *Journal of the House of Commons: volume 1: 1547–1629* (1802): 644–47.
60. Eph. 5:23.
61. See Glyn Redworth, "Matters Impertinent to Women: Male and Female Monarchy under Philip and Mary", *English Historical Review*, 112 (1997), 607–11 and Harry Kelsey, *Philip of Spain King of England. The Forgotten Sovereign* (London and New York: I.B. Tauris, 2012), 93–9.
62. "Second Treasons Act of Mary, 1555," in *Tudor Constitutional Documents 1485–1603*, ed. Joseph R. Tanner (Cambridge: Cambridge University Press, 1951), 408–411.
63. James I, "The Trew Law of Free Monarchies," in *James VI and I: Political Writings*, ed. by Johann P. Sommerville (Cambridge: Cambridge University Press, 1995), 75.
64. Reynolds, *Vox Coeli*, 38.
65. Dispatch from Gondomar to Philip III, AGS, E., Leg. 2600, doc. 65, in Francisco de Jesus, *Narrative of the Spanish Marriage Treaty*, ed. and transl. by Samuel R. Gardiner (Camden Society, 1869), 313–21.
66. Consulta by Luis de Aliaga to Gondomar, AGS, E. 2518, doc. 42, in *Narrative*, 305–13.

67. AGS, E. 2518, 305–13.
68. BL, Add. ms. 38139, fols. 71v–73r: the 1604 peace was intended to "bee observed and kept by their subiectes throughe all their Dominions." See also Santiago Martínez Hernández, (ed.), *Governo, Politica e Representações do Poder no Portugal Habsburgo e nos sues Territórios Ultramarinos (1581–1640)* (Lisbon: Centro de Historia de Alem-Mar, 2011), 177–8.
69. See Croft, *King James*, 84–5.
70. BL, Add. ms 72392, Trumbull Papers, f. 1r. On the English side, among the other advantages that could result from a Spanish Match, the author listed: "Great King daughter," "much money," and "security and safety."
71. AGS, E., Leg. 2514, doc. 41, Meeting of the Council of State, Madrid, February 14, 1615. John Keay, *The Honourable Company. A History of the English East India Company* (London: Harper Collins, 1991), 47–48.
72. On Spanish reactions to the agreement between the EIC and the VOC, see AGS, E., Leg. 2515, doc. 37; AGS, E., Leg. 437, doc. 30; AGS, E., Leg. 2516, doc. 10. See also AGS, E. Leg. 2598, doc. 94: in a letter dated September 10, 1618, Francis Cottington complained of Portuguese cruelties against the English.
73. AGS, E., Leg. 2558, doc. 136.
74. For Gondomar's conversations with James Hay, Viscount Doncaster, who had been sent to France by James between 1621 and 1624, see BPR, II/2108, docs. 23 and 27.
75. TNA, SP 14/138, f. 155, Conway to Calvert, February 27, 1622/3.
76. RAH, L-24, fols. 551v–552v.
77. DRI, vol. X, 3–4.
78. Among those influential figures, the most important was Mendo da Mota, member of the Council of Portugal since 1612. His correspondence with Bishop António de Gouveia concerning the necessity of an alliance is to be found in BL, Eg. ms 1133, fols. 258r–261r.
79. AGS, E., Leg. 2850, docs. 1, 2, James to Philip III, April 3, 1617.
80. See, for example, AGS, E., Leg. 2850, doc. 10, Meeting of the Council of State, 2 November 1617. See also discussions of Robert Mansell's expeditions against pirates in 1621, Andrew Thrush, "Mansell, Sir Robert (1570/71–1652)," *ODNB*.
81. AGS, E., Leg. 2645, unfoliated, Meeting of the Council of State, Madrid, August 19, 1623.
82. Carter defines dowry provisions as "mundane considerations" in Charles H. Carter, *The Secret Diplomacy of the Habsburgs, 1598–1625* (New York and London: Columbia University Press, 1964), 98–99.
83. TNA, SP 14/169, f.20, Chamberlain to Carleton, July 3, 1624.
84. TNA, SP 14/169, f.20, Chamberlain to Carleton, July 3, 1624.

85. See, for example, RAH, Z-8, f. 53v.
86. Especially articles 2, 3, 4, 5, 6, and 8 of the marriage treaty. See also, AGS, E., Leg. 1869, doc. 9, Duke of Albuquerque to Philip IV, Rome, October 26, 1623.
87. AGS, E., Leg. 2531, unfoliated, especially letter from the Spanish Ambassador to the king of England, May 13, 1661.

BIBLIOGRAPHY

Primary Sources

Manuscripts:
Archivo General de Simancas, Valladolid
Estado, *Legajos*: 2557; 2515; 437; 2514; 2516; 2598; 2558; 2850; 2645; 1869; 2531
Estado, *Libros*: 369
Biblioteca Nacional de España, Madrid
Manuscritos: 10794
British Library, London
Additional: 38139; 72392
Egerton: 1131; 1133
National Archives, Kew
State Papers: 14/138; 14/169
Real Academia de la Historia, Madrid
Collección Salazar y Castro: L-24; Z-8
Printed:
Ashton, Robert, ed. *James I by his contemporaries. An Account of his career and character as seen by some of his contemporaries.* London, 1969.
Notestein, Wallace, Helen Relf, Hartly Simpson, eds. *Commons Debates.* 1935.
De Jesus, Francisco. *Narrative of the Spanish Marriage Treaty.* Edited and translated by Samuel R. Gardiner. Camden Society, 1869.
Henar Pizarro Llorente, Pablo María Garrido, eds. *Fray Francisco de Jesús Jódar. Papeles sobre el Tratado de Matrimonio entre el Príncipe de Gales y la Infanta María de Austria (1623).* Madrid, 2009.
Hakluyt, Richard. *A particular discourse concerning the great necessity and manifold commodities that are like to grow to this Realm of England by the Western discoveries lately attempted.* London, 1584.
Harlow, V.T. *Raleigh's Last Voyage. Being an account drawn out of contemporary letters and relations both Spanish and English.* London, 1932.
James I. "The Trew Law of Free Monarchies", in *James VI and I: Political Writings.* Edited byJohann P. Sommerville. Cambridge, 1995.
Oldys, William and Birch, Thomas, eds. *The Works of Sir Walter Raleigh.* 8 volumes. Oxford, 1829.

Petrie, Charles ed. *The Letters, Speeches and Proclamations of King Charles I.* London: Cassell, 1968.
Questier, Michael ed. *Stuart Dynastic Policy and Religious Politics, 1621–1625.* Camden Fifth Series, 2009.
Reynolds, John. *Vox Coeli.* London, 1624.
[Scott, Thomas] (transl.) *News from Pernassvs.* 1622.
Tanner, Joseph R. ed. *Tudor Constitutional Documents 1485–1603.* Cambridge, 1951.

Secondary Sources

Carter, Charles Howard. *The Secret Diplomacy of the Habsburgs, 1598–1625.* New York and London: Columbia University Press, 1964.
Cogswell, Thomas. *The Blessed Revolution. English Politics and the coming of war 1621–1624.* Cambridge: Cambridge University Press, 1989.
Couto, Dejanira, and Loureiro, Rui. *Ormuz 1507 e 1622: Conquista e Perda.* Lisbon, 2007.
Croft, Pauline. "Trading with the Enemy 1585–1604." In *Historical Journal*, 32. (1989): 281–302.
Croft, Pauline. *King James.* Basingstoke, 2003.
Cross, Robert."Closer Together and Further Apart. Religious Politics and Political Culture in the British-Spanish Match, 1596–1625." In *Stuart Marriage Diplomacy. Dynastic Politics in their European Context, 1604–1630.* Edited by Valentina Caldari and Sara Wolfson. Boydell and Brewer, forthcoming 2017.
Disney, Anthony. *A History of Portugal.* 2 volumes. Cambridge: Cambridge University Press, 2009.
Doran, Susan, and S. Thomas Freeman *Mary Tudor. Old and New Perspectives.* London: Macmillan, 2011.
Doran, Susan, and Paulina, Kewes (eds.). *Doubtful and Dangerous. The question of succession in late Elizabethan England.* Manchester: Manchester University Press, 2014.
Duindam, Jeroen. "Dynasties." *Medieval Worlds*, 2. (2015): 59–78.
Duncan, Sarah. "He to be intituled Kinge. King Philip of England and the Anglo-Spanish court." In *The Man Behind the Queen. Male Consorts in History.* Edited by Charles Beem and Miles Taylor, 55–80. New York: Palgrave Macmillan, 2014.
Geevers, Liesbeth and Marini, Mirella eds. *Aristocracy, Dynasty and Identity in Early Modern Europe, 1520–1700.* Aldershot: Ashgate, 2016.
Jowitt, Claire. *The Culture of Piracy, 1580–1630: English Literature and Seaborne Crime.* Farnham: Ashgate, 2010.

Keay, John. *The Honourable Company. A History of the English East India Company*. London: Harper Collins, 1991.
Kelsey, Harry. *Philip of Spain King of England. The Forgotten Sovereign*. London and New York: I.B. Tauris, 2012.
Matthee, Rudi, and Flores, Jorge. *Portugal, the Persian Gulf and Safavid Persia, Acta Iranica, 52*. Leuven: Peeters, 2011.
Pursell, Brennan. "The End of the Spanish Match." In *Historical Journal*, 45. (2002): 699–726.
Redworth, Glyn. *The Prince and the Infanta. The Cultural Politics of the Spanish Match*. New Haven and London: Yale University Press, 2003.
Redworth, Glyn. "Sarmiento de Acuña, Diego, count of Gondomar in the Spanish nobility (1567–1626)." *ODNB*.
Redworth, Glyn. "Matters Impertinent to Women: Male and Female Monarchy under Philip and Mary." In *English Historical Review*, 112. (1997): 597–613.
Russell, Conrad. "The Reign of Mary I, 1553–1558." In *The Crisis of Parliaments. English History 1509–1660*. Oxford: Oxford University Press, 1971.
Samson, Alexander, ed. *The Spanish Match. Prince Charles's Journey to Madrid, 1623*. Aldershot: Ashgate, 2006.
Shami, Jeanne. *John Donne and Conformity in Crisis in the Late Jacobean Pulpit*. Cambridge: Cambridge University Press, 2003.
Sharpe, Kevin, ed. *Faction and Parliament. Essays on Early Stuart History*. Oxford: Oxford University Press, 1978.
Stone, Richard. "The Overseas Trade of Bristol before the Civil War." In *International Journal of Maritime History*, 23 (2011): 211–239.
Subrahmanyam, Sanjay. *The Portuguese empire in Asia 1500–1700: A political and economic history*. London and New York: Longman, 1993.
Thrush, Andrew. "The French Marriage and the Origins of the 1614 Parliament." In *The Crisis of 1614 and the Addled Parliament: Literary and Historical Perspectives*. Edited by Stephen Clucas and Rosalind Davies, 25–36. Aldershot: Ashgate, 2003.
Thrush, Andrew. "Mansell, Sir Robert (1570/71-1652)." *ODNB*.
Whitelock, Anna, and Alice Hunt (eds.). *Tudor Queenship: The Reigns of Mary and Elizabeth*. Basingstoke: Palgrave Macmillan, 2010.
Wormald, Jenny. "James VI and I: two Kings or one?" In *History*, 68. (1983): 187–209.
Wormald, Jenny. "James VI and I (1566–1625), king of Scotland, England, and Ireland." *ODNB*.

CHAPTER 7

"The Princesses' Representative" or Renegade Entrepreneur? Marie Petit, the Silk Trade, and Franco-Persian Diplomacy

Junko Thérèse Takeda

PROLOGUE

On March 2, 1705, Marie Petit and Jean-Baptiste Fabre boarded the royal vessel *Tridan* in Toulon, France, destined for the Levant. Fabre, who hailed from a Marseillais banking and textile trading family, had been appointed Louis XIV's first official envoy to the Safavid Shah Sultan Hosayn. After pausing in Alexandretta (Iskenderun), the pair proceeded to Aleppo, where Turkish, Jewish, and Armenian creditors waited to collect debts that the insolvent Fabre could not pay. So, Petit loaned him two thousand *livres*.[1] This was only one of many troubles for the French mission. The local pasha refused to let Fabre depart for Persia without receiving orders from Constantinople. Fabre sought the aid of his wife Anne Cataro in Constantinople to secure the Turkish Divan's permission to continue his journey, to no avail.[2] Strongly worded messages from Louis XIV's Secretary of State for the Navy, Jérôme Phélypeaux, comte de Pontchartrain, that "nothing is as contrary to the

J.T. Takeda (✉)
Syracuse University, Syracuse, USA

rapport between the two empires than to refuse passage to a Frenchman in the Grand Seigneur's lands," failed to produce results.³ So Petit and Fabre backtracked to Alexandretta, Cyprus, Rhodes, and Samos. Fabre ordered his nephew Jacques, his secretary Pierre Dubies, and the entourage to remain there with the royal gifts for the shah while he and Petit sailed to Constantinople to obtain passports to travel from Ottoman to Persian territory.

Back in Constantinople in January 1706, Petit lodged with an Armenian, while Fabre stayed "incognito" for 35 days at the Persian ambassador's residence and concocted alternative methods to complete his journey. He and Petit arranged to travel in merchants' disguise in the Persian diplomat's retinue. He sent an Armenian, Baron Suffert, to pick up his entourage and gifts from Samos, transport them to Smyrna, and connect to a caravan to Yerevan on the Persian frontier, where they would reunite with him before the final leg to Isfahan.⁴

Petit and Fabre arrived in Yerevan, on the Persian frontier, in June 1706. But Fabre died on August 16, allegedly poisoned by the Khan of Yerevan while staying at his pleasure house.⁵ Fabre's untimely death jeopardized Louis XIV's plans to "secure privileges to trade more successfully in Persia" and weaken Dutch and British commerce established with the Safavids.⁶ It was at this point that Petit emerged as the protagonist in a curious and tragic story of entrepreneurship and betrayal. The woman allegedly assumed the title, "a representative of the princesses of France," and secured an audience with Sultan Hosayn. But upon her return to France in 1709, her French enemies incarcerated her as an imposter, prostitute, apostate, and traitor.

While long treated as a subject for Orientalist romance novels, Marie Petit and her Persian adventures have only recently attracted the attention of scholars interested in the role of powerful women in early modern diplomacy and cross-cultural exchanges.⁷ By building on such studies and examining the fraught relationships among Petit, Fabre, and Fabre's eventual successor as official ambassador, Pierre-Victor Michel (1678–1718) from the perspective of transcontinental entrepreneurship, this essay engages with traditionally overlooked, yet important questions in French history. How did geopolitical conflicts among the gunpowder empires shape French overseas trade and Bourbon expansionist diplomacy? What does the transnational context of the Asian, and specifically Persian, silk trade reveal about the relationship between French mercantilism and entrepreneurship? To what degree did local and provincial individuals, resources, and interests determine French royal strategies for overseas commercial expansion? And what role did women play in these transnational commercial activities?

Fabre died; Petit failed to obtain recognition from Louis XIV for her leading role in the French mission to Persia; the treaty Michel secured with Sultan Hosayn in 1708 produced no lasting effects; the fall of the Safavid Empire in 1722 rendered Mohammed Reza Beg's subsequent Persian embassy to France (1715) meaningless. Nonetheless, a study of the failed French missions to Persia in the first decade of the eighteenth century can offer valuable insights into the symbiotic relationship between domestic social and economic changes in France and the political contests for imperial power occurring in western Asia in the eighteenth century. Petit's story can remind historians that the two significant historical processes that defined the eighteenth century— "western" democratic revolutions and the crises of Asian "gunpowder" empires—were more intertwined than historians have allowed. A study that considers the twilight of the Safavid dynasty with the dawn of French mercantilist entrepreneurialism is but one way in which scholars of France can begin to integrate Atlantic world studies with those of the Asian and Indian Ocean.

Unfortunately, Pontchartrain sabotaged Petit's efforts to publish her memoirs, but several documents describing her activities among the Safavids remain. Michel's account of his embassy provides overwhelmingly negative portrayals of Fabre and Petit's missions. Thanks to the pains he took to discredit his predecessors, he left a trail of correspondences with French missionaries, Persian officials, and the French ambassador at Constantinople, Charles de Ferriol, in addition to a collection of legal briefs prepared against Petit. Letters of support from rulers in the Persian borderlands, in addition to legal memos written on Petit's behalf, provide another dimension to her story.

While these documents present a fragmentary and inconsistent record of Petit's activities, they can be mined for valuable nuggets of information regarding the unstable world of diplomacy on the far reaches of French global activity. What becomes clear is the extent to which that world was peopled not with statist representatives with direct connections to the French Crown, but rather provincial and foreign adventurers, entrepreneurs, risk-takers, and even women, primarily interested in their own survival, status, and assets.

While the French crown customarily relied on nobles and clergymen from administrative dynasties to represent the king in permanently established, prestigious ambassadorial posts across Europe, it faced challenges enlisting qualified diplomats willing to do the king's bidding in far-flung territories that lacked standing French institutions. Constantinople was the closest place to the Safavid Empire that had a permanent French ambassadorial presence, due to Franco-Ottoman political ties established by Suleiman the Magnificent and François I. This personnel shortage was exacerbated thanks to France's late entry into the Asia trade, long after Portuguese, British and Dutch trading companies had staked out strategic positions along the African coast, the Indian Ocean, and the Arabian Sea. Despite Cardinal de Richelieu's attempts to fund expeditions to Russia, Turkey, Persia, and India, the French crown began actively encouraging expansionist overseas trade only from the tenures of Louis XIV's Controller-General Jean-Baptiste Colbert and his son, Jean-Baptiste Antoine Colbert, the marquis de Seignelay. Their efforts to challenge Dutch supremacy in the Asia trade inspired three geographically specific goals: strengthening Franco-Ottoman trade through Marseille and the Mediterranean; using the Russian-Volga route to access Persia; establishing the Atlantic passage to India.

In this context, the French monarchy's need for representatives willing to sign on to financially and physically risky embassies in the Asian theater provided chances for opportunists of lesser-rank to prove their bonafides, collect personal wealth, and upgrade their status. Provincial merchants and manufacturers particularly found the potential for self-aggrandizement offered by trans-imperial trade and diplomacy particularly enticing. Their participation became increasingly important for the French monarchy. Competition among the Ottomans, Mughals, and Safavid empires, and intensified rivalries among Europeans vying for land and sea-lanes to Asian textiles, spices, and porcelains, created a volatile environment ripe for adventurers willing to harness their personal interests, experiences or assets to statist ventures that seemed to promise positive returns. In the parlance of the time, they were *entrepreneurs*.

When the French term *entrepreneur* first appeared in Jean Nicot's *Thresor de la langue francoyse* (1606) it signified a "redemptor" and "susceptor," someone who undertook a project. By the time the word appeared nearly a century later in the first edition of the *Dictionnaire de l'Académie française* (1694), it had acquired new meanings. The dictionary specified that entrepreneurs oversaw construction of public buildings and ships, projects useful to civic life and to the state.⁸ Between the dictionaries' publications, the term began appearing regularly in correspondences among controller-generals, royal intendants, provincial merchants, and manufacturers. In such letters, an *entrepreneur* was understood as someone who risked private assets on commercial, industrial, or martial ventures beneficial to the public good. The development of this terminology during the height of Colbert's influence at court coincided with the appearance of new trade laws that reevaluated the role of merchants and commerce in French society and opened up opportunities for the Third Estate. In his ground-breaking *Parfait négociant, ou instruction generale pour ce qui regarde le commerce,* Jacques Savary, co-author of Colbert's *Code Marchand* (1673) highlighted that entrepreneurship, wholesale, and international commerce involved "risks" and "dangers" surmountable only by the most "noble and honest" civil servant. An entrepreneur required the best traits of an Old Regime aristocrat and a modern citizen: nobility and virtue.⁹

The Fabre brothers, Petit, Michel, and the individuals who impacted their missions—the Armenian adventurer Philippe de Zagly, Georgian regent Vakhtang VI, and Fabre's Armenian aids and minders Suffert and Cocurdoulon—were entrepreneurs according to the dictionaries' definitions. They pushed the boundaries of corporate hierarchies and pursued royal protection by developing enterprises useful for statist commercial expansion. But France's failures to secure direct trade with Persia, and on a personal level, the misfortunes that befell several of these individuals reveal the dangers involved in *négoce* and *entreprise*. Moreover, the question of whether they acted in the interests of the state and remained virtuous and noble haunted these entrepreneurs regardless of their successes or failures, because ultimately, what drove entrepreneurship was personal. The veil of virtue and nobility draped over their activities could be shredded in a volatile environment where individuals exposed to unforeseen contingencies and the unpredictable effects of personal choice wielded the language of public-mindedness as a weapon to question the motives of competitors. Entrepreneurship remained dangerous and life-threatening in the early modern world. And it was particularly so for Petit, a commoner and a woman.

Petit, Silk Merchants, and Missionaries in Persia

The impetus behind Fabre's mission to Persia was silk and local manufacturing. Silk became the most coveted symbol of wealth and power in seventeenth-century Europe. The majority raw silks annually imported into Europe—86% of 200–2,50,000 kilograms—came from Persia, where sixteenth- and seventeenth-century Safavid conquests of Ottoman and Uzbek silk-growing territories sustained unprecedented economic growth. By the early seventeenth century, Persia annually produced over 2200 tons of raw silk.[10]

This silk trickled into France through Turkey. The southern seaport of Marseille emerged as France's entrepôt for Ottoman, Indian, and Persian raw silks since France's first trade capitulation with the Turks (1569).[11] Silk, in addition to dyes, became vital to the development of Marseillais and Languedocian manufacturers. Following a slump that saw Franco-Levantine commercial activity plummet 90% between the 1630s and 1660s, Colbertist reforms implemented on the heels of Louis XIV's conquest of Marseille (1660) liberalized French trade of Turkish and Persian goods through the city. Raw silks poured in through Smyrna, Tripoli, Aleppo, Cyprus, and the Greek Archipelagos.[12] The French, however, lacked treaties with the Safavids for direct trade, so relied on Ottoman middlemen who charged exorbitant costs to transport Persian products.

Nonetheless, Marseillais merchants and bankers profited from these developments, if not in money, then in expanded networks and mid-level administrative appointments. The Fabres were a case in point. Sons of *négociant* Jourdan Fabre, Jean-Baptiste Fabre and his four brothers secured positions in trade, banking, and textile manufacturing around the Mediterranean. The most successful, royal favorite Joseph Fabre, elected to consulship (municipal aldermen) in 1657, was a merchant entrepreneur and silk manufacturer, banker for the prince of Savoy and French ambassador in Constantinople, Marseille's treasurer of the marines, director of French consulates in the Levant, and head of the *Compagnie de la Mer Méditerranée*. Along with his brother Matthieu, he served as Marseille's representative at the Council of Commerce in Paris and negotiated the 1703 reinstatement of Marseille's free-port status for direct trade with the Levant. Another brother, Louis-Marseille, served as French consul in Smyrna (Izmir) and directed the family's silk depots in Adrianople (Edirne) and Constantinople.[13]

Given their extensive Mediterranean connections, the Fabres realized the importance of Persian silk and technologies, and the potential for direct trade with France. They employed hundreds of skilled craftsmen and thousands of workers of foreign origin in their silk factories. The workforce in Joseph Fabre's factory in Marseille included employees from Naples, Turkey, Holland, and Persia.[14] But power contests among the Ottomans and their neighbors, in addition to Louis XIV's continental wars, disrupted Levantine trade and ran up costs of materials and salaries of foreign workers. The Fabres reported losses in Marseille over 260,000 *livres* by the turn of the century. Such deficits were at the center of Joseph Fabre's mind when he assumed his role as Marseille's deputy at the Council of Commerce in Paris, and joined by his brothers Matthieu and Jean-Baptiste at the capital. It was he who approached Pontchartrain with the idea for the French king to pursue direct trading with Persia by sending his brother Jean-Baptiste as an envoy to the Safavids.[15] With Jean-Baptiste planted in Persia, he could recruit "workers and locate equipment necessary to produce [silks] like those made in the Indies and China that our own French are incapable of creating."[16] The diplomatic appointment would signal a financial and political coup for the Fabres, and particularly for Jean-Baptiste: in addition to social prestige, it would come with the privilege of sidestepping custom duties and trade restrictions imposed on French merchants in Persia.[17] The family could make the leap from banking, commerce, and consulships into the elite world of ambassadorial diplomacy.

While France's alliance with the Ottomans, the Safavid's political adversary, impeded cooperation with Persia, the strategy to build on France's historical strengths in the Mediterranean and use a Marseillais family experienced in Ottoman trade to break into direct commerce further eastward seemed logically sound.[18] After all, apart from missionaries, southern French merchants had brokered the initial contacts between France and Persia in the seventeenth century. The first efforts to establish a direct Franco-Persian commercial link had materialized under Louis XIII when he sent the Marseillais Louis Deshayes de Courmenin to Persia to negotiate trade privileges for French merchants surpassing those of the British and Dutch, freedom to establish Catholic missions, and security for Christian minorities. The mission failed due to Ottoman obstructionism and the opposition of the French ambassador to Constantinople. Just prior to Fabre and Petit's departure for Persia, in 1700, Pontchartrain dispatched to Persia another Marseillais cloth merchant, Jean Billon de Canserilles. Billon hoped to connect overland Persian trade to the well-established Levant route to Marseille. Despite his audience with Sultan Hosayn in 1704, no official trade treaty materialized.[19]

Pontchartrain hoped that Jean-Baptiste would convince the Persians to devote a share of their trade to France and allow textile trafficking beyond the expensive Smyrna-Aleppo-*l'echelle de Constantinople* overland corridor.[20] From the crown's vantage point, the Fabres' connections in the Levant and in Paris, in addition to Jean-Baptiste's history of textile trading in Constantinople, made him more likely to conduct a fruitful mission. He had spent considerable time in the Ottoman capital as a merchant, factory owner, general-agent for Marseille's trade, and a *chargé d'affaires* following the death in 1685 of French ambassador Gabriel-Joseph de Lavergne, Vicomte de Guilleragues. "Experienced in Turkish ways, fluent in the language," and acquainted with the powerful, he showed himself "capable of the most considerable negotiations."[21] Louis XIV "strongly approved" of the decision to dispatch him to Isfahan, and floated the idea of establishing French consulates in Iran.[22] He ordered Pontchartrain to contact Louis-Marie Pidou de St. Olon, bishop of Babylon—the crown's primary liaison in Persia—requesting information on the Safavids and asking him to "urge [Fabre] to exercise prudence and restraint to foster a positive opinion of our nation."[23]

But Fabre was not a prudent and restrained man. As early as 1685, the French ambassador's wife, Anne-Marie de Guilleragues complained to the marquis de Seignelay of Fabre's "extraordinary expenses" and indecent relationships in Istanbul, including a 5-years long affair with a Greek woman, "the daughter of a tavern-keeper and a slave." Fabre had a history of going rogue, she insinuated, producing evidence of his failure to wait for royal letters to initiate negotiations with the Grand Vizier and his lieutenant Kaimakan.[24] More problematic, by his ambassadorial appointment to Persia, Fabre had accrued massive debts that frustrated his ability to fund his mission. The "considerable sums" advanced by his brother Joseph being insufficient to cover expenses, he searched for other means of support.[25] He turned to Petit.

Petit had encountered Fabre in 1702. The merchant from Constantinople had arrived in Paris to conduct business at court and took up residence near her *maison de jeu* on rue Mazarine.[26] Her home being a place where "people of quality" came for entertainment, Fabre visited her "when time allowed." When he solicited her help to finance his journey, she agreed, assuming that "an individual whom His Majesty had honored with the title of Ambassador would not lack the means to reimburse her." She loaned him 8000 *livres* to cover food, valet service, and travel costs, which he promised to repay prior to leaving Paris. He failed to produce the sum then, but assured her that she would see the money a month after he arrived in Isfahan. Petit signed a promissory note to follow him until everything was returned.[27] She advanced more funds between his departure from France and arrival on the Persian border, all totaling 12,200 *livres.* He died before producing a penny.[28]

Focused on safeguarding her investments after Fabre's death, Petit distinguished herself as an advocate for members in Fabre's entourage and secured an audience with Shah Sultan Hosayn. But her role in the incidences that caught the Shah's attention also laid the groundwork for her enemies' eventual lawsuits against her. The most significant of these was what her allies and foes alike described as "the affair of the orange," where a dinnertime altercation between Petit and a servant, Justiniani, who threatened her with physical violence, escalated into "a great disorder" among the French delegation and prompted the khan of Yerevan to intervene.[29] The khan determined that "there was no reason to excuse the violent acts imputed to [Justiniani], nor his insolence toward the woman to whom he should have expressed deference." He threw the servant in prison.[30]

Tensions between the French and Persians flared when Fabre's entourage from Samos was seized upon arrival in Persia. Jacques Fabre and a Jesuit, Father Maunier, leaned on Petit to use her connections to the khan to secure their release, which she did. But when these men helped Justiniani escape from prison, the khan sent his forces to pillage the French lodgings. Petit lost more than 800 *livres* worth of effects, two Persians died, and the French and Armenians were taken into custody. The khan freed Petit, and when she slipped him 4000 *livres,* he released all of her compatriots, except for the Armenians Suffert and Cocurdoulon, Justiniani and Maunier, the latter whom he condemned to death. Petit pleaded for the Jesuit's life, offering to die by his side. Moved by her bravery, the khan spared him and formally acknowledged Petit's investments. The Armenians lost their heads. Justiniani died in prison.

The shah, hearing of Petit's courage, expressed that "he would be delighted to meet such a Frenchwoman who had facilitated the late Fabre's passage into Persia." He summoned her and the Frenchmen to court, providing them with a crew and per diem.³¹ She arrived outside of Qazvin at the end of December 1706. The atamadoulet, or prime minister, ordered the vizier to grant her an audience with the ruler, the shah's drogman, and court. Eunuchs conducted her to the seraglio to meet the shah's wife. She received "all honors possible," and "when the Atamadoulet...expressed that the King had granted her Farewell, she [was told] to return through Georgia as requested." The minister withdrew 1800 *livres* from his treasury for her travels, and the shah's drogman delivered her farewell leave, with an order to the khan of Yerevan "to execute the Judgment rendered for her 8000 *livres* and additional 4200."³²

While the Shah allegedly considered Petit the "facilitator" of Fabre's mission and regional khans offered her protection, her status as leader of the French delegation did not go unchallenged. Petit's legal advocate, Monsieur Eydoux, would eventually claim upon her return to France that she "rendered service to the State and loaned money in Service of the King." He would insist that the responsibility she assumed guarding the gifts from her king to the Shah and the lengths she went to protect French nationals and Catholics in the Shah's territories established her as a veritable public servant.³³ But Charles de Ferriol and his undersecretary Michel, whom the former selected as Fabre's official successor, refused to acknowledge her as a legitimate representative of the French nation. Upon news of Fabre's death, Ferriol hastily sent Michel to Persia in October 1706 to thwart Petit. Convinced "that it would take too long to wait for the French court's response," he chose not to wait for the French king to appoint a new ambassador to Persia. Michel "accepted His Excellency's orders as those of the king's," and left Constantinople with a drogman, valet, and janissary. He reached Persia within 38 days.³⁴ But the cat and mouse hunt to track down Petit, efforts by the khans to suspend Michel's mission, the Atamadoulet's death, the Shah's pilgrimages to Mashhad and Qom, and delays in obtaining proof of credentials drew out Michel's journey. Petit met Sultan Hosayn in the winter of 1706. Michel's audience with him did not occur until June 1708; they finalized a commercial treaty in October of that year.

Michel's appearance on the diplomatic stage was much more fortuitous than Jean-Baptiste Fabre's. The son of a Marseillais carpenter, Michel had placed himself in Ferriol's service at a young age, honed his skills on the battlefield and distinguished himself in Transylvania prior to climbing the rungs of his patron's office.³⁵ Unlike the aging Fabre, who benefited from his family's half-century long royalist and mercantile activities, the novice Michel depended on his connection to Ferriol to cultivate his alliances—primarily with missionaries. Fabre could afford to skirt Ferriol, with whom he had a complicated relationship; Michel remained beholden to him, given his subordinate position.

Michel arrived in Persia as a merchant traveling without an entourage, carrying no official papers authenticating his status as Fabre's successor. Michel's memoir and correspondences reveal an interesting tension: building credibility among the Persian elite required him to convince them that he was the rightful successor of the very person he disavowed as a national embarrassment. He cultivated an alliance with Jacques Fabre to strengthen his case against Petit, while disassociating himself from the elder Fabre, whom he portrayed as a self-interested, insolvent merchant led astray by a whore. He relied on Capuchin and Jesuit missionaries to underscore his commitment to public service and to his Catholic king; he used the language of public good to frame his diplomatic mission as one essential to recovering France's religious and commercial interests in Asia, while denouncing Fabre and Petit as existential threats to Catholicism and to France.

As Michel's 2-years wait to see the shah revealed, France's position in the Safavid Empire—like his own—was tenuous. As the French role in the Ottoman and Mediterranean carrying trades rose across the seventeenth century, the Dutch and British, who were not bound to a treaty with the Turks, had benefited from the defeat of the Portuguese at Hormuz in 1622 and dominated commerce along the Persian Gulf and the Indian Ocean. The influence they wielded in Persia becomes evident in Michel's complaints that "the Persians received representatives from the least important princes of Europe, and those of our enemies, while they were not interested in seeing one from the greatest Christian monarch." The British, Dutch, and Portuguese, he reported, gave 7000 gold *toman* to the Atamadoulet and "the most powerful lords" to refuse him an audience with the Shah. They, together with Armenian heretics, paid the Atamadoulet to raid the French lodge after the "affair of the orange." While it remains possible that Michel fabricated these allegations to exaggerate his obstacles, they reveal his cognizance of how western Asian geopolitics were tangled with European contests for power.[36]

With France taking a backseat to Dutch and British influence in Persia, Michel insisted that Fabre and Petits' debaucheries threatened to destroy its reputation irrevocably. He stressed that France's status in

Persia suffered due to reports circulating of Fabre, "the compromised merchant," "the bankrupted trader from Constantinople," who "committed a thousand follies with a whore that he passed as a representative of the princesses of France." But while he took every opportunity to malign Fabre and Petit in his memoir, Michel found himself having to defend Fabre to his Persian hosts to bolster France's position, and his own. When pressed by Persian officials about Fabre's legitimacy, he produced facsimiles of Fabre's letters of credence from Louis XIV and one for himself from Charles de Ferriol. When asked why France could not send representatives "more meritorious" than "dishonorable" merchants, he countered that the British and Dutch sent no one but merchants as emissaries.[37]

While pressures to protect France's position in Persia forced him to defend Fabre, Michel had nothing good to say of Petit. He claimed that she personified the debauchery that doomed the man and his operation: "This concubine was the source of all the disorders and scandals since her departure from France." She was a debauched "whore" contracted to "serve Fabre like a servant" and "launder his clothes" while she arranged "tête-à-tête's" with the son of the Nazir (Khan's superintendent) of Yerevan. Besotted by the temptress, whom they mistook to be the French king's daughter, the khans of Yerevan and Tauris, and their subordinates, favored "the courtesan," detained him using various pretexts, and impeded his efforts to lead the French delegation.[38]

The longer regional governors blockaded his attempts to reach the Shah, the more Michel sharpened his rhetorical attacks against Petit, arguing that his legitimacy was a matter of national and religious security.[39] He begged the Bishop of Babylon to extradite her to France. It was critical, he insisted, "for me to speak with authority to stop the woman from proceeding to the Court, where she has repeatedly claimed she will turn Turk and defeat all the missionaries in Persia." Michel accused her of authorizing the deaths of Suffert and Cocurdoulon, "who had placed themselves under the protection of France."[40] He suggested that Petit had more blood on her hands. She had assassinated Jean-Baptiste Fabre: "the woman wanted to strangle Fabre to plunder his effects." In short, she committed crimes of lèse-majesté: murder, apostasy, and treason to her king and god.[41]

While accusations of lèse-majesté were original to Michel, the criminalization of Petit's sexuality could be traced to her arrival with Fabre in Aleppo. Missionaries nervous about the safety and reputation of

Catholics in the Ottoman Empire had circulated reports of Petit entertaining Fabre's excessively large entourage on board ship with drunken debaucheries, gambling, and dancing.⁴² By fall of 1705, Pontchartrain had received a memoir containing "very disturbing allegations" of sexual misconduct. The Secretary of the Navy forwarded it to consuls in Aleppo with an order that were such accusations confirmed, the king would "interdict Fabre from continuing his voyage." Louis XIV signed an order on November 11, 1705 to recall Fabre to Marseille, "having learned of his bad conduct on board *Le Toulouse* in Aleppo, and not desiring him to continue his voyage." Pontchartrain described how "the Consul, all the Missionaries, and some merchants wrote unanimously regarding [Fabre's] bad conduct and scandalous debauchery with the named Petit, which is hard to doubt." Should he refuse to return Petit and the majority of his "useless men" to France, he warned, the king would "punish him severely as an example to others."⁴³ The orders went ignored.

Missionary criticisms of Petit's promiscuity crescendoed in Persia, where the Bishop of Babylon complained that her "extravagant proceedings and imprudence" were "unutterably prejudicial to the honor of France and interests of the Catholic religion."⁴⁴ While the Jesuit Maunier tried unsuccessfully to name the Bishop of Babylon as Fabre's successor, Petit headed the French delegation and cultivated relations with Safavids who persecuted Uniate Armenians. Chief among them, Imām Qoli Beg, Petit's *memainder* and drogman, forced conversions and swindled missionaries and the prominent Julfan Catholic Shahriman family with fraudulent claims totaling 28,000 *toman* (400,000 *livres*).

Qoli Beg was no ordinary drogman. The son of a bankrupt Armenian goldsmith from Julfa, he had traveled to Europe, where between 1660 to 1700, he adopted the monikers Khwaja Phillip'os, Comte de Siry, Comte Philippe de Zagly, and Husayn Beg Talish. He appeared at the French court around 1675, claiming to be a son of a Safavid official. With none other than Louis XIV's brother, the Duc d'Orleans, serving as godfather, he was baptized Catholic and honored with a pension and position in the Musketeers. After marrying the sister-in-law of gem merchant Jean-Baptiste Tavernier, he turned his attention toward Latvia (Kurland), Sweden, Brandenburg, Poland, and Moscow, where he brokered trade concessions and religious liberties for Armenian merchants who were redirecting Persian silk through the Caspian-Volga-Baltic trade routes.⁴⁵

By Petit's arrival in Persia, the Armenian had converted to Shi'a Islam and reemerged in Yerevan as Imām Qoli Beg. The credentials of the multilingual former French musketeer secured him positions as the khan's inspector of troops and Petit's guide and drogman. He accompanied Petit to the shah's court and played a leading role in the scuffle with the French that left two Persians killed, two Armenians executed, and Justiniani dead. After Petit's departure, Qoli Beg provided services for Michel, but hearing that "he repeatedly insulted the French," "overtly declared himself against Catholics," pursued "diabolic projects with Petit," forced the Shahrimans to "take the Turban," and spied for the British, the Frenchman vowed to kill him. Michel immediately requested Qoli Beg's death upon entering into the khan's good graces. When the khan delivered him Qoli Beg's decapitated head (he was executed in Tabriz on August 2, 1707), the missionaries celebrated. The Bishop of Babylon credited Michel for "expelling the infamous concubine; having the dangerous renegade Zagly, enemy of our nation, decapitated; and for reestablishing our Jesuit mission in Erivan."[46]

Certainly, religious persecution and conflict played major roles in the contests between Jean-Baptiste Fabre, Petit, Qoli Beg, and Michel. But if we look at the linguistic violence leveled at the former three individuals by Michel and his supporters, what seems also to have driven it is a deep apprehension toward an explicitly self-interested mixture of entrepreneurialism and renegadism that they came to represent. Their cross-cultural code-switching in itself was not unique. European travelers, including Michel, traveled in disguise, assumed alternate identities, and adopted local customs upon crossing into Iran. But in a world of trans-imperial trade and diplomacy, where legitimate French entrepreneurialism involved aligning your personal interests with the public good, Fabre, Petit, and Qoli Begs' behaviors could be interpreted by their Catholic and royal adversaries as an overt betrayal of public interests for personal ones. Fabre's bankruptcy, Petit's alleged promiscuity, and Qoli Beg's swindles became a synecdoche for a brand of entrepreneurial renegadism fueled by unrestrained avarice, immorality, and desire that invited accusations of disloyalty and treason. Much as the slippage from early modern privateering to piracy saw state-sanctioned ship-stealing transform into unlawful robbery at sea, Fabre, Petit and Qoli Begs' cultural code-switching, unlicensed and unbridled, skated into the criminal space of lèse-majesté. Michel, more than anyone, understood the unstated rules of entrepreneurship—that everyone's virtue remained suspect, and that the individual who used the language of public-mindedness most convincingly and ferociously could hold on to legitimacy. And so he did.

Petit, Vakhtang VI and the Politics of Identity at the Edge of Empire

Despite the accusations leveled against her by Michel, Ferriol, and the French missionaries in Iran, Marie Petit succeeded in finding some supporters. Following her audience with the shah, she traveled through Tabriz and Yerevan, arriving at the court of Vakhtang VI, regent of Kartli, in Tiflis (Tbilisi) in July 1707. In September, she proceeded to Akhalzikhé, where the pasha's wife furnished her with an escort to Trebisond (Trabzon), from where she continued to Constantinople then to France in 1709.[47] Petit's Georgian episode offers a fascinating window into the politics of religious identity in the Safavid borderlands, and how they became intertwined with French diplomacy at the end of Louis XIV's reign. Petit capitalized on Vakhtang VI's desire to secure the Sun King's protection and obtained the Georgian regent's patronage critical to dispute negative portrayals of her character and actions.

In a letter addressed to the French king in 1707, Vakhtang waxed poetic of Louis XIV, "our father, and master, who loves God and the Holy Trinity." "Having shed blood for Christianity, your name has reached the corners of the world," he praised. After apologizing for taking liberties to pen such a missive, Vakhtang described how Georgia and France enjoyed "such a friendship, that when we see a French person, we render them all services possible." He described how he extended hospitality to Petit, "delighted to see a lady in these barbaric lands, far from France, so firm in her Catholic faith." He begged the king not to believe "false reports" maligning her character; Petit, he insisted, "is a wise lady of good spirit...a good Catholic lady," who had saved a Jesuit priest and several Frenchmen in Persia. Such evaluations mirrored those in a message he sent to Ferriol, attesting her "good mores" and "admirable conduct."[48]

Sandwiched between the Ottoman, Safavid, and Romanov empires, the Caucasian territories of Georgia and Armenia had experienced for centuries the challenges of retaining political and religious autonomy. The Peace of Amasya between Suleiman and Shah Tahmasp (1555) had carved a border that handed western Armenia and Georgia to the Ottomans, and eastern and southern Georgia to the Persians. The Safavids punished Georgian struggles for independence with invasions, deportations, and forced conversions, while relying on loyal Georgian rulers to provide military force to keep the Russians, Ottomans, and Afghans at bay. Like his father Levan (Shah Quli Khan, 1653–1709), regent of Kartli, Vakhtang VI outwardly made concessions to the Safavids while exploring strategies to recover religious and political freedoms.[49] Sultan Hosayn tolerated Vakhtang's flirtation with Orthodoxy and provided him with a royal subsidy because he provided service on the Afghan front. Petit's arrival at Vakhtang's doorstep provided him the perfect opportunity to initiate overtures to Louis XIV to request the Catholic monarch's aid against his Islamic overlord.

Such support became critical in 1714, when the shah summoned Vakhtang to confirm him as king of Kartli on condition that he embrace Islam. When he refused, Sultan Hosayn imprisoned him and canceled his subsidy. Hoping that Louis XIV would pressure the shah to release him, Vakhtang sent his uncle, Sulkhan Saba Orbeliani, a Catholic monk, to Rome and Versailles to negotiate on his behalf. In two memoirs on Georgia, Sulkhan Saba detailed how "Georgia is in imminent danger of completely becoming *mahométane*...24 well-populated provinces and neighboring states will be plunged into idolatry." Imploring Louis XIV to come to their aid, Sulkhan Saba requested 300,000 *écus* to return Vakhtang from Isfahan, establish missions, and mount a military challenge to Shah Sultan Hosayn's religious imperialism.

Letters from Vakhtang in hand, Sulkhan Saba offered privileges for transit trade in textiles through Georgia to Persia in exchange for political and religious protection. In two audiences with Louis, he proposed a French consulate in Tiflis; safe passage for French merchants to and from Persia; and concessions to transport merchandise to the Black Sea, to open warehouses and stores, and trade silks, cotton, and wax with the Circassians and Mingrelians. Opening the Georgian corridor would mean diverting three-quarters of the expensive caravan traffic through Smyrna to the cheaper Black Sea route. If economic incentives were not sufficient to convince Louis, Sulkhan Saba produced a brief from Pope Clement XI, who had resolved to protect Georgia in the interests of expanding Catholicism in the east.[50]

Pontchartrain urged Jean-Baptiste Colbert de Torcy, Secretary of State of Foreign Affairs, to "develop and conduct these projects in great secrecy." A trade treaty with Georgia would reduce silk trafficking costs by half and cut the caravan trek from 105 to 26 days. The Persia-Georgia-Black Sea route would help textile merchants avoid the dangers of piracy, weaken Venetian, British, and Dutch trade in the region, and result in "extraordinary advantages for France's manufacturers." Sulkhan Saba added the possibility of founding a *Collège français* in Georgia that would send sons of nobility to train with the French navy in Marseille, to eventually lead a Christian fighting force in the midst of Islamic Eurasia. Given its "incalculable advantages" for France, Louis XIV and Pontchartrain considered the Georgian trade deal one of the state's "largest projects." The king promised to work with his consuls to facilitate Vakhtang's liberation.[51]

But the project crumpled. The requested funds did not materialize and French missionaries never arrived in Georgia. The Georgian trade corridor was not included in Louis XIV's commercial treaty with Sultan Hosayn concluded with Mohammed Riza Beg's Persian embassy to Versailles (1715). Louis died a few months later, and the regent Philippe II, Duc d'Orléans proved uninterested in pursuing Catholic expansion in far-flung Eurasian territories. Vakhtang remained in captivity until 1719; the shah did not release him until he converted to Islam. The collapse of the Safavid Empire a few years later freed Vakhtang from the Shah's hold, only to thrust him into the chaos of war among Ottomans, Russians, and Persians that left him exiled and Georgia destroyed.

Vakhtang's Franco-Georgian diplomacy only resulted in one small victory. His statements of Petit's good conduct helped invalidate Michel's claims against her. Upon her return to France in 1709, Michel had obtained a *lettre de cachet* to incarcerate her in Marseille's Maison de Refuge for repentant prostitutes. Pontchartrain granted her a trial and freed her from the Maison in 1713, but she lost her claim to the 12,000 *livres*. Relying in large part on Vakhtang's positive letters of support, she acquired an Arrêt de Conseil from the *cour de cassation* (court of last resort) in 1719 to revoke earlier judgments rendered against her. But her financial state in ruin, her health broken, the "representative of the princesses of France" accused of "prostituting the French nation" was never heard from again.[52]

Conclusion

Petit was not a queen. Neither was she born into nobility. She was a common, ordinary woman from Moulins. Were it not for the large amounts of money she accumulated, presumably at her gambling house that made her an attractive source of funds for the bankrupt Jean-Baptiste Fabre, her life, like those of the vast majority of her female contemporaries, would have remained invisible to history. What made her exceptional was the written record left of her travels, scant and scattered though they may be, that allows us to reconstruct a remarkable part of her life.

Those records fail to reveal her motivation for going to Persia, aside from collecting Fabre's debts owed to her. They fail to expose what led her to believe that traveling 1700 miles to a distant land was a risk worth taking for a woman. Perhaps she calculated that were she to stay in Paris and wait for Fabre's return, she would have several thousand *livres* to lose. Perhaps as a madam of dubious status and background whose assets were financial, and not familial, she had everything to lose by staying in Paris. Or, she and the married Fabre had something more than a creditor-debtor relationship, as her enemies intimated. We will never know. What we can glean from the records is that her financial capital provided Petit with a significant source of mobility to leave France. It allowed her to wield enough power and leverage in the Persian and Georgian contexts to survive and return intact to her home country, where it turned out, the powers that be restricted her options and further success.

While she may have existed on the fringes of proper French society, and her choices and experiences may seem unusual compared to other French commoners of her sex, the Mediterranean space into which she entered was populated with men and women like her who transgressed boundaries. As Eric Dursteller has recently demonstrated, the relative ease of "seaborne communications" created an early modern Mediterranean world not characterized exclusively by binaries and "cultural collision," but rather by shared attitudes, behaviors, and values. Historians have described the sea and surrounding areas as a borderless space disposed to cultural contact and intermingling, where hundreds of thousands of individuals fashioned and refashioned their lives in ways that challenged fixed ideologies and identities. In other words, the space was fertile for renegadism: as Dursteller suggests, an act understandable not only as the breaking of religious conventions, but political, gender, or social ones as well.[53] While early modern religious and secular authorities assigned pejorative readings to renegadism, recent scholarship has shown how it permitted historical subjects to exercise agency, however limited. Renegadism allowed men and women an opportunity to escape socioeconomic or political instability in their regions of origin, or provided more options to achieve physical security, financial gain, or social mobility.

Renegadism, it can be argued, was not simply something limited to the fringes. The Mediterranean was hardly a periphery. One of the major arguments of this essay is that we should consider it central to statecraft, and particularly, to the economics of early modern statecraft that we call mercantilism. Historians have increasingly disputed the assumption that mercantilism was a doctrine premised on dirigisme and micromanagement.[54] Growing European states with outsized imperial ambitions and limited resources relied on individuals, communities, and institutions at local and provincial levels. The story of Fabre, Petit, and Michel's adventures in Persia fits into these reconsiderations of mercantilism. It can help cast doubt over absolutism's absoluteness and centrifugal direction. It underscores how mercantilism—even the French variant—was linked with entrepreneurial opportunism connected to renegadism.

This is not to defend mercantilism. Certainly, with it appeared some kernels of modern democratic equality and citizenship. The notion that universal rights, rather than particularistic privileges, ought to be the foundations for good governance sprouted as global trade relaxed entrenched social hierarchies. Seeking to augment its international standing by developing a commercial and industrial society, the French Crown introduced policy innovations aimed at centralizing power while weakening feudal society and its vertical structures. But the economic theory that equated the prosperity of the nation with its ability to capture the largest percentage of the allegedly fixed amount of worldly wealth gave rise to the fiscal-military state, monopolies in armed trading, racialized slave markets, and underground commerce.[55] Mercantilism played a foundational role in the ugly birth of modernity. Violence was central to its development.

Part of this violence directly impacted Petit. While the disinclination of privileged nobility to embrace the privilege of risking their necks in chancy missions proffered opportunities for members of the Third Estate, competition among them to turn a profit and earn royal protection could turn ruthless. Fabre, Petit, and Michel viciously declared and defended their diplomatic legitimacy precisely because their claims to it remained shaky and insecure. Fabre and Michels' financial shortages, impromptu appointments to ambassadorship, and personal feuds threatened to sabotage their missions. Petit did not share the pecuniary woes of her male counterparts, but the self-appointment of a daughter of a master cobbler and a laundress to a position of diplomatic authority remained unconventional and easily assailable.[56] The ways in which she transgressed norms of gender and estate, traveled with the married Fabre and won the admiration of Muslims, and Armenian heretics opened her to charges of depravity. In an environment where missionaries caught in explosive confessional struggles with heretics and non-Christians moonlighted as royal representatives, informants, and unofficial diplomats, Petit's eccentricities, interpreted as moral failings, made her particularly vulnerable.

Ultimately, neither Fabre, nor Michel, nor Petit, as official or semi-official French representatives to Persia, found the French crown to be a source of reliable support. As in other remote corners of French commercial and colonial activities, mercantilism on the ground and across the waters, for all of Louis XIV's aspirations to and claims of centralized governance, remained un-centralized and chaotic. Slowness of communication to and from Versailles forced Ferriol, Fabre, Petit, and Michel to make decisions and act independently of the crown. They were left to their own devices to navigate the labyrinth of local alliances and animosities, gather information for survival, arrange travel privileges, collect financial backing and broker agreements beneficial for king and state. The extent to which they could do so was limited by personal conditions and circumstances beyond their control. Fabre's debts led him to rely on Petit, which provoked the ire of Jesuits and Capuchins. Petit's ambiguous relationship with Fabre and the latter's conflicts with Ferriol left her little option but to turn to non-Christians— tributary lords, princes, translators, and guides—for support, which furthered accusations of renegadism. Michel, a relatively inexperienced diplomat, whose status as Fabre's successor remained unconfirmed for over a year, did not share his predecessor's history of financial and moral failings. Consequently, he was able to curry the favor of ecclesiastics who shunned Fabre and Petit. With fault lines drawn between Petit and her Persian and Georgian supporters on one end, and Michel and the ecclesiastics on the other, existent confessional disputes flared and fated Petit to her ruin.

Though Michel succeeded in neutralizing his political competition, bad timing doomed Franco-Iranian and Georgian diplomacy. By the time official contacts materialized between the French, Persians, and Georgians, Safavid political and economic powers had deteriorated. Borderland conflicts had unsettled Iranian stability, commercial activity, and silver supplies. This process predated the French missions to Persia by decades. Plague and famine killed over 70,000 inhabitants in Isfahan between 1678 and 1679, and 80,000 in 1685.[57] Financial crises forced Sultan Hosayn's predecessor, Sulayman and his grand vizier, Shaykh Ali Khan to search for strategies to increase revenues. Zagly and Vakhtang's gambles on Europe's receptiveness to Persian trade aligned with such imperial initiatives. But while seeming to prop up Safavid economic interests, the political havoc that their entrepreneurial adventurism wrecked hastened the decline of the weakened empire. Sultan Hosayn's trade concessions with France—one of his final attempts to free the Safavids from Dutch and British influence, resist Ottoman encroachments, and shore up economic stability—could do little to prevent his fall, and with it, the end of a dynasty.

Gunpowder geopolitics—particularly the tensions between Ottoman Turkey and Safavid Iran—elevated costs of raw materials, destabilized markets, and created the tense economic environment in the Mediterranean world that propelled Marseillais merchants like the Fabres in the first place to search for alternative trade routes, recruit foreign workers, and forge diplomatic ties. It offered opportunities for personal gain that attracted Petit, Michel, Philippe de Zagly, and other ambitious individuals from humble origins. But gunpowder geopolitics also played a major role in limiting the scope and success of French mercantilism east of the Ottoman trade zone. It rendered entrepreneurial activities and cultural code-switching risky and deadlier. An analysis that considers jointly, the crises of Eurasian empires and transitions of European old regimes to modern democracies, can allow historians to more fully appreciate global interconnectedness in the long eighteenth century. And it can remind us that that which we moderns celebrate as cosmopolitanism has in the historical past, been fueled and shaped by the dark realities of un-belonging, desperation, and violence.

Notes

1. Monsieur Eydoux, *Mémoire pour servir d'instruction au procès de Demoiselle Marie Petit* (Henri Brebion, 1710), 490.
2. Archives Étrangères [AE] Corr. Pol. Turquie 43, fols. 95–96. Cataro lived by the French embassy in Constantinople. The French ambassador Charles de Ferriol claimed that he advanced 2000 ecus for Cataro to secure Fabre's transit permission. But biographers have highlighted the fraught relationship between Ferriol, Cataro, and Fabre, suggesting that Cataro was Ferriol's lover and that Ferriol intended to sabotage Fabre's mission, having hoped that his undersecretary Pierre Victor Michel would be tapped for the Persian embassy: "Dissatisfied with the preference for Fabre, he sought to thwart it...Ferriol secretly undermined his spouse's efforts." See "Marie Petit," in Michaud, *Biographie universelle, ancienne et moderne*, vol. XXXII (Paris), 594–597.
3. Archives Nationales de France [AN] MAR/B/7/73/187–189, 201. Plans to get Fabre to Persia as a merchant charged by the Compagnie des Indes Orientales to inspect French trade in Iran and Surat fell through.
4. Eydoux, *Mémoire*, 490.
5. Eydoux, *Mémoire*, 490. Fabre fell ill at "Carpoula, maison de plaisance du Kam d'Erivan."
6. AN/MAR/B7/71/221, Lettre, January 9, 1704, à M. l'Evesque de Babylone.
7. See Matthew Lauzon, ""In the Name of the Princesses of France": Marie Petit and the 1706 French Diplomatic Mission to Safavid Iran," in *Journal of World History*, 25 (2014): 341–371; Katherine McDonald, "Marie Petit's Persian Adventure (1705–8): The Eastward Travels of a French 'Concubine,'" in *Prostitution and Eighteenth-Century Culture: Sex, Commerce and Morality*, eds. Ann Lewis and Markman Ellis (London: Pickering and Chatto, 2012), 59–70.
8. Jean Nicot, Tresor de la langue francoyse (1606), and Dictionnaire de l'Académie française, 1st Edition (1694), Accessed at http://artflsrv02.uchicago.edu/cgi-bin/dicos/pubdico1look.pl?strippedhw=entrepreneur.
9. Jacques Savary, *Parfait négociant*, 408.
10. Marika Sardar, "Silk along the Seas," in *Interwoven Globe*, ed. Amelia Peck (New Haven: Yale University Press, 2013), 67.
11. Rémy Kerténian, "Apparences baroques et production textile à Marseille, 1600–1750," *Revue Marseille* 192 (2000), 85–92; Junko Takeda, "French Mercantilism and the Early Modern Mediterranean: A Case Study of Marseille's Silk Industry," in Special Issue: "France and the Early Modern Mediterranean," *French History*, 29.1 (2015), 12–17.

12. Archives de la Chambre de Commerce de Marseille [ACCM] B3, 587–92; 47–51; Takeda, "French Mercantilism," 12–17.
13. Junko Takeda, *Between Crown and Commerce: Marseille and the Early Modern Mediterranean* (Baltimore: Johns Hopkins University Press, 2011), 23, 44–49.
14. AN/M/B7/589. Lettre, 15 juillet 1693.
15. Joseph put a good word in for Jean-Baptiste as early as 1685, when he reminded Pontchartrain how "our entire family is committed to the service of the king and his grandeur." AE/B/III/259, 25 avril 1685.
16. Archive de la ville de Marseille [AVM] HH 432. Lettre, 18 octobre 1708.
17. Lauzon, 343.
18. The Ottomans relied on France to invade Persia in 1547 when they took Tabriz. French diplomats repeatedly suggested that cooperation with Persia would damage the Franco-Ottoman alliance crucial to hold back the Hapsburgs. While Shah Abbas I approached Henri IV, the French turned down his overtures to maintain Ottoman trade privileges. Missionaries, most notably the Capuchin Raphael du Mans, who lived in Isfahan between 1647 and 1696, helped the French gain a minor foothold among the Safavids. The bishop of Babylon also served as Louis XIV's representative in Persia. See Jean Calmard, "The French Presence in Safavid Persia: A Preliminary Study," in *Iran and the World in the Safavid Age*, ed. Willem Floor and Edmund Herzig (London: I. B. Tauris, 2005), 309–315.
19. Calmard, 310.
20. AN/MAR/B/7/71/153, Letter, October 17, 1703.
21. AN AE/B/3/259/2, Letter, April 25, 1685.
22. AN MAR/B/7/71/230. Letter, January 23, 1704.
23. AN MAR/B/7/71/221.
24. AN AE/B/1/379, Letter, September 12, 1685.
25. AN Mar/B/7/73/279.
26. Michaud, *Biographie universelle*, 594–597.
27. Fabre, quoted in Henri Aurenche and Louis Coquet, *La Brelandière; Ambassadrice du Roi Soleil* (Paris: Nouvelles Éditions Latines, 1945), 153; Michaud, *Biographie universelle*, 594, quotes her oath: "I the undersigned, will follow Fabre in his travels to Constantinople and elsewhere, whether it be for the king or his own affairs, and assist him with my care without claiming remuneration, Marie Petit."
28. Eydoux, *Mémoire*, 489–490.
29. The "affair" was so-named due to Petit throwing an orange at Justiniani.
30. Eydoux, *Mémoire*, 490–491.
31. Eydoux, *Mémoire*, 492.
32. Eydoux, *Mémoire*, 494; Lauzon, 353.

33. Eydoux, *Mémoire*, 488.
34. Michel, *Mémoire du sieur Michel…en Perse*, 5.
35. Monsieur Brosset, "Documens originaux sur les relations diplomatiques de la Géorgie avec la France vers la fin du règne de Louis XIV," *Nouveau Journal Asiatique*, Tome IX (Paris, 1832), 200.
36. Brosset, 30–31.
37. Brosset, 25, 28–29, 31–32, 41–43.
38. Michel, "Mémoire," 8, 12–18, 25.
39. Michel claimed that Petit had "done infinite harm to the nation and to religion." Michel, "Mémoire," 21.
40. Michel, "Mémoire," 25.
41. Michel did not retract this claim, even after hearing rumors that the khan of Yerevan had poisoned Fabre. The Persian ambassador who had helped Fabre and Petit enter the territory was an enemy of the Atamadoulet and the khan. The latter believed that if Fabre obtained an audience with the shah, he would urge him to promote the ambassador to Beylerbey. When the shah agreed to an audience with Fabre, the khan had him poisoned. Michel, *Mémoire*, 28–31.
42. "Marie Petit," in Michaud, *Biographie universelle, ancienne et moderne*, vol. XXXII (Paris), 594–7; Lauzon, 364–65.
43. AN/MAR/B/7/73/206, 210, 279, 312.
44. Bishop of Babylon, in *A Chronicle of the Carmelites in Persia*, ed. Herbert Chick (London: I. B. Tauris, 2012), 535.
45. Robert Gulbenkian, "Philippe de Zagly, Marchand Arménien de Julfa et l'établissement du commerce Persan en Courlande en 1696," *Revue des etudes arméniennes 7* (1970): 361–399; Rudolph Matthee, *The Politics of Trade in Safavid Iran: Silk for Silver, 1600–1730* (Cambridge: Cambridge University Press, 2006), 200–201; Philip Curtin, *Cross-Cultural Trade in World History* (Cambridge: Cambridge University Press, 2002), 202–204; Sebouh Aslanian, *From the Indian Ocean to the Mediterranean: The Global Trade Networks of Armenian Merchants from New Julfa* (Berkeley: University of California Press, 2011), 82–85; Edmund Herzig, "A Response to one Asia, or Many? Reflections from connected history," in *Modern Asian History* 50.1 (2016), 44–51.
46. Michaud, *Biographie universelle*, 337–8; Michel, *Mémoire*, 50–51, 62–64, 72, 82–84.
47. Brosset, "Documens originaux sur les relations diplomatiques de la Géorgie," 203–204.
48. Brosset, 206–08, 213.
49. Vakhtang VI's father Levan (1653–1709) became regent of Kartli in 1675, when the Safavids named his brother Georgi XI (Gurgin Khan), king of Kartli, leader of a military offensive against Afghan tribes.

Levan's conversion to Islam secured him as naib of Kerman, and later, divanbeg, or justice, in Persia.
50. Sulkhan Saba, "Mémoire présenté à M. le C de Pontchartrain, minister d'état du très-grand empereur de France pour remette à sa majesté imperial," in Brosset, 347–353; Louis Coquet, "Une ambassade géorgienne en France au Grand Siècle," in *Revue Mensuelle, Prométhée, organe de défense nationale des peuples du Caucase et de l'Ukraine et du Turkestan*, No. 4. (1927) 17–25; Donald Rayfield, *Edge of Empires: A History of Georgia* (London: Reaktion Books, 2013), 222–226.
51. Pontchartrain in Coquet, "Une ambassade géorgienne," 22–25.
52. Michel, 36.
53. Eric Dursteller, *Renegade Women: Gender, Identity and Boundaries in the Early Modern Mediterranean* (Baltimore: Johns Hopkins University Press, 2012), ix, 108–109, 112.
54. See for example, *Mercantilism Reimagined: Political Economy in Early Modern Britain and its Empire*, eds. Philip Stern and Carl Wennerlind (Oxford: Oxford University Press, 2014).
55. Michael Kwass, *Contraband: Louis Mandrin and the Making of a Global Underground* (Cambridge: Harvard University Press, 2014).
56. Lauzon, 354; H. Dussourd, *La Brendalière, une adventurière d'origine moulinoise* (Moulins, 1966), 5–6. There remains speculation over whether her real father was her godfather, Jean Fromental, a legal prosecutor whose laundry was done by Petit's mother. See Brosset, "Documens originaux sur les relations diplomatiques de la Géorgie avec la France vers la fin du règne de Louis XIV," in *Nouveau Journal Asiatique*, Tome IX (Paris, 1832), 200.
57. Matthee, *Politics of Trade*, 177.

Bibliography

Primary Sources

Manuscripts:
Archive de la ville de Marseille. HH 432.
Archives Étrangères. B/III.
Archives Étrangères. Corr. Perse 2–4, Corr. Pol. Turquie 43.
Archives Nationales de France. MAR/B7.

Printed:
Monsieur Eydoux. *Mémoire pour servir d'instruction au procès de Demoiselle Marie Petit*. Henri Brebion, 1710.

Secondary Sources

Aslanian, Sebouh. *From the Indian Ocean to the Mediterranean: The Global Trade Networks of Armenian Merchants from New Julfa*. Berkeley: University of California Press, 2011.

Aurenche, Henri, and Coquet, Louis. *La Brelandière; Ambassadrice du Roi Soleil*. Paris: Nouvelles Éditions Latines, 1945.

Calmard, Jean. "The French Presence in Safavid Persia: A Preliminary Study." In *Iran and the World in the Safavid Age*. Edited by Willem Floor and Edmund Herzig, 309–326. London: I. B. Tauris, 2005.

Curtin, Philip. *Cross-Cultural Trade in World History*. Cambridge: Cambridge University Press, 2002.

Dursteller, Eric. *Renegade Women: Gender, Identity and Boundaries in the Early Modern Mediterranean*. Baltimore: Johns Hopkins University Press, 2012.

Gulbenkian, Robert. "Philippe de Zagly, Marchand Arménien de Julfa et l'établissement du commerce Persan en Courlande en 1696." In *Revue des études arméniennes* 7. (1970): 361–399.

Kerténian, Rémy. "Apparences baroques et production textile à Marseille, 1600–1750." In *Revue Marseille* 192. (2000): 85–92.

Kwass, Michael. *Contraband: Louis Mandrin and the Making of a Global Underground*. Cambridge: Harvard University Press, 2014.

Lauzon, Matthew. ""In the Name of the Princesses of France": Marie Petit and the 1706 French Diplomatic Mission to Safavid Iran." In *Journal of World History*, 25. (2014): 341–371.

Matthee, Rudolph. *The Politics of Trade in Safavid Iran: Silk for Silver, 1600–1730*. Cambridge: Cambridge University Press, 2006.

McDonald, Katherine. "Marie Petit's Persian Adventure (1705–8): The Eastward Travels of a French 'Concubine.'" In *Prostitution and Eighteenth-Century Culture: Sex, Commerce and Morality*. Edited by Ann Lewis and Markman Ellis, 59–70. London: Pickering and Chatto, 2012.

Sardar, Marika. "Silk along the Seas." In *Interwoven Globe*. Edited by Amelia Peck, 66–81. New Haven: Yale University Press, 2013.

Takeda, Junko. *Between Crown and Commerce: Marseille and the Early Modern Mediterranean*. Baltimore: Johns Hopkins University Press, 2011.

Takeda, Junko. "French Mercantilism and the Early Modern Mediterranean: A Case Study of Marseille's Silk Industry." Special Issue: "France and the Early Modern Mediterranean." In *French History*, 29.1. (2015): 12–17.

PART III

Exotic Encounters

CHAPTER 8

"I would not have given it for a wilderness of monkeys": Turquoise, Queenship, and the Exotic

Carole Levin and Cassandra Auble

Michael Radford's 2004 film version of *The Merchant of Venice* largely adheres to Shakespeare's narrative, but it ends with a scene not specified in the play. The character Jessica, played by Zuleikha Robinson, stands alone outside of Portia's palace at Belmont; she gazes across the water

---

Earlier versions of this paper were presented at the Shakespeare at Kalamazoo session of the Medieval Congress, May, 2013, and the Society for Renaissance Studies at Southampton University July, 2014, and in Venice in July 2016 as part of the University of Warwick's program to accompany the production of The Merchant in Venice held in the Jewish Ghetto, Carole would like to thank Carol Rutter for her great hospitality during that time. The authors are deeply grateful to Jo Eldridge Carney for her help with this essay.

C. Levin (✉)
University of Nebraska, Lincoln, NE, USA

C. Auble
West Virginia University, Morgantown, WV, USA

toward Venice where she fled from her father, Shylock, when she eloped with Lorenzo. This scene parallels the previous one in which Shylock also stands alone; he is on the street, exiled from his place of worship. As the film closes, Jessica looks down at her hand and on her finger is a large turquoise ring set in gold, presumably the ring her mother had given her father when they were betrothed. Within the confines of Shakespeare's play, it is assumed—on the power of hearsay—that Jessica took the beloved ring and traded it away. In Radford's iteration, the revelation that Jessica in fact kept the turquoise does not so much rewrite the play as it clarifies a textual uncertainty. In so doing, Radford emphasizes the play's themes of dislocation, miscommunication, and loss, and exposes its incomplete resolution.

Shakespeare's *The Merchant of Venice*, in keeping with the heterosexual conventions of generic comedy, ends with the newly married couples going off to couple, the single Antonio being the conspicuous outlier. Radford's decision to conclude instead with a distressed and solitary Jessica challenges the lighter romantic paradigm and points to the play's more troubling religious and sexual politics. In a play that swiftly establishes binary oppositions—Christian/Jew, heterosexual/homosocial, usury/generosity—only to complicate them, it is Jessica, even more than Antonio, who occupies a disconcerting liminal space. Her problematic and uncertain position by the play's end, glossed over by Shakespeare's text, has been acknowledged and emphasized by scholars as well as numerous contemporary performances.[1] While Shakespeare's play challenges many circumscribed boundaries between Christian and Jewish categories, Jessica is the one character who firmly but uneasily inhabits both worlds.

Jessica is a merchant's daughter, not a queen. Shakespeare, writing in London in the 1590s, could observe both a queen and merchants' daughters, and queens in the Renaissance also greatly valued turquoise, and in some cases, turquoise rings had great significance. The turquoise, coming from Persia and Arabia, was a valuable stone in sixteenth-century Britain. It was worn by queens and also given as gifts to and from queens such as Mary I and Elizabeth I. Particularly for Mary Stuart, there were turquoise rings at critical moments of her life, including her abdication. While today usually turquoise are set in silver, in Renaissance England they were set in gold, exotic from a faraway land, and highly prized. Turquoise had other potential values, however, that included powerful protection. In this essay, Shakespeare's play works as a frame to explore the value of turquoise, from where it was traded, its ownership by queens and others of high status, and its supposed magical properties in English Renaissance culture. Thus, we can understand its value at the time.

In *The Merchant of Venice*, rings play a central role, both literally and metaphorically, as numerous critics have demonstrated.[2] In contrast, the turquoise ring is mentioned only briefly in the play, but its symbolic import is profound—so much so that Radford allows the camera to linger on it, giving the ring the filmic version of "the last word." The presence of the turquoise ring redeems Jessica and returns some of our sympathies to Shylock, but it also reminds us of the ambiguous relationship between father and daughter, and that the play's larger ethnic and religious conflicts are left unresolved. It also serves as a touchstone for questions of trade and exoticism.

Shylock's Ring

Why does such a small material object carry so much resonance? In *The Merchant of Venice*, Jessica lives alone with her father, Shylock, the Jewish moneylender, in a rigid, constrained household. Their home is where Shylock keeps his wealth, in the form of currency, gold, and precious jewels, including a diamond worth two thousand ducats. When Shylock goes out on business, he insists that Jessica keeps the house securely locked: "Hear you me, Jessica,/ Lock up my doors … Do as I bid you. Shut doors after you./ Fast bind, fast find" (2.5. 27–28, 51–52).[3] One evening, Shylock is invited to supper with some Christians, but he feels ambivalent about attending because of a disturbing dream: "There is some ill a-brewing towards my rest,/ For I did dream of money-bags tonight" (2.5. 17–18).

Shylock's ill-ease is well founded, for Jessica, who has described her house as "hell" (2.3.2), is already plotting her escape, and she does not intend to go empty-handed. Her Christian lover Lorenzo tells his friends, "She hath directed/ How I shall take her from her father's house,/ What gold and jewels she is furnish'd with" (2.4. 29–32). Indeed, Jessica ably executes the plan, disguising herself as a page and taking as much of Shylock's wealth as she can physically manage. Recent productions have shown a Lorenzo more entranced with the plunder than with the woman he has promised to marry: Jessica "furnished" with caskets of gold and jewels is one thing; Jessica without is quite another.[4]

Shylock is distraught at Jessica's elopement, but he is also furious that she absconded with his property. We first hear of Shylock's outrage through a second-hand report from Salerio, one of Lorenzo's friends:

> I never heard a passion so confused,
>
> So strange, outrageous, and so variable
>
> As the dog Jew did utter in the streets.
>
> 'My daughter? O, my ducats! O, my daughter!
>
> Fled with a Christian! O, my Christian ducats! …
>
> And jewels, two stones, two rich and precious stones,
>
> Stol'n by my daughter! Justice! (2.8. 12–21)

While Salerio's account is cruelly delivered, it may not be exaggerated, for the expression of anger we hear directly from Shylock is equally intense. Shylock has asked his compatriot Tubal to go to Genoa to pursue Jessica. When Tubal returns, he tells Shylock, "I often came where I did hear of her, but cannot find her" (3.1. 69). In Radford's film, we see flashbacks of Jessica enjoying herself in Genoa as Tubal tells Shylock about her extravagant activities, spending on just one night "fourscore ducats"—perhaps a plausible act of rebellion given the parsimony of her father's household. Shylock is outraged: "I would my/ daughter were dead at my foot, and the jewels in her ear! Would/ she were hearsed at my foot, and the ducats in her coffin!" (3.1. 74–76). Shylock's response to Jessica's elopement, particularly his conflation of the loss of his daughter and his wealth, is often cited in assessments of his character and seldom to his benefit.[5] It is not clear whether Shylock is most upset about his daughter's clandestine marriage, her conversion to Christianity, or the theft of his property, but he is portrayed here at his stereotypical worst: a miser who cares more about his money than his only child. But as we find out at the end of the film, Tubal's reporting may not have been truthful, and in the film, it appears that for whatever reasons of his own, Tubal is deliberately enraging Shylock, and whenever Shylock begins to calm down, Tubal has something else to say that will stir him up. What is the most upsetting for Shylock is when Tubal claims that one of Antonio's creditors "showed me a ring that he had of your daughter for a monkey" (3.1. 98–99). Shylock is devastated, immediately assuming that it must have been his turquoise ring. "Out upon her! Thou torturest me, Tubal. It was my/ turquoise; I had it of Leah when I was a bachelor: I would not/ have given it for a wilderness of monkeys" (3.1. 100–102). While Shylock's previous rant cast him in a most unflattering light, his reaction to his wife's gift renders him sympathetic and humane: he valued the ring for its personal history, not its financial worth. As Catherine Richardson points out, Shylock's response to the traded ring connects "the rhetoric of humanity with the capacity for deep emotion … The ring actually wounds him, as though it was used by his daughter as a weapon against him. Brief as it is, its mention is crucial to the tension Shakespeare maintains between the stock comic Jew who rants of daughters and ducats and Shylock the individual, the man with a past." [6]

And what of the fact that Jessica allegedly exchanged the turquoise ring for a monkey? Monkeys, along with parrots and lapdogs, were in vogue as expensive household pets; they also had a reputation for being lecherous animals.[7] Jessica's purported exchange of the ring for a monkey could be seen as an assertion of her independence: sexually, financially, and emotionally. Bruce Boehrer argues that Jessica's decision to exchange the ring for the expensive, exotic, and impractical monkey "repudiates a particular symbolic investment that Shylock holds dear, for it transforms the Jew's turquoise ring, the enduring emblem of his dead wife's love, into a purely economic commodity, significant only with respect to its exchange value."[8] In divesting herself of the ring, Jessica would appear to be turning her back on her emotional ties with both her father and her mother and establishing her own autonomy.

But according to Radford's film, Jessica did *not* trade away the ring, the implication being that Tubal was misinformed or invented the anecdote and that Jessica has kept her mother's ring all along. As Samuel Crowl argues, "Unlike Bassanio, she does not give it away; in fact, she wears it as a sign of her divided loyalties. Her melancholy thus ends the film as Antonio's began it, and the experience of Radford's *Merchant* has been to make us understand why we are so sad."[9] This one cinematic gesture demands our reassessment of Jessica, for it seems that she has neither repudiated nor forgotten her parents and her past. Indeed, Jessica's final, desolate expression suggests that she has finally realized the ramifications of her behavior: she has bound herself to an opportunistic husband who continues to criticize her Jewish past and to a community who just imposed a draconian financial and religious sentence on her father. Rather than verbally articulating Jessica's regrets, Radford conveys her complex emotions with the simple display of the turquoise ring.

Love tokens, often rings, were frequently exchanged by courting couples in the Renaissance. Most common were poesy rings, plain gold rings engraved with brief inscriptions and made for mass consumption. Indeed, in *The Merchant of Venice*, the character Gratiano tries to defend giving away his ring from Nerissa by describing it as just "a hoop of gold, a paltry ring/ … whose posy was/ For all the world like cutlers' poetry/ Upon a knife" (5.1. 146–149). Of these simple poesy rings, Charles Oman explains, "a young man might give his girlfriend a *ring* when his modern descendant might find it safer to present a box of *chocolates*."[10] While these plainer and less expensive poesy rings could signify a lesser level of commitment, rings set with gems, including turquoise, were more expensive and were typically used as betrothal or wedding bands. In the early modern period, as now, marriages were solemnized in a public ceremony with an exchange of vows and rings. Rings were integral to Christian marriage rituals but were an important part of Jewish marriage customs as well.[11] Jacqueline Marie Musacchio suggests that Jewish betrothal rings were "ritual objects," and "were preserved and used for several generations." She notes that both women and men, as Shylock did, received rings.[12]

Why does Jessica's possession of this ring matter so much, and why did Shakespeare specify a *turquoise* ring? Is it significant that Shakespeare determined that the ring would be turquoise, rather than diamond, ruby, or emerald? The previous critical discussion has briefly touched on the possession of turquoise and its accompanying lore, but this essay explores the extensive presence and powers of this exotic stone in early modern England and Europe, its value both financially and magically, and Shakespeare's deliberate use of it to convey cultural contentions in *The Merchant of Venice*. Shylock's ring is the only time turquoise is mentioned in any Shakespeare play.

The Value of Turquoise

Although today turquoise is considered a semiprecious stone, less valuable than diamonds, rubies, sapphires, and other precious stones, it was highly valued in the early modern period. In 1609, Anselmus de Boot, court physician of Emperor Rudolph II, stated that the turquoise "was so highly regarded by men that no man considered his hand to be well adorned unless he wore a fine turquoise."[13] Diana Scarisbrick notes that of the many semiprecious stones available in early modern England, "the turquoise seems to have been the most valued" and were often worn in rings with larger stones set as solitaires and smaller ones banded across the finger.[14] The fact that Leah gave Shylock a ring of such worth speaks to her commitment to him even if Shylock came to prize it more for its emotional than its market value.

Turquoise was valued enough to be specifically listed in inventories, most often as rings set in gold. An inventory of royal accounts from 1514 lists the payment of £10 for a turquoise ring to John Baptista de Consaloveris, merchant of Milan, and a 1527 inventory valued a turquoise ring at £10; one pound then worth about £500 today.[15] In England, two turquoise rings were listed in Thomas Cromwell's inventory of 1527. One was "a great gold turquoise ring" that appears to be the ring he chose to wear when he had his portrait painted by Hans Holbein.[16] This ring, worth £7, is the second most expensive piece of jewelry listed in the inventory after a gold ring with a rock ruby valued at £13. A second gold ring "with a turquoise like a heart" was valued at £6 and at the making of the inventory was one of two rings worn upon Cromwell's finger. It may be that this ring was given to Cromwell by his wife.[17] Those in Cromwell's employ also knew of his interest in turquoise. In 1532, his servant Thomas Upton "sent [him] the best turquoise [he] could meet with" while in Antwerp, a trading center.[18]

Specific references to turquoise rings in numerous wills also testify to their value. When he died in 1513, Robert Fabyan, author of chronicles, left his daughter Mary "a ryng of gold, sett w^t a turques, a dyamaunt, and a ruby;" a will from 1523 described "3 rings of fine gold, whereof is 2 turquoises and a sapphire;" and a will from 1542 listed "a rynge of golde with a turquays."[19] In 1548, Jane Strelley left two rings in her will, one diamond and the other turquoise.[20] In his will of 1565, John Horton left "to the right honourable and my singular good Lord the Lord Ewerye for a token, one golde ringe w 11 $^{\prime}$ a turkes in itt, desyringe him to be good Lord and ffrend unto my wiffe and childringe." Also in 1556, Rowlande Swynborn, the clerk for the Master of Clare Hall Cambridge, left his brother John "one ring of golde with a turkeys stone in it."[21]

The value turquoise held is also evidenced in its use by high nobility and royalty, especially in rings, which played a role in diplomacy. When Henry VIII made the decision to invade France in 1513,

Louis XII's queen, Anne of Brittany, sent James IV of Scotland a gold ring set with a large turquoise with the request that James help the French. Despite being Henry's brother-in-law, James was glad to oblige, the Scots for centuries being in frequent conflict with the English. As part of his chivalric code, James gave the English a month's notice of his invasion, and Catherine of Aragon, as regent, sent Thomas Howard, Earl of Surrey, with an army to meet the challenge. The English army defeated the Scots at Flodden field and James was killed. Howard, promoted to Duke of Norfolk after the victory, was rewarded with the dead Scottish king's sword, dagger, and the turquoise ring that Queen Anne had sent him.[22] This ring was kept in the Howard family as a treasure for centuries. William Howard, Viscount Stafford was executed on December 29, 1680, due to the lies of Titus Oates and the Popish Plot; the night before his death he bequeathed to his niece James IV's sword and turquoise ring.[23]

Another turquoise in this period was also a royal gift. After Thomas, Cardinal Wolsey was forced to turn over the great seal and was confined to his house, Henry was still ambivalent about how he felt about his former closest advisor. In February 1530 to reassure Wolsey, he sent Master Russell to bring him "a great ring of gold with a turquoise for a token." He told Wolsey, "The King commendeth him unto you and will you to be of good cheer, who loveth you as well as ever he did, and is not a little disquieted for your trouble."[24] The same year the victor of Flodden field's son, Thomas, third Duke of Norfolk, sent a ring with a turquoise as a way of showing his support for a prospective candidate seeking the office of burgess of Oxford.[25] In 1538, Honor Plantagenet, Viscountess Lisle, received a package of several rings while she was living with her husband in Calais. The package contained two gold rings with diamonds, a ring with a sapphire and one with a turquoise, each of which came from a different acquaintance. That the Viscountess received such sparkling jewels is not surprising, as she was known for her contacts with important figures, including Anne Boleyn, Thomas Cromwell, and Edward Seymour. The bejeweled rings were tools by which her friends hoped to remain in her thoughts and benefit from her patronage network.[26] Jewelers and goldsmiths carefully kept account of their turquoise, another indicator of its financial worth. In Henry VIII's reign, Humphrey Newton purchased from a goldsmith a turquoise, a sapphire, a ruby, and a diamond, for which he paid in installments.[27]

The Suggestive and Curative Powers of Turquoise

In his *Utopia*, Sir Thomas More satirizes those who wear ostentatious jewels and excessively prize precious metals that "have no function with which we cannot easily dispense." The inherent value of physical objects is subjective, More insists, for unlike iron which serves multiple purposes, gold, silver, and other jewels have no practical value. Rather, "human folly has made them precious because they are rare. But in fact nature, like a most indulgent mother, has placed her best gifts out in the open, like air, water, and the earth itself; vain and unprofitable things she has hidden away in remote places."[28] While More clearly failed to influence his countrymen's possession and display of jewels, his clever social critique encourages us to consider what qualities made turquoise so valuable.

The appearance of turquoise, especially its color, seems to account for much of its appeal—indeed, contemporary descriptions of the stone are often poetic. Thomas Browne called the turquoise as "an obscure Gem," describing the color as "bluish ... yet somewhat inclining to a green."[29] The physician and lexicographer John Bullokar referred to the turquoise as a "precious stone of a silke blew collour," while Antoine Le Grand called it as a "precious stone, of a Sky colour mixt with Green."[30] Others cited Pliny as an authority, who stated that "the best Turquois is that which approcheth nearest to the grasse green of an Emeraud."[31] Early in the seventeenth century, traveler Lewes Roberts described the turquoise as being of "thick green colour, *or between a green and skie-colour*," adding that the turquoise is also held in good esteem in India.[32] Perhaps, the most interesting description is the French Protestant writer Pierre de la Primaudaye's: he styles the turquoise as "garnished with the colour of heaven ... for it is of a skie colour and celestriall blewe, and verie bright."[33]

Turquoise was not only described as beautiful, but also thought to hold suggestive and curative properties. Shakespeare most likely would have been aware of the suggestive and curative powers turquoise was believed to possess, as turquoise lore was ubiquitous in popular and literary discourse. The goldsmith Richard Martin noted that wearing turquoise would help "to preserve the eye sight," and in the mid-seventeenth century, Daniel Lakin argued that turquoise could be of great help in stopping bleeding: "I my selfe too have found the like efficacie of this stone in an over much *Haemorrhagie*," including those who suffered from nose bleeds. Lakin goes on to describe the cure of a serious case: a seventy-year-old man who had long suffered from bloody urine and weakness, began to feel better within an hour after Lakin convinced him to wear turquoise rings.[34] The French humanist Pierre Boaistuau stated that according to most philosophers, turquoise would "chase awaye thoughtes and troubles of the braine."[35] Thomas Browne believed the turquoise "recreats the heart and sight."[36] Perhaps had Shylock still had his turquoise ring, he would not have been so uncontrolled in his rage and grief over Jessica's abandonment of him.

In addition to curative powers, the turquoise was thought to be prophetic and was especially efficacious in warning or keeping one from imminent danger: Boaistuau wrote that "The Turkeys doth move when there is any peril prepared to him that weareth it."[37] Belief in the turquoise's magical properties can be dated back to 1250, when a German, possibly named Volmar, composed a medical lapidary written in verse in the vernacular. There are numerous extant manuscript copies, and it was first printed in 1495 and again in 1498. George Frederick Kunz suggests it is "probably the earliest notice" of another impressive and magical quality of the stone. According to this lapidary, "Whoever owns the true turquoise set in gold will not injure any of his limbs where he falls, whether he be riding or walking, so long as he has the stone with him."[38] This view is further described in *The Sanctuarie of Salvation*, originally by Levinus Lemnius in Latin, and translated into English by one H.K. "Turquoyse saueth and preserueth from slipping, falling, and rushing against any thing, or if any such thing doe happen, it keepeth the body safe from hurt." The sixteenth-century natural philosopher John Maplet also noted that turquoise kept someone from falling and added that to save its wearer, "it would receyue the daunger of the fal itself, and to breake and burst in sunder, rather than the man should fall and miscarie."[39] Charles Oman also suggests that one reason the turquoise "became so popular at the close of the Middle Ages, is that it protects riders from falling off their horses."[40]

Turquoise could also warn its wearer of coming illness by changing color. This quality is noted in a number of seventeenth-century texts, such as William Basse's *A Helpe to Memory and Discourse* and Basse's newly corrected and enlarged version of the thirteenth-century Michael Scot's *The Philosopher's Banquet*. "The Turcoyse-stone, if the wearer of it bee not well, changeth his colour, and looketh pale and dimme, but increaseth to his perfectnesse as he recovereth to his health."[41]

John Donne refers to this belief about the efficacy of the turquoise in his *An Anatomy of the World*:

> As a compassionate Turcoyse which doth tell
>
> By looking pale, the wearer is not well.[42]

Perhaps, most powerful of all was the belief that turquoise prevented grave and even fatal harm. Michael Drayton wrote that one who wore turquoise "is often kept from peril,"[43] and some lapidaries argued that it was a shift in the color of the turquoise that would warn someone not only of possible illness but of "any peril" that might be awaiting him.[44] De la Primaudaye stated that some reported the turquoise's "virtue and propertie" were marvelous, including giving the wearer the ability to "resist poysons."[45] Surely, Leah would have considered that not only was the ring she gave her beloved of great financial value but would also protect him as well, and also a sign of how she loved him. In his 1615 text *A Discourse of Marriage and Wiving*, Alexander Niccholes argued the idea that the changing color of turquoise to reflect the health of the wearer could be a metaphor for a loving wife in marriage: "A true wife should bee like a *Turcoyse* stone, cleere in heart in her husbands health, and clowdy in his sickenesse."[46]

Amidst so many positive powers, turquoise was also said to have what might be called in today's medical parlance "a side effect"—if a woman wore it she could not conceive.[47] Had Jessica traded away the ring, perhaps its sterilizing quality contributed to her decision; keeping the ring in spite of its reputed effect on reproduction casts the prospects of a fruitful marriage in even greater doubt. Nonetheless, since many women owned turquoise, this particular characteristic may not have been as widely accepted.

Not everyone believed in the spectrum of powers attributed to the turquoise, but even their skepticism testified to the wide-spread fascination with the stone. In his 1653 book, *A Cabinet of Jewels*, Thomas Nichols scoffed that many believed that the turquoise "doth participate with all its masters dangers, perils, and evils, and that it doth receive his injuries, and the harm of his blows, falls, and contusions into itself."[48] The same doubt was shown by the Emperor Charles VI's jester, Perico de Sant Erbas; when a knight asked him about the virtues of the turquoise, he replied, "Why if you have a turquoise about you, and should fall from the top of the tower be dashed to pieces," at least the turquoise would not break.⁴⁹ In her recent novel, *Bring Up the Bodies*, Hilary Mantel refers to the popular Tudor association of turquoise and magic when Sir Edmund Bedingfield shows his wife Grace his turquoise ring: "You see this? The late cardinal gave it to me, and I am known to wear it." Grace asks him "Is that it, the magic one? ... Melts stone walls, makes princesses fall in love with you?" Bedingfield assures her that it is.⁵⁰

Turquoise as Exotic

Finally, turquoise was valued, even more than other gems, for its association with the exotic. Many in England believed that most turquoise came from Turkey, and it was in fact often known as the turkey stone. The noted Jacobean goldsmith Richard Martin, in his manuscript *The Goldsmiths Storehouse*, stated that the "Turchois stone ... taketh his name from the place where it grows," a point also made by the natural philosopher, John Maplet, "It is called a *Turches* for that it is onely found in Turkland or amongst the Turkes."⁵¹ Boaistuau, on the other hand, noted that the best turquoise "come from a towne in *Persia*, called *Balascha*, where there is greate store."⁵² The Oxford scholar Samuel Clarke, who was fascinated by the foreign and exotic, added "Arabia and Indostan" as excellent sources for turquoise.⁵³

As the early modern English traveled the world, they often saw beautiful turquoise. In the mid-seventeenth century, Samuel Clarke describes an English ambassador in the Persian Empire entertained by the local duke in the city of Shyraz. Thirty young men dressed gorgeously and wearing "chains of Gold, of Pearl, of Rubies, Turquoises, and Emeralds," ushered in the duke to see the ambassador.⁵⁴ In a more wide-ranging text, Clarke describes beautiful turquoise around the world. In Ethiopia, the Emperor owns many priceless gems including "turquoises." In Cusco, the imperial city of the Incas, which is a Temple of the Sun, there are images "all set with *Turkesses*, and *Emeralds*." In Venice at the Treasury of St. Mark, there are enough gems "to pay six Kings Ramsomes" and "There you may see an Armour all of massie Gold, beset all over with great *Pearles, Turkies, Rubies*."⁵⁵ Thomas Herbert also described his travels and experience with trade in Africa, India, and the Middle East. He explained that on the coast in India from September to March, there were booths, tents, and straw houses in great numbers where they would sell calico and other beautiful fabrics, translucent ceramics, cabinets, gems such as agate, turquoise, and cornelians, as well as a range of food and drinks. He also traveled through Persia and saw wealthy, powerful men wearing their rings set with turquoise.[56]

Though we cannot know if Shakespeare was aware of it, Persian and Arabian mythology included stories of fabulous wealth coming to someone after a dream about turquoise, and Hindu mystics believed that if one looked upon a turquoise right after seeing the new moon, he was "destined to enjoy immeasurable wealth."[57] Jackson Boswell argues that it "seems reasonable" that Shakespeare would have been acquainted with turquoise origins and folklore "for many writers he might have known had noted its peculiar properties."[58] If Shakespeare was aware, this would have made Leah's present to Shylock all the more remarkable; she was hoping that the ring would bring him wealth as well as protection and being a thing of beauty.

But if the early modern English associated the turquoise with Turkey, then the gem had distinct associations with "otherness," which accounts for Shakespeare's decision to link Shylock with this particular stone. Turkey, in turn, evoked the Muslim Ottoman Empire, and as Kim Hall explains, "English fears of Ottoman religious and political domination in the early modern period coalesced in the figure of the Turk … a generic term with a wide range of references: it conflated Turkish people, Muslims, and the Ottoman state in almost entirely disparaging ways."[59] Furthermore, as Daniel Vitkus demonstrates, Muslims and Jews were often lumped together as the foreign "other" to the English "self": "Several long-standing traditions, both learned and popular, linked Muslims and Jews."[60] The most prominent of these traditions were religious and economic, particularly in areas of trade.

Nabil Matar argues that the Elizabethan view of Muslims was more forgiving than their attitude toward the Jews because the English were actually involved in "an extensive commercial, diplomatic, and social engagement with the Turks and Moors of the Muslim empires." In short, Elizabethans were more likely to have met or encountered a Muslim than a Jew; however, Muslims, like Jews, were clearly seen as alien and depicted as such, particularly in literary and theological discourse, and the English "transformed contact into conflict, engagement into stereotyping."[61] England's economic relations with Muslims were as fraught as Shakespeare's depiction of the Venetians' economic relations with the Jews: mutual need and benefit were accompanied by suspicion.

QUEENS AND TURQUOISE

As we discussed before, turquoise was valued at the court of Henry VIII, and Katherine Howard, who loved jewelry, had many. Some she was willing to part with. She had a serious quarrel with Henry's daughter Mary, telling Henry that she did not treat Katherine with due deference owed her as queen. Henry dismissed two of Mary's ladies, and to his daughter's great anguish, one died soon after. But Mary realized this was a battle she could not win and made her peace with Katherine. Katherine then gave her a pomander with a clock decorated with many small rubies and turquoise. The chain that went with it, gold links with many pearls, Katherine reserved for herself. Mary did not keep the pomander long. In 1542, she passed it on to her young half-sister Elizabeth, perhaps because she did not care for Katherine, perhaps because she did not care for turquoise. In her privy purse accounts of the 1540s, she had listed a great deal of jewelry, with diamonds, rubies, emeralds, pearls, and other gems, but only one turquoise bracelet.[62]

In 1562 when Margaret, Countess of Lennox was secretly negotiating a marriage between her son, Henry, Lord Darnley, and his cousin Mary Queen of Scots, she sent him a turquoise ring, whether for him or as a gift to Mary is not clear. The ring was considered significant enough that when Elizabeth's government was investigating the Countess's machinations, it was mentioned twice. It may have been that the ring was intended for Mary because of her fondness for turquoise: the Scottish queen had a portrait painted with a gold and turquoise necklace.[63] But Darnley may also have been fond of turquoise rings, and Francis Yalxley, who was sometimes a spy for English and European Catholics, admired Darnley so much he sent him a turquoise ring as a token of friendship.[64]

Another turquoise ring was given to Mary Stuart, but in more trying circumstances. After the successful rebellion against her, Sir Robert Melville brought her a turquoise ring as a gift from several Scottish lords, but stated that the ring authorized their message that the only way she could save her life was to abdicate. Otherwise, they would either have her murdered or put on trial with a foregone verdict of guilty.[65] When the Scottish lords offered Mary Stuart the turquoise ring if she would abdicate, it might also have held the implication that she would be protected as a former ruler, a compelling notion given that most monarchs who were forced to give up their thrones met untimely and violent deaths.

Another individual closely connected to Mary Stuart used turquoise to carry a message. In December 1571, while imprisoned in the Tower for his connection to the Ridolfi Plot, John Leslie, Bishop of Ross, asked his servant Cuthbert Reid to acquire "ane propir ring with a turcas stone, and wreit within it '*Pro principe*'," and two other rings with stones that included the phrases "*Pro patria*" and "*Plurima passus*" (for the prince/leader, for country, and many suffered). Perhaps, Leslie intended the rings as a sign of his continued loyalty and support for her cause.[66]

Elizabeth I, whose love of fine clothing and jewelry is legendary, also appreciated turquoise. In the 1580s, a number of cameo portraits of Queen Elizabeth were created; as Scarisbrick points out, the jewelry was "meticulously rendered," and the stones often used were "sardonyx, garnet, sapphire, and turquoise."[67] In the 1590s, Elizabeth gave as a christening gift a small turquoise cameo portrait of herself, surrounded by rubies and diamonds.[68] John Mabbe, a London goldsmith in service to Queen Elizabeth, listed in a 1576 inventory "eightene Ryngs enameled white and black with Turcas in every Ryng." Given that black and white were colors favored by Elizabeth, perhaps Mabbe hoped the rings would catch the Queen's eye. While we do not know whether she purchased the rings from the goldsmith, the Queen's 1587 inventory lists nine turquoise rings, suggesting she found the stone appealing enough to add to her jewelry collection.[69]

Elizabeth received one turquoise ring that had particular political meaning. In 1580, Sir John Fitzgerald, better known as John of Desmond, joined his cousin James fitz Maurice Fitzgerald, in another rebellion in Ireland. Desmond was killed in a skirmish in January 1582. His body was sent to Cork and for several years after his corpse, in chains, hung over the city gates, a horrific sight. His fine gold ring, set with turquoise, was sent to Elizabeth.[70]

Radford's bold "ring trick" does not subvert Shakespeare's play—it brings to the forefront existent textual anxieties and tensions. The play already demonstrates that Shylock's response to the turquoise ring speaks to a loving relationship with his wife. The film's revelation that Jessica kept the turquoise ring as a reminder of her parents' marriage and her own origins is a poignant but troubling indication that the work of reconciling her Jewish and Christian selves is still to be done, just as her community is still reckoning with religious and ethnic tensions. In her new life, Jessica, like the turquoise ring, is a prized and valuable commodity who will always be marked by a sense of otherness.

The precious stones the Elizabethans possessed—diamonds, rubies, emeralds, sapphires, and pearls—came from foreign countries, but turquoise in particular represented the mysterious and the unusual. Elizabeth loved turquoise just as she was "so fascinated by things Islamic that she requested from her ambassador in Istanbul some Turkish clothes."[71] By wearing turquoise, she was clearly signaling her openness to trade and expansion of the empire. Like pet monkeys and parrots, spices, and silks, turquoise was enthusiastically absorbed into English material culture but maintained its air of exoticism. Shakespeare's decision to link Shylock with turquoise—instead of the diamonds and other jewels he owned—is a fitting indicator of Shylock's own ambiguous social position as both economically valuable and alien. Elizabeth, an unmarried woman ruling alone, is also in some senses an outsider and alien, perhaps linking her to both Shylock and Jessica. For all of them, turquoise held importance.

Notes

1. See Carole Levin, "Converting the Daughter: Gender, Power, and Jewish Identity in the English Renaissance," in *Shakespeare's Foreign Worlds: National and Transnational Identities in the Elizabethan Age*, ed. Carole Levin and John Watkins (Ithaca: Cornell University Press, 2009), 85–110; Mary Janell Metzger, "'Now by My Hood, A Gentle and No Jew': Jessica, *The Merchant of Venice*, and the Discourse of Early Modern England Identity," *PMLA*, 113 (1998): 52–63; and Lisa Lampert, *Gender and Jewish Difference from Paul to Shakespeare* (Philadelphia: University of Pennsylvania Press, 1994).
2. See Karen Newman, "Portia's Ring: Unruly Women and the Structure of Exchange in *The Merchant of Venice*," *Shakespeare Quarterly*, 38 (1987): 19–33; Suzanne Penuel, "Castrating the Creditor in *The Merchant of Venice*," *Studies in English Literature, 1500–1900*, 44.2 (Spring 2004): 255–275.
3. Textual references are from *The Norton Shakespeare*, 2nd ed., ed. Stephen Greenblatt, et al. (New York: W.W. Norton & Co., 2009).
4. The 1999 production at the Shakespeare Theatre in Washington, D.C., staged Lorenzo on his knees ecstatically running the gems and gold through his fingers, ignoring Jessica—one of many recent productions that highlight Lorenzo's financial agenda.
5. Scholarship on Shylock is extensive. Among the many excellent analyses, see James Shapiro, *Shakespeare and the Jews* (New York: Columbia

University Press, 2007). Also, Michael Ephraim, "Jephthah's Kin: The Sacrificing Father in *The Merchant of Venice*," *Journal of Early Modern Cultural Studies*, 5.2. (2005): 71–93 and Anita Gilman Sherman, "Disowning Knowledge of Jessica, or Shylock's Skepticism," *Studies in English Literature, 1500–1900*, 44.2 (Spring 2004): 277–295.
6. Catherine Richardson, *Shakespeare and Material Culture* (Oxford: Oxford University Press, 2011), 42. Richardson's analysis of the significance of rings within the "webs of discourse" in *The Merchant of Venice* is excellent.
7. http://www.oed.com.library.unl.edu/view/Entry/121265?rskey=UMR0rW&result=1#eid, accessed May 4, 2013.
8. Bruce Boehrer, "Shylock and the Rise of the Household Pet: Thinking Social Exclusion in *The Merchant of Venice*," *Shakespeare Quarterly* 50 (1999), 158.
9. Samuel Crowl, "Looking for Shylock: Stephen Greenblatt, Michael Radford, and Al Pacino," in *Screening Shakespeare in the Twenty-First Century*, ed. Mark Thornton Burnett (Edinburgh: Edinburgh University Press, 2006), 121.
10. Charles Oman, *British Rings: 800–1914* (Totowa, NJ: Rowman and Littlefield, 1974), 38.
11. http://www.metmuseum.org/toah/hd/cour/hd_cour.htm; Deborah L. Krohn, "Rites of Passage: Art Objects to Celebrate Betrothal, Marriage, and the Family," *Art and Love in Renaissance Italy*, ed. Andrea Bayer (New York: The Metropolitan Museum of Art, 2009), 63. See also, Teresa McNally, "Shylock's Turquoise Ring and Judaic Tradition," *Notes and Queries* (September 1992): 320–21.
12. Jacqueline Marie Musacchio, "Jewish Betrothal Ring," *Art and Love in Renaissance Italy*, 102.
13. De Boot, "Gemmarum et lapidum historia," Lug. Bat, 1636, 270 in George Frederick Kunz, *The Curious Lore of Precious Stones* (Philadelphia and London: J. B. Lippincott Co., 1913), 111.
14. Diana Scarisbrick, *Tudor and Jacobean Jewellery* (London: Tate Publishing, 1995), 91. As early as the fourteenth century, a London jeweler created a ring which had "oval sapphire and an amethyst set between two turquoises." Oman, *British Rings: 800–1914*, 21.
15. *Letters and Papers, Foreign and Domestic, of the Reign of Henry VIII*, ed. J.S. Brewer and R. H. Brodie (London: H. M. Stationery Office, 1862–1920), Volume I, Part 2, 1495.
16. Currently in the Frick Collection, http://collections.frick.org/view/objects/asitem/items$0040:101.
17. Robert Hutchinson, *Thomas Cromwell: The Rise and Fall of Henry VIII's Most Notorious Minister* (New York: Thomas Dunne Books, 2007), 121.

18. *Letters and Papers, Foreign and Domestic, of the Reign of Henry VIII*, Volume V, 504.
19. *Letters and Papers, Foreign and Domestic, of the Reign of Henry VIII*, Volume III, Part 2, 1324; Herbert Norris, *Tudor Costume and Fashion* (Mineola, New York: Dover Publications, 1938), 144.
20. Maria Hayward, *Rich Apparel: Clothing and the law in Henry VIII's England* (Burlington, VT: Ashgate, 2009), 242.
21. http://www.archive.org/stream/catalogueoffinge00brituoft/catalogue-offinge00brituoft_djvu.txt.; http://archive.org/stream/northcountry-will00surtuoft/northcountrywill00surtuoft_djvu.txt.
22. Mary F. S. Hervey, *The Life, Correspondence & Collections of Thomas Howard, Earl of Arundel* (Cambridge: University Press, 1921), xxxiii.
23. Agnes Strickland, *Lives of the Queens of Scotland and English Princesses Connected with the Regal Succession of Great Britain* (Edinburgh and London: W. Blackwood and Sons, 1850–1859), I, 89n2.
24. John Strype, *Ecclesiastical Memorials: Relating Chiefly to Religion, and the Reformation of it, and the Emergencies of the Church of England, under King Henry VIII, King Edward VI, and Queen Mary the First* (London: J. Osborn, 1721–33), I, 178–9; George Cavendish, *Two Early Tudor Lives: The Life and Death of Cardinal Wolsey*, ed. Richard Standish Sylvester (New Haven: Yale University Press, 1962), 114.
25. *Letters and Papers, Foreign and Domestic, of the Reign of Henry VIII*, Volume IV, Part 3, 3180.
26. "Plantagenet, Arthur, Viscount Lisle (*b.* before 1472, *d.* 1542)," David Grummitt in *Oxford Dictionary of National Biography*, ed. H. C. G. Matthew and Brian Harrison (Oxford: OUP, 2004); online ed., ed. Lawrence Goldman, January 2008, http://0-www.oxforddnb.com.library.unl.edu/view/article/22355 (accessed February 9, 2016); *Letters and Papers, Foreign and Domestic, of the Reign of Henry VIII*, Volume XIII, Part 2, 389.
27. Deborah Youngs, *Humphrey Newton (1466–1536): An Early Tudor Gentleman* (Woodbridge, United Kingdom: Boydell & Brewer, 2008), 152.
28. Sir Thomas More, *Utopia*, eds. George M. Logan and Robert M. Adams (Cambridge: Cambridge University Press, 1989), 151.
29. Sir Thomas Browne, *Nature's cabinet unlock'd wherein is discovered the natural causes of metals, stones, precious earths, juyces, humors, and spirits, the nature of plants in general, their affections, parts, and kinds in particular* (London, 1657), 43.
30. J. B., *An English expositor teaching the interpretation of the hardest words vsed in our language. With sundry explications, descriptions, and discourses. By I.B. Doctor of Phisicke* (London, 1616), n. p.; Antoine Le Grande,

An entire body of philosophy according to the principles of the famous Renate Des Cartes in three books, (I) the institution ... (II) the history of nature ... (III) a dissertation of the want of sense and knowledge in brute animals ... / written originally in Latin by the learned Anthony Le Grand; now carefully translated from the last corrections, alterations, and large additions of the author, never yet published ... by Richard Blome (London, 1694), 198.

31. *The historie of the world Commonly called, the naturall historie of C. Plinius Secundus. Translated into English by Philemon Holland Doctor in Physicke. The first tome* (London, 1601) II, 619.
32. Lewes Roberts, *The merchants map of commerce wherein the universal manner and matter relating to trade and merchandize are fully treated* (London, 1700), 29.
33. Pierre de La Primaudaye, *The third volume of the French academie contayning a notable description of the whole world,* .... Written in French by that famous and learned gentleman Peter de la Primaudaye Esquier, Lord of the same place, and of Barree: and Englished by R. Dolman. (London, 1601), 427.
34. Daniel Lakin, *A miraculous cure of the Prusian swallow-knife being dissected out of his stomack by the physitians of Regimonto, the chief city in Prusia : together with the testimony of the King of Poland, of the truth of this wonderfull cure : likewise the certificate of the lords the states and all the physitians of Leyden/ translated out of the Lattin; whereunto is added a treatise of the possibility of this cure with a history of our owne of the consolidation of a wound in the ventricle; as also a survay of the former translation, and censure of their positions* (London, 1642), 21.
35. Pierre Boaistuau, *Certaine secrete wonders of nature containing a descriptio[n] of sundry strange things, seming monstrous in our eyes and iudgement, bicause we are not priuie to the reasons of them.* Trans. E. Fenton. (London: 1569), 41r.
36. Browne, *Nature's cabinet unlock'd*, 43.
37. Boaistuau, *Certaine secrete wonders of nature*, 51v.
38. Volmar, "Steinbuch," ed. Hans Lambel, Heilbronn, 1877, p. 19 in Kunz, *Curious Lore of Precious Stones*, 109. For more on Volmar, see John Greenfield, "A Sermon on Stones: A Note on Volmar's Daz Steinbuoch" *Revista da Faculdade de Letras* "Linguas e Literaturas" Porto XII, (1995): 293–300.
39. Levinus Lemnius, *The sanctuarie of saluation, helmet of health, and mirrour of modestie and good maners wherein is contained an exhortation vnto the institution of Christian, vertuous, honest, and laudable life, very behoouefull, holsome and fruitfull both to highest and lowest degrees of men ... /* written in Latin verie learnedly and elegantlie by Leuinus Lemnius of Zirizaa, physitian, and Englished by H.K. for the common commoditie

and comfort of them which understand not the Latine tongue (London, 1592), 207; John Maplet, *A greene forest, or A natural historie wherein may bee seene first the most sufferaigne virtue in all the whole kinde of stones & mettals* (London, 1567), 23.
40. Oman, *British Rings*, 60–61.
41. William Basse, *A Helpe to memory and discourse with table- talke as musicke to a banquet of wine : being a compendium of witty, and vsefull propositions, problemes, and sentences / extracted from the larger volumes of physicians, philosophers, orators and poets* (London, 1630), 58; Michael Scot, *The philosophers banquet Newly furnished and decked forth with much variety of many severall dishes, that in the former service were neglected. Where now not only meats and drinks of all natures and kinds are served in, but the natures and kinds of all disputed of. As further, dilated by table-conference, alteration and changes of states, diminution of the stature of man, barrennesse of the earth, with the effects and causes thereof, phisically and philosophically. Newly corrected and inlarged, to almost as much more. By W.B. Esquire* (London, 1633), 223.
42. John Donne, *An anatomy of the vvorld Wherein, by occasion of the vntimely death of Mistris Elizabeth Drury the frailty and the decay of this whole world is represented* (London, 1611), B4.
43. Michael Drayton, *The Muses Elizium lately discouered, by a new way ouer Parnassus*, 2nd edn. (London, 1630), 79.
44. Boaistuau, *Certaine secrete wonders of nature*, 52.
45. Primaudaye, *The third volume of the French academie contayning a notable description of the whole world*, 427.
46. Alexander Niccoles, *A discourse, of marriage and wiving and of the greatest mystery therein contained: how to choose a good wife from a bad. An argument of the dearest use, but the deepest cunning that man may erre in: which is, to cut by a third betweene the greatest good or evill in the world. Pertinent to both sexes, and conditions, as well those already gone before, as shortly to enter this honest society* (London, 1615), 49.
47. *Le Lapidaire du XIVth siecle*, ed. Is. del. Sotto (Vienna, 1862), 109 in Boswell, "Shylock's Turquoise Ring," 482n3.
48. Thomas Nicols, *Arcula gemmea: or, A cabinet of jewels* (London, 1653), 30.
49. Kunz, *The Lore of Precious Stones*, 24; Dr. Doran, *The History of Court Fools* (London: R. Bentley, 1858), 320.
50. Hilary Mantel, *Bring up the Bodies* (New York: Henry Holt and Co., 2012), 92.
51. Richard Martin, *The Goldsmiths Storehouse*, 93v Folger MS V.a. 179 (1604?); John Maplet, *A greene forest, or A naturall historie vvherein may bee seene first the most sufferaigne vertues in all the whole kinde of stones & metals* (London, 1657), 23.

52. Boaistuau, *Certaine secrete wonders of nature containing a descriptio[n] of sundry strange things*, 41v.
53. Samuel Clarke, *A geographicall description of all the countries in the known world as also of the greatest and famousest cities and fabricks which have been, or are now remaining* (London, 1657), 193.
54. Clarke, *A geographicall description of all the countries in the known world*, 16.
55. Samuel Clarke, *A mirrour or looking-glasse both for saints and sinners held forth in about two thousand examples wherein is presented as Gods wonderful mercies to the one, so his severe judgments against the other* (London, 1654), 619, 622, 626, 627.
56. Sir Thomas Herbert, *Some Years Travels into divers Parts of Asia and Afrique Some yeares travels into divers parts of Asia and Afrique Describing especially the two famous empires, the Persian, and the great Mogull: weaved with the history of these later times as also, many rich and spatious kingdomes in the orientall India, and other parts of Asia; together with the adjacent iles. Severally relating the religion, language, qualities, customes, habit, descent, fashions, and other observations touching them* (London, 1638), 37–8, 124.
57. Boswell, "Shylock's Turquoise Ring," 482; Surindro Mohun Tagore, "Mani Mala," t II, Calcutta, 1881, p. 883 in Kunz, *The Curious Lore of Precious Stones*, 345.
58. Boswell, "Shylock's Turquoise Ring," 483.
59. Kim Hall, *Othello: Texts and Contexts* (New York: Bedford/St. Martin's, 2007), 205.
60. Daniel Vitkus, *Turning Turk: English Theatre and the Multicultural Mediterranean, 1570–1630* (New York: Palgrave Macmillan, 2003), 182.
61. Nabil Matar, *Turks, Moors, and Englishmen in the Age of Discovery* (New York: Columbia University Press, 1999), 14.
62. *Privy Purse Expenses of Princess Mary, daughter of King Henry the Eighth, afterwards Queen Mary*, Frederic Madden, ed. (London: W. Pickering, 1831), 178. Elizabeth as queen also had a turquoise clock that could be worn but from its description it does not appear to be same one.
63. Lionel Cust and George Scharf, *Notes on the Authentic Portraits of Mary, Queen of Scots, based on the researches of the late Sir George Scharf* (London: J. Murray, 1903), 125.
64. Morgan Ring, *So High a Blood: The Story of Margaret Douglas, the Tudor that Time Forgot* (London: Bloomsbury Publishers, 2017), 157.
65. Adam Blackwood, *Martyre de la Royne d'Escosse* (Paris, 1587), 146–48. Agnes Strickland, *The Life of Mary Queen of Scots* (London: G. Bell, 1873), 30.

66. "John Lesley (1527–1596)," Rosalind K. Marshall in *Oxford Dictionary of National Biography*, ed. H. C. G. Matthew and Brian Harrison (Oxford: OUP, 2004); online ed., ed. Lawrence Goldman, May 2007, http://www.oxforddnb.com/view/article/16492; *Calendar of State Papers relating to Scotland and Mary, Queen of Scots, 1547–1603.Vol. 4. :1571–1574*. Entry Number: 87, Page Number: 69 Date: Dec. 20 1571 "Bishop of Ross to Cuthbert Reid"
67. Scarisbrick, *Tudor and Jacobean Jewellery*, 61.
68. Joan Evans, *English Jewellery: From the Fifth Century AD to 1800* (London: Methuen & Co., Ltd., 1921), 96.
69. Thomas Rymer, *Foedera, conventiones, literæ, et cujuscunque generis acta publica, inter reges Angliæ, … ab anno 1101–[1654]*, Vol. 15 (London, 1728), 759; BL, Royal MS, Appx 68, f. 23 as cited in Diana Scarisbrick, *Jewellery in Britain 1066–1837: A Documentary, Social, Literary, and Artistic Survey* (Norwich: Michael Russell Ltd., 1994), 149.
70. *Calendar of the State Papers Relating to Ireland, of the reigns of Henry VIII, Edward VI, Mary and Elizabeth*, ed. Hans Claude Hamilton, Ernest G. Atkinson, and Robert Pentland Mahaffy (London: Longman, Green, Longman, & Roberts, 1860–1912), II, 340.
71. Matar, *Turks, Moors, and Englishmen in the Age of Discovery*, 34.

Bibliography

Primary Sources

Basse, William. *A Helpe to memory and discourse with table- talke as musicke to a banquet of wine : being a compendium of witty, and vsefull propositions, problemes, and sentences / extracted from the larger volumes of physicians, philosophers, orators and poets.* London, 1630.

Boaistuau, Pierre. *Certaine secrete wonders of nature containing a descriptio[n] of sundry strange things, seming monstrous in our eyes and iudgement, bicause we are not priuie to the reasons of them.* trans. E. Fenton. London: 1569.

Browne, Sir Thomas. *Nature's cabinet unlock'd wherein is discovered the natural causes of metals, stones, precious earths, juyces, humors, and spirits, the nature of plants in general, their affections, parts, and kinds in particular.* London, 1657.

Calendar of the State Papers Relating to Ireland, of the reigns of Henry VIII, Edward VI, Mary and Elizabeth. Edited by Hans Claude Hamilton, Ernest G. Atkinson, and Robert Pentland Mahaffy. London: Longman, Green, Longman, & Roberts, 1860–1912.

Cavendish, George. *Two Early Tudor Lives: The Life and Death of Cardinal Wolsey.* ed. Richard Standish Sylvester. New Haven: Yale University Press, 1962.

Clarke, Samuel. *A geographicall description of all the countries in the known world as also of the greatest and famousest cities and fabricks which have been, or are now remaining*. London, 1657.

Clarke, Samuel. *A mirrour or looking-glasse both for saints and sinners held forth in about two thousand examples wherein is presented as Gods wonderful mercies to the one, so his severe judgments against the other*. London, 1654.

de La Primaudaye, Pierre. *The third volume of the French academie contayning a notable description of the whole world, ...* Written in French by that famous and learned gentleman Peter de la Primaudaye Esquier, Lord of the same place, and of Barree: and Englished by R. Dolman. London, 1601.

Donne, John. *An anatomy of the vvorld Wherein, by occasion of the vntimely death of Mistris Elizabeth Drury the frailty and the decay of this whole world is represented*. London, 1611.

Drayton, Michael. *The Muses Elizium lately discouered, by a new way ouer Parnassus*, 2nd edn. London, 1630.

Herbert, Sir Thomas. *Some Years Travels into divers Parts of Asia and Afrique Some yeares travels into divers parts of Asia and Afrique Describing especially the two famous empires, the Persian, and the great Mogull: weaved with the history of these later times as also, many rich and spatious kingdomes in the orientall India, and other parts of Asia; together with the adjacent iles. Severally relating the religion, language, qualities, customes, habit, descent, fashions, and other observations touching them*. London, 1638.

J. B. *An English expositor teaching the interpretation of the hardest words vsed in our language. With sundry explications, descriptions, and discourses*. By I.B. Doctor of Phisicke. London, 1616.

Lakin, Daniel. *A miraculous cure of the Prusian swallow-knife being dissected out of his stomack by the physitians of Regimonto, the chief city in Prusia : together with the testimony of the King of Poland, of the truth of this wonderfull cure : likewise the certificate of the lords the states and all the physitians of Leyden/ translated out of the Lattin; whereunto is added a treatise of the possibility of this cure with a history of our owne of the consolidation of a wound in the ventricle; as also a survay of the former translation, and censure of their positions*. London, 1642.

Le Grande, Antoine. *An entire body of philosophy according to the principles of the famous Renate Des Cartes in three books, (I) the institution ... (II) the history of nature ... (III) a dissertation of the want of sense and knowledge in brute animals ... / written originally in Latin by the learned Anthony Le Grand; now carefully translated from the last corrections, alterations, and large additions of the author, never yet published ... by Richard Blome*. London, 1694.

Lemnius, Levinus. *The sanctuarie of saluation, helmet of health, and mirrour of modestie and good maners wherein is contained an exhortation vnto the institution of Christian, vertuous, honest, and laudable life, very behoouefull, holsome and fruitfull both to highest and lowest degrees of men ... /* written in Latin verie learnedly and elegantlie by Leuinus Lemnius of Zirizaa, physitian, and Englished by H.K. for the common commoditie and comfort of them which understand not the Latine tongue. London, 1592.

Letters and Papers, Foreign and Domestic, of the Reign of Henry VIII. Edited by J.S. Brewer and R. H. Brodie. Vol. I. London: H. M. Stationery Office, 1862–1920.

Letters and Papers, Foreign and Domestic, of the Reign of Henry VIII. Edited by J.S. Brewer and R. H. Brodie. Vol. III. London: H. M. Stationery Office, 1862–1920.

Letters and Papers, Foreign and Domestic, of the Reign of Henry VIII. Edited by J.S. Brewer and R. H. Brodie. Vol. IV. London: H. M. Stationery Office, 1862–1920.

Letters and Papers, Foreign and Domestic, of the Reign of Henry VIII. Edited by J.S. Brewer and R. H. Brodie. Vol. V. London: H. M. Stationery Office, 1862–1920.

Letters and Papers, Foreign and Domestic, of the Reign of Henry VIII. Edited by J.S. Brewer and R. H. Brodie. Vol. XIII. London: H. M. Stationery Office, 1862–1920.

Maplet, John. *A greene forest, or A natural historie wherein may bee seene first the most sufferaigne virtue in all the whole kinde of stones & mettals.* London, 1567.

Martin, Richard. *The Goldsmiths Storehouse.* 93v Folger MS V.a. 179 (1604?).

More, Sir Thomas. *Utopia.* Edited by George M. Logan and Robert M. Adams. Cambridge: Cambridge University Press, 1989.

Nicols, Thomas. *Arcula gemmea: or, A cabinet of jewels.* London, 1653.

Niccoles, Alexander. *A discourse, of marriage and wiving and of the greatest mystery therein contained: how to choose a good wife from a bad. An argument of the dearest use, but the deepest cunning that man may erre in: which is, to cut by a third betweene the greatest good or evill in the world. Pertinent to both sexes, and conditions, as well those already gone before, as shortly to enter this honest society.* London, 1615.

Oxford Dictionary of National Biography.

Privy Purse Expenses of Princess Mary, daughter of King Henry the Eighth, afterwards Queen Mary. Edited by Frederic Madden. London: W. Pickering, 1831.

Roberts, Lewes. *The merchants map of commerce wherein the universal manner and matter relating to trade and merchandize are fully treated.* London, 1700.

Scot, Michael. *The philosophers banquet Newly furnished and decked forth with much variety of many severall dishes, that in the former service were neglected. Where now not only meats and drinks of all natures and kinds are served in, but the natures and kinds of all disputed of. As further, dilated by table-conference, alteration and changes of states, diminution of the stature of man, barrennesse of* the earth, with the effects and causes thereof, phisically and philosophically. Newly corrected and inlarged, to almost as much more. By W.B. Esquire. London, 1633.

Strickland, Agnes. *Lives of the Queens of Scotland and English Princesses Connected with the Regal Succession of Great Britain.* Edinburgh and London: W. Blackwood and Sons, 1850–1859.

Strype, John. *Ecclesiastical Memorials: Relating Chiefly to Religion, and the Reformation of it, and the Emergencies of the Church of England, under King Henry VIII, King Edward VI, and Queen Mary the First.* London: J. Osborn, 1721–1733.

The historie of the world Commonly called, the naturall historie of C. Plinius Secundus. Translated into English by Philemon Holland Doctor in Physicke. The first tome. London, 1601.

Secondary Sources

Boehrer, Bruce. "Shylock and the Rise of the Household Pet: Thinking Social Exclusion in *The Merchant of Venice*." In *Shakespeare Quarterly* 50. (1999): 152–170.

Crowl, Samuel. "Looking for Shylock: Stephen Greenblatt, Michael Radford, and Al Pacino." In *Screening Shakespeare in the Twenty-First Century.* Edited by Mark Thornton Burnett, 113–127. Edinburgh: Edinburgh University Press, 2006.

Ephraim, Michael. "Jephthah's Kin: The Sacrificing Father in *The Merchant of Venice*." In *Journal of Early Modern Cultural Studies*, 5.2. (2005): 71–93.

Gilman Sherman, Anita. "Disowning Knowledge of Jessica, or Shylock's Skepticism." *Studies in English Literature, 1500–1900*, 44.2. (Spring 2004): 277–295.

Hayward, Maria. *Rich Apparel: Clothing and the law in Henry VIII's England.* Burlington, VT: Ashgate, 2009.

Hervey, Mary F. S. *The Life, Correspondence & Collections of Thomas Howard, Earl of Arundel.* Cambridge: University Press, 1921.

Hutchinson, Richard. *Thomas Cromwell: The Rise and Fall of Henry VIII's Most Notorious Minister.* New York: Thomas Dunne Books, 2007.

Krohn, Deborah L. "Rites of Passage: Art Objects to Celebrate Betrothal, Marriage, and the Family." In *Art and Love in Renaissance Italy.* Edited by Andrea Bayer, 60–68. New York: The Metropolitan Museum of Art, 2009.

Kunz, George Frederick. *The Curious Lore of Precious Stones.* Philadelphia and London: J. B. Lippincott Co., 1913.

Lampert, Lisa. *Gender and Jewish Difference from Paul to Shakespeare.* Philadelphia: University of Pennsylvania Press, 1994.

Levin, Carole. "Converting the Daughter: Gender, Power, and Jewish Identity in the English Renaissance." In *Shakespeare's Foreign Worlds: National and Transnational Identities in the Elizabethan Age*. Edited by Carole Levin and John Watkins, 85–110. Ithaca: Cornell University Press, 2009.

Mantel, Hilary. *Bring up the Bodies*. New York: Henry Holt and Co., 2012.

Matar, Nabil. *Turks, Moors, and Englishmen in the Age of Discovery*. New York: Columbia University Press, 1999.

McNally, Teresa. "Shylock's Turquoise Ring and Judaic Tradition." In *Notes and Queries* (September 1992): 320–21.

Metzger, Mary Janell. "'Now by My Hood, A Gentle and No Jew': Jessica, The Merchant of Venice, and the Discourse of Early Modern England Identity." In *PMLA*, 113. (1998): 52–63.

Musacchio, Jacqueline Marie. "Jewish Betrothal Ring." In *Art and Love in Renaissance Italy*. Edited by Andrea Bayer, 29–43. New York: The Metropolitan Museum of Art, 2009.

Newman, Karen. "Portia's Ring: Unruly Women and the Structure of Exchange in The Merchant of Venice." In *Shakespeare Quarterly*, 38. (1987): 19–33.

Norris, Herbert. *Tudor Costume and Fashion*. Mineola, New York: Dover Publications, 1938.

Oman, Charles. *British Rings: 800–1914*. Totowa, NJ: Rowman and Littlefield, 1974.

Penuel, Suzanne. "Castrating the Creditor in *The Merchant of Venice*." In *Studies in English Literature, 1500–1900*, 44.2. (Spring 2004): 255–275.

Richardson, Catherine. *Shakespeare and Material Culture*. Oxford: Oxford University Press, 2011.

Ring, Morgan. *So High a Blood: The Story of Margaret Douglas, the Tudor that Time Forgot*. London: Bloomsbury Publishers, 2017.

Scarisbrick, Diana. *Tudor and Jacobean Jewellery*. London: Tate Publishing, 1995.

Shapiro, James. *Shakespeare and the Jews*. New York: Columbia University Press, 2007.

The Norton Shakespeare, 2nd ed., ed. Stephen Greenblatt, et al. New York: W.W. Norton & Co., 2009.

Youngs, Deborah. *Humphrey Newton (1466–1536): An Early Tudor Gentleman*. Woodbridge, United Kingdom: Boydell & Brewer, 2008.

CHAPTER 9

A Vision on Queen Elizabeth's Role in Colonizing America: Stephen Parmenius's *De Navigatione* (1582)

Erzsébet Stróbl

The 1580s witnessed the first attempts of the English to establish a colony in the New World. While the explorations and circumnavigation of the globe by Francis Drake (1577–1580) proved to be profitable, several other endeavors—especially Frobisher's 1578 fiasco—showed that the English did not have easy access to the wealth of the new continent. The repeated journeys had to be well-advertised, and a great amount of promotional literature was published to accompany the new projects, more than in any other European country.[1] The Hungarian scholar Stephen Parmenius of Buda contributed to this endeavor with one of the first works on the role of Queen Elizabeth I in colonization. His Latin poem *De navigatione* (1582)[2] depicted a humanistic vision about the importance of colonial ventures and actively promoted the 1583 expedition of Sir Humphrey Gilbert to North America. As an outsider who arrived in England only a few years earlier, he had a keen sense to register the common excitement about the new explorations, as well as to record the emerging insular pride of the English in their

E. Stróbl (✉)
Károli Gáspár University, Budapest, Hungary

country and their queen. As a scholar, he had the means to integrate these ideas with his classical learning and record them in the pretentious form of poetry. He was also the first learned scholar to accompany a journey to North America with the deliberate aim to record its glory and achievements for posterity, and one—dying in a shipwreck off the shores of Sable Island—who sacrificed his life for his vision and hope of becoming North America's first poet.

The following essay will highlight the significance of Parmenius's *De navigatione* in the early colonial writings of the English and will attempt to reconstruct his possible Hungarian heritage in order to explain the text's unique stance and divergence from other similar pamphlets. It will also shed light on the workings of colonial propaganda by emphasizing the enhanced role of the poet in pre-settlement texts besides that of the scholar and courtier adventurer. Furthermore, an analysis of the tropes of Parmenius's poem will illustrate its connection to the humanistic discourse of service of the commonwealth which emerged parallel to a strong national pride in late sixteenth-century England. The work is also an outstanding contribution to Queen Elizabeth's early cult, which prescribes her a leading European role as a prince of Protestants.

STEPHEN PARMENIUS OF BUDA

Little is known about Stephen Parmenius's life before he arrived in England around 1581. What can be better reconstructed are the years when he settled in Oxford, became part of a circle of prominent scholars, such as Richard Hakluyt, William Camden, and Thomas Savile. He was also granted access to influential courtiers such as Sir Henry Unton and Sir Humphrey Gilbert, which attests to his exceptionally warm welcome probably due both to his breadth of learning and his religious sympathies.[3] While Parmenius was favorably received by Englishmen, the Hungarian poet also seems to have been open and ready to embrace all the new friendships, knowledge, and opportunities offered to him. He was so overwhelmed by the bounties of England, the liberality of her government, and the excellence of scholarship found there as to claim that "it had so exceeded all my expectations that now ... the delightful friendship of the English has almost dispelled my longing for Buda and the Hungary which I am bound to call my homeland."[4] To better understand Parmenius's admiration expressed in his works one needs to look at the situation of Hungary in the second half of the sixteenth century which influenced his upbringing and religious outlook.

The best sources about Parmenius's early years are the scattered remarks about his home and country in his two works published in London.[5] In the preface to his *De navigatione,* he claims that he was born in Buda, where he obtained some education from his "erudite teachers" who are mentioned both proudly and lovingly as "such as have always been the pride of my native Hungary (and are particularly so now, among her still surviving relics)."[6] The boast is offset by the melancholy tone which claims that he was born "in the servitude and barbarism of the Turkish empire," although of Christian parents. This dichotomy between the flourishing of learning and Christianity on the territory of the former medieval kingdom of Hungary, on the one hand, and the struggle against the oppression and "barbarity" of Turkish occupation of the central one-third of the country, on the other, best describes the climate of sixteenth-century Hungary. For Parmenius, his country became the easternmost outpost to defend Christianity and western humanistic ideas against the unquenchable tide of the conquest of the Ottoman Empire that subdued most of southeastern Europe during the course of the century.

The capital Buda—where Parmenius was born—fell in 1541, and further Turkish expansion continued until 1566 with the central territories becoming part of the Ottoman Empire for the rest of the sixteenth and most of the following century. The remaining parts were torn into two as a consequence of the civil war and the election of two rival kings after the death of the young King Louis II in the Battle of Mohács in 1526. The northwestern areas were gained by the Austrian Archduke and Hungarian-Bohemian King Habsburg Ferdinand, while the eastern country—mostly the territory of Transylvania—obtained a separate identity through its resistance to the influence of the Habsburgs and its high level of religious liberty.[7]

The country's religious orientation by the end of the century was mostly Protestant, with the overwhelming majority of the population belonging to one of the new reformed creeds,[8] among which Lutherans and Calvinists were the most dominant, although in Transylvania there was a large following of Anti-Trinitarians. It was among the members of this latter denomination that the admiration for the English Queen as a leader of European Protestantism appeared. At Cluj in a surviving copy of the Anti-Trinitarian manifesto *De falsa et vera unius Dei* (1568), the original dedication to John Sigismund is missing and the book contains a second dedication to Elizabeth Tudor dated 1570.[9] The author tries to establish an intimate relationship with the English monarchy by comparing the two countries as places where Protestant monarchs reign and by associating the virtues of Elizabeth's brother Edward VI to those of the young Protestant Hungarian King John Sigismund. The dedication styles the English Queen as a successful leader of a peaceful Protestant country, envisions her as the fountain of learning and true religion and a possible patron of the true reformed Church in Europe. The eulogy of the Anti-Trinitarian community attests to the positive reputation of Elizabeth Tudor's reign in East Central Europe in the late 1560s and early 1570s during the formative years of Parmenius's life. This led Tibor Klaniczay to conclude that Parmenius may have spent some time at the Anti-Trinitarian college at Cluj before starting on his European trip, although there is no further evidence to support the theory.[10]

Parmenius's home, the central part of the country—though devastated by the Turks—maintained a relatively vigorous intellectual life in the first few decades of its occupation. Although all higher educational opportunities ceased after the city fell into enemy hands, the peregrination of students to the cultural centers of Europe from the region continued. The tradition to visit universities abroad and to maintain active contact with the intellectual circles of Europe already characterized the country in the Middle Ages with approximately 9200 registered Hungarian students at various European centers of learning. During the period 1526–1600, this number did not decrease; on the contrary, in this short time span it reached 3375, excluding the French and English territories.[11] Yet the city of Buda and its nearby settlements Pest and Óbuda sent altogether only 14 students to European universities between 1526 and 1582 and none again until 1700, which indicates a significant decline in the prospects of education in the Buda region by the time Parmenius reached England.[12] However, the intellectual climate of the area around the former capital before 1580 is well exemplified by the two famous scholars István Szegedi Kis and Máté Skaricza teaching and preaching in Ráckeve, situated just thirty-eight kilometers south of Buda. They were active during the childhood and adolescence of Parmenius—Szegedi between 1563 and 1572 and Skaricza in 1564, 1568 and between 1572 and 1591—so their theological outlook and work may have exerted an important influence on Parmenius, a possibility that has to be taken into account as the two scholars were among the most revered intellectuals of the region.

After studying in Vienna, Krakow and Wittenberg, István Szegedi Kis—an active proponent of the Helvetic confession in the Danubian basin—became one of the key figures of the Reformation in Hungary.[13] He was admired by outstanding scholars like Theodore Beza to whom he sent his writing *Assertio Vera De Trinitate* and who later published it in Geneva in 1573 accompanied by a warm letter addressed to the author. The book refuted the doctrines of the Anti-Trinitarians and corresponded well with the need of Beza, who faced the problem of the spreading of similar doctrines. Szegedi's other works were also printed in the centers of European Protestantism: Geneva, Basel, Schaffhausen, and London.

Szegedi's student Máté Skaricza is one of those few scholars who left an account of his peregrination in Europe. His writing—attached to the biography of his master *Vita Stephani Szegedini* (Basel 1585)[14]—describes his travels between 1569 and 1572 and shows the interests, routes, possibilities, and hardships a Protestant student had during his trip, thus providing the closest example to the available choices Parmenius had a decade later. Skarica visited Italy—in spite of the warning of his master and other friends of the dangers to a Protestant in a Catholic country—as he believed that the best knowledge of Aristotle and Plato was accessible there. He depicted the suspicion of the Italians who searched the luggage of every foreign-looking traveler and how he was forced to destroy all the papers he collected. He gave an account of his joyful arrival in Geneva where he could speak his mind freely and of the meeting of several renowned scholars, among them Beza, in whose home he spent 6 days. On his travels in the North he visited Basel, spending 6 months studying Hebrew, stopped at Strasbourg and Heidelberg on his way to Wittenberg, where he spent a further 4 months among a thriving community of Hungarian students.[15] After touring the cities of Germany, the Low Countries and staying at Paris, Skarica even visited England, stopping in London and Cambridge where he met John Foxe and Edward Dering. Skarica calls Queen Elizabeth a person of "rare virtues"[16] and speaks about the "noble magnanimity" with which he was received in scholarly circles, thus describing a similar reciprocal respect between Hungarians and English as can be detected in the reception of Parmenius. This openness toward the plight of the Hungarians already could be seen in an official call for common prayer of the English to be used "through the whole Realme, to excite and stirre all godly people unto God for the preservation of those Christians and their

Countreys, that are now invaded by the Turke in Hungary or elsewhere" on every Sunday, Wednesday, and Friday.[17] The prayer appeared at the time of the great Turkish campaign of 1566 a few years before Skarica's visit, and his warm welcome by the famous martyrologist John Foxe and the scholar and radical theologian Dering could have been inspired by the general sympathy for the Hungarians.

Skarica's arrival back to Hungary in 1572 coincided with Parmenius's years of study in the region, and he presumably heard about the travels of Skarica. Similarly to Skarica he spent 3 years wandering around Europe starting in about 1578/9, and stopped at Wittenberg—the only place where his name survives on a list of students for the year 1579[18]—where Skarica also studied. Skarica's rare example of visiting England could have inspired Parmenius, and his positive account of the friendliness of the English may have encouraged him.[19] Much like Szegedi and Skarica, Parmenius is more likely to have belonged to the Reformed (Calvinist) branch of Protestantism than to the Anti-Trinitarian, as Anti-Trinitarianism was deemed heretical by the Church of England by the late 1570s, and between 1579 and 1589 six of their proponents were burnt at the stake.[20] His close relationship with some of the chief courtiers of the time, such as Henry Unton—whom he may have already met during his journeys on the Continent[21]—would have been impossible had he adhered to views denying the Trinity.

Parmenius's aim on his travels was not only to visit centers of culture but also to see "wisely constituted states" and "the impeccable administration of many branches of the Church,"[22] which was an approach that comprised both the broadening of knowledge in the classics as well as a heightened interest in the workings of governmental systems and the multiplicity of religious creeds. Arriving from a country torn by war and religious diversity, his fascination with the peaceful country of England where religion was officially uniform must have been profound. Yet—like Skarica—he intended to return to his mother country as he claims in his poem: "Fate ... [summoned me] to sing reluctantly of sad defeats / In Danube lands: the Fates must keep me back / For tasks like that."[23] Thus, he felt the duty and urge to serve his native homeland, as Skarica did, who remained in the territory of Turkish occupation and died in a Turkish onslaught in 1591. But Parmenius's destiny lay elsewhere.

By the autumn of 1581, Stephen Parmenius of Buda had arrived in Oxford and took up residence with Richard Hakluyt, a senior member of Christ Church.[24] Through Hakluyt Parmenius was introduced to Sir

Humphrey Gilbert about whose colonizing expedition, he wrote and published his poem *De navigatione*. By the time this expedition was launched on June 11, 1583, he was aboard the *Swallow* to be taken to the New World to eternalize in Latin poetry the fame of English exploration. Unfortunately, he never lived to fulfill his wishes, as on August 29, 1583, his ship ran aground and broke up.[25] In his eyewitness account Edward Haies mentions his name as one of the greatest losses:

> Amongst whome was drowned a learned man, an Hungarian, borne in the Citie of Buda, called thereof Budaeus, who of pietie and zeale to good attemptes, adventured in this action, minding to record in the Latin tongue, the gests and things worthy of remembrance, happening in this discoverie, to the honour of our nation, the same being adorned with the eloquent stile of this Orator, and rare Poet of our time.[26]

Elizabethan Views on Explorations and Colonization

Parmenius's fortune to reside with Richard Hakluyt in Christ Church, Oxford, brought him into the center of discussion and knowledge about naval exploration and colonization. Hakluyt and his elder cousin, Richard Hakluyt, the lawyer, a member of Middle Temple—an institution to which the leading figures of English seafaring, Walter Raleigh, Martin Frobisher, and John Hawkins also belonged—shared an interest in the new science of geography, and in collecting maps and information on voyages.[27] By 1577, the younger Hakluyt, a theologian and ordained priest, took up giving public lectures about geography showing "both the olde and imperfectly composed, and the new lately reformed Mappes, Globes, and Spheares" to his audience for the first time.[28] He encouraged the translation of travel accounts, such as John Florio's rendition in 1580 of Jacques Cartier's journey of 1534, and published the first collection of documents about English exploration under the title *Divers Voyages Touching the Discoverie of America* (1582). While for Parmenius Hakluyt's activity must have been an introduction to this new field of study, the frenzy for naval adventure had already started in England a few years before his arrival. The late 1570s and early 1580s saw the first attempts at the systematical exploration of the northern parts of America and the printers of London brought forth an unprecedented number of tracts on the necessity of discovery and settlement, as well as travel accounts. Parmenius's *De navigatione* of 1582 was among these early pre-settlement pamphlets.

Tudor England was late to embark on the discovery of overseas land. Though Henry VII encouraged the building of an English fleet and employed John Cabot, who in 1497 explored the shores of North America, no royal initiative was undertaken to colonize and settle the land of the American continent. It was not until the Elizabethan years that there were more substantial efforts made to search for both the northeast and northwest passage to China. The chief propagator of the idea of a British Empire was John Dee, advisor to the Queen, who in his *General and Rare Memorials Pertayning to the Perfect Arte of Navigation* (1577) set down the many advantages of a strong British fleet, a "Pety-Navy-Royall" which he saw as instrumental for the security of the nation. Dee advocated an expansionist policy and the right for the English to settle the territories lying north of Florida, a claim that was founded both on Cabot's discoveries as on accounts of the mythic dominions of Arthur and legends of the Welsh prince Madoc.[29] Dee intended his book—with only a hundred printed copies—for a restricted and select audience who would understand and share his vision illustrated on the front cover about the urgency of transforming England into a naval power. Entitled "Hieroglyphicon Brytanicon," an elaborate engraving on the front cover depicts Queen Elizabeth sitting in a ship named Europe, and Lady Occasion standing on a rock pointing to her forelock and urging the Queen "to catch hold on" and seize the opportunity offered to her country.[30] A further female figure, "RES-PUBL. BRYTANICA" kneels in supplication on the mainland pleading with the Queen to send forth a sailing expedition. While the image openly propagates the country's active participation in naval enterprises, the positioning of the Queen at the helm of the ship decorated by the royal arms assigns her a new role as the monarch to realize this dream. Furthermore, the Queen is also portrayed as the leader of the Protestant cause in Europe: "Sitting at the HELM of this Imperiall Monarchy, or rather, at the Helm of the IMPERIALL SHIP, of the most parte of Christendome: if so, it be her Graces Pleasure," as it is explained in Dee's ekphrasis later in the text.[31] The conditional tense used by Dee seems to provide room for manoeuvre for the Queen, yet Dee makes no secret that she is expected to become the head of the reformed part of Europe and he tops her ship on the engraving with the Chi-Rho christogram. Furthermore, the presence of another vessel with a Dutch flag on the river argues for the Queen's military involvement in the Dutch War of Independence. Thus, in this early pamphlet on propagating the overseas expansion of England, naval exploration gets associated with the question of religion and the success of Protestantism.

Another conspicuous aspect of Dee's frontispiece is the prominence of female figures in a maritime context, as it goes against the traditional association of seafaring with manly traits. On the illustration of the front cover of *General and Rare Memorials,* there is the contrast between the two parts of the image along a slanting axis drawn from the upper right corner to the lower left corner. While the upper right half is allegorical featuring God's glory, the archangel Michael, the hermetic signs of Sun, Moon, and ten stars, and the representations of Occasion, Britannica and Europe on the Bull; the lower left is crammed with signs of human power: soldiers with drawn swords, episodes of a possible treaty negotiation, castles and ships. At the top right side heavenly and female symbols dominate, at the bottom left side earthly and masculine ones. Queen Elizabeth appears on the side of hermetic symbols with three of her councilors placed further below in the ship. She enjoys the rays of God's glory, and her position at the helm of the ship and the archangel protecting her with drawn sword argue for her prophetic role. Dee's composition presents a powerful picture of his envisioned English expansionist policy delivered in terms of female agency. Very rarely would later tracts on naval exploration return to this feminized image, but among the few would be Parmenius's poem 6 years later.

Among the formal treatises on colonization, the first pamphlet that intended to persuade a wider public was Sir Humphrey Gilbert's *A Discourse of a Discoverie for a New Passage to Cataia* (1576) in which he advocated the possibility of a Northwestern passage to China. Written 10 years earlier and perhaps inspired during his service in France where he may have encountered the Huguenot interests in similar projects, the publishing of the work was meant to lend force to Gilbert's expedition of 1578, to which he gained the first ever Letters Patent for settlement from the Queen. The treatise lists the "commodities" to be had from such a discovery, laying down the arguments to be echoed in many further works. Apart from the promised gain from the direct trade routes to the Orient, gold, silver, and other precious merchandise, Gilbert underlines the importance of colonization as a solution to social ills. He envisions the newly settled lands as the homes of those "needie people of our Countrie, which now trouble the common welth, and through want here at home, are inforced to commit outrageous offenses, whereby they are dayly consumed with the Gallowes,"[32] and argues that colonization provides a possibility for employment of the poor and vagrant. In close correspondence with Dee's view, he sees naval travel as a means to increase the number of English ships and trained sailors as well.[33]

The significance of Gilbert's pamphlet also lies in its way of presentation: Gilbert employed the service of a poet to advertise his planned project. The text is not directly imparted by its author, but it is rendered by the poet George Gascoigne who is claimed to have persuaded Gilbert to let him print it and who introduces the work and attaches a sonnet about Gilbert. That Gilbert felt the need of a literary advocate to promote his ventures may shed light on the origin of Parmenius's later involvement to produce a text promoting the second planned voyage of Gilbert 6 years later, perhaps taking over the role from Gascoigne who died in 1577. It may also explain Gilbert's predilection for humanists establishing his fame through poetry and his decision to invite Parmenius on his 1583 journey to later sing the glory of the expedition.

In 1578, Thomas Churchyard also published two poems to praise the two then most prominent figures of English exploration: Gilbert and Martin Frobisher.[34] The compositions examine the old question of why noble men of wealth, having a family and enjoying the monarch's favor, would leave all behind and start on a journey to the unknown. Churchyard provides the classical answer: to achieve virtue through the service of the commonwealth. His lines about the lack of "greedy hope of gain" and the "noble fire that burnes in brest"[35] echo the morality of Cicero's *De officiis* that places selfless service as the noblest aim in life. In such a context a contrast is drawn between the experience of going abroad and staying at home, while the first promises wealth, experience, knowledge, wisdom, service, and honor, the other is seen as idleness, waste of time, folly, shame, and the pursuit of worthless pastimes. The first underlines manliness while the second is seen as womanly weakness:

> You are not ruld by love of babes,
>
> > nor vvomens vvilles yevvus.
>
> But guided by such grace,
>
> > as God himselfe hath sent,
>
> And that you do, is done indeede
>
> > vnto a good intent.[36]

This masculine character of the pre-settlement colonial literature has been already noted by Howard Mumford Jones,[37] and it mostly appears as a form of service where physical strength and endurance is combined with knowledge and courage. The prominence of manly virtue also appears in Churchyard's other pamphlet of the same year about the second voyage of Frobisher which decries those that oppose exploration: "the coward Spirite of those that dare attempt no hazardes comes from a feble iudgement, or a weak womanish bodie, that trembles to take in hande any stoute or manly exercise."[38] Frobisher becomes the *par excellence* of manly virtue by the end of the 1570s, and he is compared to Ulysses, Jason, Heracles, Hector, and other antique heroes in three further travel accounts published in 1578 and 1579. Especially his third journey of 1578 where a fleet of 15 vessels brought home two hundred tons of ore that promised to contain gold—though it later turned out to be worthless iron pyrite—was hailed as a new journey for the Golden Fleece: "The glittering fleece that he doth bring, / in value sure is more, / Than Iasons was, or Alcides fruite, / whereof was made suche store."[39]

The reports of Dionyse Settle and Thomas Ellis both add a laudatory poem by Abraham Fleming—the translator of Virgil's *Eclogues*—to enhance the effect of their texts. Ellis, a sailor, even appends a further four poems that both serve as a eulogy of Frobisher and as an apology of the style and learning of the author. The preface of Ellis hints at the unease of the writer about his ability of following the expected literary conventions:

> … my simple wit and iudgement, cannot attaine and reache unto the flowing style of great *Plutarch*, not yet the eloquence of the noble *Tullie*: I being a Sailer, more studied and used in my Charde and Compasse, and other things belonging to Navigation, than trained up in Minerva's Court, or taught by the sage philosophers, the fathers of eloquence whose sweete and sacred sappe I never sucked.[40]

The employment of Fleming and the addition of the four poems endeavor to make up for Ellis's presumed lack of learning, and demonstrate the insistence of contemporary exploration literature on using classical parallels and employing the service of poets in advocating journeys. As most of the active promoters of discovery were members of the intellectual life of the sixteenth century, such as Thomas Smith, Philip Sidney, Humphrey Gilbert, or Walter Raleigh, the language of humanism became a hallmark of early colonization discourse.[41] The praise of an active life—*vita activa*—in the form of finding new land and extending trade was depicted as service and duty instead of the pursuit of personal interest and gain. The "Epistle Dedicatorie" of a further account of Frobisher's voyages written by George Best expounds this view and echoes John Dee's standpoint that the English have a unique opportunity that they should grasp, though—as opposed to Dee—it emphasizes the masculinity of the enterprise: "It is not unknown to the world, that this our native country of England in al ages hath bred up (and especially at this present aboundeth with) many forward and valiant knights, fit to take in hand any notable enterprise."[42]

However, there is unease detectable in all these writings about conquest and the taking of new land, which is counterbalanced by Gilbert and Dee in their social arguments about providing new employment and homes for the poor. Further justification for colonization is offered by the religious claim of Christianizing the savages, first appearing in Churchyard's tract of 1578 where the "purpose of manifestyng Gods mightie woorde and maiestie among those that feed like monsters (and rather live like dogges than like men) doeth argue not only a blessed successe, but persuadeth a prosperous and beneficiall retourne."[43] Although the accounts of the voyages of Frobisher call the natives "cannibals," they include some positive traits about their personality by describing them as fierce in struggle and cunning in warfare and heroic in their willingness to cast themselves down from a rock rather than become captives. George Best's remark that "they beganne to growe more civill, familiar, pleasaunt, and docible among us in a verye shorte time" promises little difficulty in converting them and Dionyse Settle forecasts a heavenly and earthly reward for "who so ever can winne them from their infidelitie and service, hee or they are worthy to receive the greatest rewarde at Gods hands, and the greatest benefites of those countries, which he hath discovered."[44] While these texts use the Christianizing of pagans as one of the arguments to justify territorial conquest, by the early 1580s, the emphasis on the question of true faith becomes a major theme and is associated with the image of just government. The question of religion appears as a central theme in two further influential writings, both systematically discussing the advantages of colonization: the introduction of John Florio's translation of Cartier's journey (1580) and the dedication to Philip Sydney of Richard Hakluyt's *Divers Voyages* (1582). In Florio, it follows right after the first argument about the abundance of the land and claims that "the people, though simple and rude in manners, and destitute of the knowledge of God or any good lawes, yet [are] of nature gentle and tractable and most apt to receive the Christian religion, and to subject themselves to some good government."[45] Hakluyt adds a further point to the case when accusing the Spanish and Portuguese of conquering land with the pretext of converting the infidels, yet they "in deed and truth sought not them, but their goods and riches."[46] Thus as a theologian, he brings forth the issue of true religion. This marks the first seed of the emergence of the Black Legend about Spanish cruelty and inhumanity that will be used to justify Protestant colonization in the New World and which will be fully expounded in the poem of Parmenius.[47]

Richard Hakluyt's *Divers Voyages* displays a close correspondence to the themes of Parmenius, which indicates that the Hungarian scholar actively participated in the ongoing debates about founding a colony and agreed with the views of his friend.[48] *Divers Voyages* asserts the appropriateness of the time for the English to take a share of conquest and planting while free land is still available,[49] enlists social reasons for it, like the overpopulation of England—a common belief among late Elizabethans based perhaps on the increasing number of the poor and vagrant—the problem of overcrowded prisons,[50] and highlights the importance of converting "those gentile people to Christianity."[51] The only point not mentioned by Parmenius is Hakluyt's reasoning about the economic benefits of trade that the poet perhaps deemed inappropriate for his theme and genre of a laudatory poem in Latin.

THE VISION OF A GOLDEN AGE

While Parmenius's Latin poem promoting the planned 1582 voyage of Humphrey Gilbert—that finally sailed only in 1583—fits into the climate of Elizabethan exploration literature with its humanist rhetoric, the writer's Hungarian background adds a new dimension to its language that discusses England and America as sister countries. The two regions are united by the metaphor of the Golden Age as Parmenius treats savage America as a pre-historical ageless land of innocence, on the one hand, and depicts England as a country of peace, plenty, learning, and true religion if compared to other parts of Europe, on the other. While the first image reflects the poet's classical learning, the second can be regarded as the opinion of a person who came from a country stricken by war and one who traveled around Europe and is able to form a balanced opinion about England's state and government. Thus, the long eulogy of the country and her Queen is given authority and appeal by being contrasted to other countries, among them three times to the pitiful condition of Hungary.

The central trope of the poem is the reference to the Golden Age, with the word "gold" or "golden" appearing seventeen times in the poem of 330 lines. In the first part of the work, it describes the continent and people of America who live in a state of blessedness in sylvan lands, which seems timeless and ageless as it is distanced from history: "A world which has not felt the weight / Of Babylon, the Persian's might, nor known / Victorious Macedon, and never was / Subdued by Rome."[52] The distinctness of America is foregrounded by comparing it to contemporary European countries (among them Hungary) suffering from the brutal reign of Muslims, the falsehood of Italian priests, and the bloody conflicts of France and Spain, circumstances that Parmenius—using the Ovidian categories—claims to be a deterioration from the Golden Age into the Age of Iron and even beyond that into an Age of Rock. While the early Continental accounts on discoveries mostly emphasized the savagery of the New World, there were some early tracts portraying the people and their conditions as an earthly paradise.[53] For instance, in Peter Martyr's description of the second journey of Columbus (first translated and published in English in 1555 and reprinted in 1577), the people are depicted as living in a Golden Age:

> So that if we shall not be ashamed to confesse the truthe, they seeme to lyve in that goulden worlde of the which owlde wryters speake so much: wherin men lyved simplye and inocentlye without inforcement of lawes, without quarrellinge Judges and libelles, contente onely to satisfie nature, without further vexation for knoweledge of thinges to come.[54]

Montaigne in his essay "Des Cannibales" ("Of Cannibals"), published in 1580, also sees the natives of America as benevolent and happy members of a simple and content society that "not only surpass all the pictures with which the poets have adorned the golden age, and all their inventions in feigning a happy state of man, but, moreover, the fancy and even the wish and desire of philosophy itself."[55] For Parmenius, the simile serves to associate the New World with England, a country which he pronounces to be the place where the Golden Age returned, and to promote the English initiative to take this "sister" land destined to her as it is "unruled by kings [and] has been preserved for you through many centuries."[56] Parmenius transforms John Dee's argument about the fit time and good occasion for Britain to embark on exploration into a mythical image of gods, nature, and sea creatures benevolently supporting the opportunity of the English:

Good Fortune walks the land

In open view, and all the Nereid tribe

Are prancing gleefully about the waves

While Father Nereus soothes the docile deep

With his propitious wand . . .

The dolphins spring ...

... just as though their backs

Were offered to the ships to carry them

Through kindly waters.[57]

The middle section of the poem sets out to prove that England is the new land of Saturn, substantiating it by five arguments: with its right worship of God, the reign of a Queen that is just, the conditions of being free from tyrants and from enemies, and of living peacefully with neighbors. The poem consists of five declarative sentences of equal length repeating five times the phrase "arguit aurum" ("it proves that it is a Golden Age").[58] This section is so emphatic with its repetitions that it becomes the main thesis of the poem, as if Parmenius were setting out to prove and persuade the English about their mighty role which is so obvious to him as a foreigner. For Parmenius, the embodiment of this "golden race" is Humphrey Gilbert, whose enumerated valiant feats exemplify the courage of the nation. As a scholar interested in the workings of government, he sketches out a utopian dream of America governed by Gilbert where

... people, innocent

Of crime and falsity, will rather wear

The crown of lasting purity than sink

Their minds and bodies into sinful lust

Freedom and the use

Of talents will not be repressed by wealth

... based on the claim that all

Are citizens. Each man will take the part

> That duly falls to him. Then Mother earth
>
> Will yield to all, from little effort, rich
>
> Provisions from her ample store of goods
>
> No care will then oppress the youth with age,
>
> And laboring will not deprive a man
>
> Of time to make a living through his own
>
> Abilities.[59]

The imagery of these lines is truly paradisiacal: It is not just an innocent world of bounty, but also one where there are no differences of wealth and a world in which talent matters rather than wealth.[60] The poem spans past, present, and future and connects all to the idealized English and their Queen.

The praise of Elizabeth Tudor receives the longest passage within the work. Parmenius seems to have been sensitive to the developing language of the Queen's cult which was about to move over from the world of pageantry into the field of the literature with John Lyly's comprehensive summary of its tropes being published in 1580 in his *Euphues and His England*. From the mid-1570s onward, the Queen's public appearances were celebrated by a growing number of shows, pageants, and literary devices that coupled her laudation with elements of myth and legend. As the Queen was reaching an age when she could not bear children, and as England was faced by the increasing threat of war with Spain, the English began to apply to their Queen's public eulogy a cult language informed by ancient mythology and local folklore. The first examples of poetic allusions that celebrated the queen as a deity were the shows staged during her annual summer progresses. In 1575, two crucial entertainments mark the early stages of the development of the Queen's cult discourse: the "princely pleasures" organized at Kenilworth Castle, and her reception at Woodstock a month later. While the first placed her amid ancient goddesses and contained an unperformed masque by George Gascoigne associating her with Juno; the second—within a story of chivalrous romance—commended her as a virgin who places her country's interest before her personal happiness.[61] Within a few years, this second image of the Virgin Queen emerged as the central trope of the courtly praise of Elizabeth Tudor. In 1579, Edmund Spencer's *The Shepheardes Calender* introduced a further layer of praise to the Queen's expanding cult: the pastoral tradition that extolled her as queen of the golden age of Saturn.

The Hungarian scholar fully absorbed this new manner of discourse and predating many literary works in his poem painted a vivid image of Queen Elizabeth as a deity, for instance, as Athene giving her blessings on the quest of the Argonauts. The Queen is compared to nymphs, the Graces, Diana, and applauded as the mother of demigods. Elizabeth is also likened to the virgin goddess of peace and justice, Astraea, which makes *De navigatione* one of the earliest poems to apply this later well-known epithet of the Queen: "Quod tam chara Deo tua sceptra gubernat Amazon / Quam Dea, cum nondum coelis Astraea petitis / Inter mortales regina erat" ("Your mighty Queen / is reigning, dear to God as Justice was / When holding sway as goddess over men / before she sought the Heavens").[62] The Latin original associates Elizabeth both with an Amazon, a strong and forceful female leader, and with Astraea, the just ruler of a golden age of prosperity. The twin image recalls Dee's vision of the English Queen's role as elaborated in his *General and Rare Memorials*, but goes further as it uses a militant virgin's persona, an Amazon—a figure rarely used in Elizabeth's encomium—to justify the urgency of female agency. However, the associations of the just government of Astraea receive a more emphatic accent within the poem, as they offer an opportunity for hailing the outstanding Humanistic education of the Queen:

> Your authority
>
> Does not depend on lashes, rods and threats
>
> Of punishment: your royalty derives
>
> From much beneficience, and Mercy stands
>
> To guard your open gate, without a sword.
>
> … you have drunk the Muses' spring so deep
>
> That artistry can flow in golden streams
>
> From your poetic tongues.[63]

The eulogy finishes with describing Elizabeth as a leader who is respected by the whole of Europe—among them the Hungarians—creating for her a mission and a role to found an empire that recalls the frontispiece of John Dee's *Arte of Navigation*. Such a sustained poetic vision about the Queen and her country was unique at the beginning of the 1580s, and it stands as a harbinger of later dramatic works by John Lyly of the mid 1580s and the grand narrative of Edmund Spenser's *The Faerie Queene* (1590, 1596).

De navigatione also differs from early colonial literature as—instead of masculine virility—it praises a female monarch whose figure is equated with the achievements of her country. Furthermore, it creates a feminine identity for the new continent America, whose voice and supplication comprises the last quarter of the epic poem. She is not directly called a maiden, yet her virginity is implied by the lines: "A world which has not felt the weight / Of Babylon, the Persian's might, nor known / Victorious Macedon, and never was / Subdued by Rome," images alluding to lands being untouched by masculine aggression.[64] This virgin America addresses her sister a feminized Britannia ruled by a Queen—and not Humphrey Gilbert—and asks for help. In a moving image, with tears running on her face she stretches out her hand toward England and calls upon her: "Please do not ignore my tears, fair sister, but feel for me in my misfortune."[65] It is the words of this allegorical maiden which give an account of the valiant deeds of English captains—enlisting them in the exact order as mentioned on the second page of Hakluyt's *Divers Voyages*—and outline all the reasons for colonization that appeared in earlier pamphlets: the overpopulation of cities, the mildness of the climate, and most importantly her longing for God's true light. It is thus remarkable that as opposed to previous colonial writing which hails seafaring as manly prowess sharply distinguishing it from womanly weakness, Parmenius's poem positions the achievements of English sailors within a feminine frame: accounted by the words of America and enabled by the blessing of the English Queen.

In the work of Parmenius, spreading the Protestant faith becomes a crucial aspect of initiating colonization with a reference to the Black Legend and to the idolatrous falsehood of the Catholic religion:

> Are you not aware
>
> What times and what disasters I have seen
>
> After the Spaniards' endless appetite
>
> For gold had spurred them on to infiltrate
>
> My lands? (For certainly they were not moved

> By any moral zeal or holiness.) ...
>
> They make me raise altars to mortal men
>
> And pray to silent idols or trees,
>
> In madness honouring I know not what
>
> Catholic deity.⁶⁶

This deep religious concern about the "altars to mortal men" and "silent idols" worshipped by the Spanish is central to the argument that persuades through appealing both to the Protestant conviction and to the chivalry of its learned audience. The device conflates the imagery of the ancient Golden Age and the Black Legend through depicting the threat to Indians posed by their affiliation with the Spanish, calling for the active participation of Elizabethan England in (re-)establishing their purity.

The Black Legend associated Catholicism with savage barbarity and its claims were founded on the book of the Dominican missionary Bartolome de las Casas who in his tract *Brevísima relación de la destrucción de las Indias* to the later Philip II wrote about all the misdeeds the Spanish committed on their colonies which ultimately led to the introduction of regulations protecting the native population. The work was originally scripted in the Castilian language in 1542 and published in 1552, but its various translations became very popular especially in Protestant countries in order to illustrate the brutality and godlessness of the Spanish. As a propaganda piece, it was published thirty-three times in Dutch between 1578 and 1648, and in 1598 was illustrated by Theodore de Bry with the visual images of brutality, for instance, with scenes of the Spanish feeding their dogs on native children. The English translation was published in 1583—a year after Parmenius's poem—and underscores the currency of the topic in England during the early 1580s. It also may explain the centrality of the theme in *De navigatione*, a work by a committed Protestant.

The poem ends with the allegorical figure of America raising an issue unprecedented in other tracts on promoting colonization: Even the greatest and most renowned empires fall apart if injustice and tyranny are allowed:

> Cyrus' throne was won
>
> In clemency, but inhumanity
>
> Lost it to his successor. Macedon

> Subdued a widespread kingdom leniently,
>
> But later harshness broke it bit by bit
>
> Away from what had been acquired before.
>
> So, even when paternal Romulus
>
> Has laid foundations for an empire's rise,
>
> The men like Nero come and tear it down.[67]

The Latin original's last word "Nero" stands as an ominous warning to those participating in colonial ventures. Taking a truly humanist stance against greed and avarice, Parmenius casts the shadow of anxiety on the nature of imperial conquest. But his lines also reflect his own experience whose once famous home country had fallen apart as a result of civil war, and explain this unparalleled ending of the poem. The emphatic use of a feminine imagery within the poem counterbalances the aggressive masculinity of seafaring: representing the peaceful and just rule of Queen Elizabeth and the maiden America peopled with benevolent savages creates a harmonic connection between the two "sister" lands and justifies England and her Queen's claim in the New World.

De navigatione was not the only pamphlet to further the aims of Humphrey Gilbert's project of colonization. In 1583, an account by George Peckham was printed about the journey, at a time when the only surviving ship already arrived back in England, yet the *Squirrel* in which Gilbert traveled—and disappeared—was still expected to return. The *A True Report of the Late Discoveries and Possessions Taken in the Right of the Crowne of England* sets out to support and popularize Gilbert's plans "to plant themselves and theyr people in the continent of the hether part of America."[68] It imitates—as so many other pamphlets will—Parmenius's vision of the innocent savages and the religious argument, as natives are "living in ignoraunce and Idolatry . . . [and] thristing after Christianitie."[69] It is also striking how its author thrives to create a learned paratext for its pamphlet with ten poems by courtiers, military leaders, scholars, and merchant explorers—among them Francis Drake, John Hawkins, and Martin Frobisher—commending the work. Yet most of Peckham's tract consists of a systematical analysis of the advantages to be expected from trade and plantation. In this respect, it already belongs to those pamphlets—like Thomas Hariot's *A Briefe and True Report of the New Found Land of Virginia* (1588)—that are informed by the real experience of planting a settlement and persuade their audience by the exact description of plants, minerals, and possible commodities. Parmenius's text about the same voyage is still a pre-settlement discourse that relies in its form and language on classical and poetic devices.

Conclusion

The poem *De navigatione* attests to the cooperative effort of three different classes of people in Elizabethan England to promote colonization: the courtier, the scholar, and the poet. While the voyage (and the poem about it) was enabled by the political connections and financial means provided by Sir Humphrey Gilbert the courtier and encouraged by the knowledge and practical experience gathered by Richard Hakluyt the scholar, the poet, Stephen Parmenius was invited to provide a celebratory account of the glory and fame of the enterprise. The ambitions of these three people—all sharing a common Humanistic education—attest to the nature of early naval exploration which became a humanistic project with political, scientific, and poetic aspirations.

De navigatione sheds light on the vision of America of the English at a very unique moment in 1582, just before the first real attempt at colonization by Walter Raleigh in 1585. However, the theme is filtered through the sensibilities of a Hungarian who as a foreigner reflects on his own experiences within England as well as that of his home country. The work is also a significant first example of eulogizing England and her Queen by creating a humanistic, Protestant justification about English territorial expansion and ascribing England the role of spreading the bounties of her new Golden Age to the remote parts of the Globe.

Compared to both the early and later exploration literature, Parmenius's *De navigatione* represents a rare historical moment when the discourse on trade, business, and science was expressed in a poetical vision.

Notes

1. Andrew Fitzmaurice, *Humanism and America: An Intellectual History of English Colonisation, 1500–1625* (Cambridge: Cambridge University Press, 2007), 9.
2. Parmenius Stephanus, *De navigatione illustris et magnanimi equitis aurati Humfredi Gilberti, adducendam in novum orbem coloniam susceptâ, carmen epibatikos Stephani Parmenii Budeii* (London: Thomas

Purfoot, 1582). The poem was edited, translated, and published by David B. Quinn and Neil M. Cheshire, *The New Found Land of Stephen Parmenius* (Toronto and Buffalo: University of Toronto Press, 1972), 74–105.
3. The most complete biography is provided in Quinn and Cheshire eds., *The New Found Land of Stephen Parmenius*, 3–67. See also Tivadar Ács, "Egy tengerbe veszett magyar humanista költő a XVI. században" ("A Sixteenth Century Hungarian Humanist Poet Who Drowned at Sea") *Filológiai Közlöny* 8 (1962): 115–122; Tibor Klaniczay, "Jegyzetek Budai Parmenius Istvánról" ("Notes on Stephen Parmenius of Buda") in *Hagyományok ébresztése* (Budapest: Szépirodalmi Könyvkiadó, 1976), 225–242.
4. Quinn and Cheshire eds., *New Found Land*, 77. ("Accedit quod praeter omnem expectationem meam ... suavissimae Anglorum amicitiae ferme aboleverint desiderium et Pannoniarum et Budae meae, quibus patriae nomen debeo." Ibid, 76).
5. The other known work is *Paean* (London: Thomas Vautroullier, 1582).
6. Quinn and Cheshire, *New Found Land*, 77. (" ...quibus tum Pannoniae nostrae tum imprimis salvae adhuc earum reliquiae florescent ..." Ibid. 76).
7. The principality of Transylvania emerging between 1541 and 1570 became a vassal state of the Ottomans. See also Bryan Cartledge, *The Will to Survive: A History of Hungary* (London: Hurst & Company, 2011), 81–94.
8. Although it is difficult to esteem exact percentages, scholars agree that more than three-quarters of the population was Protestant, with Gábor Almási putting the figure to be 90%, Tamás Faragó 80%, and Katalin Péter between 75–80%. Gábor Almási, *The Uses of Humanism: Johannes Sambucus (1531–1584), Andreas Dudith (1533–1589), and the Republic of Letters in East Central Europe* (Leiden: Brill, 2009), 22; Tamás Faragó, *Bevezetés a történeti demográfiába (Introduction to Historical Demography)* (Budapest: Corvinus Egyetem, 2011), 347; and Katalin Péter "Reformáció és művelődés a 16. században" ("Reformation and Culture in the Sixteenth Century"), *Magyarország története: 1526–1686* (Budapest, Akadémia, 1987), I: 520.
9. Mihály Balázs, "About a copy of De falsa et vera unius Dei... cognitione: Additional data to the history of the English connections of the Antitrinitarians of Transylvania," *Odrodzenie i Reformacja w Polsce XLVII* (2003): 53–64.
10. Klaniczay, "Jegyzetek Budai Parmenius Istvánról," 232–233.
11. Most registrations were at German universities (ca. 1700), but there was a substantial number of enrollments at Vienna and in Polish universities (632 and 394 respectively). László Szögi, "A külföldi magyar egyetemjárás a kezdetektől a kiegyezésig" ("Hungarian Peregrination Abroad

from the Beginnings until the Compromise [1867])," *Educatio* 2 (2005), 249.
12. László Szögi, *Budai, pesti, és óbudai diákok külföldi egyetemjárása I. 1526–1867 (The Peregrination of Students from Buda, Pest and Óbuda I: 1526–1867)* (Budapest: Budapest Főváros Levéltára, 2004), 37.
13. For a recent study on his life in English see Stanko Jambrek, "Stephen Kis of Szeged: A Baranyan Reformer with a European Influence," *KAIROS—Evangelical Journal of Theology* 4.1 (2012): 77–98.
14. See its modern publication in Géza Kathona, *Fejezetek a török hódoltsági reformáció történetéből (Chapters from the History of the Reformation under Turkish Occupation)* (Budapest: Akadémia, 1974), 90–116.
15. Between 1555–1614, a famous Hungarian Coetus with its own special rules existed in Wittenberg which exerted a great influence on the Hungarian Reformation. Andrew Pettegree, Alastair Duke and Gillian Lewis, *Calvinism in Europe, 1540–1620* (Cambridge: Cambrige Universtity Press, 1996), 215. See also András Szabó, "Coetus-Natio-Respublica-Politica-Societas-Congregatio-Collegium-Gens: A wittenbergi magyar diákegyesület au újabb kutatások fényében, 1555–1613" ("The Wittenberg Coetus of Hungarian Students in the light of New Research, 1555–1613"), *Irodalomtörténeti Közlemények* 115.2 (2011): 229–234.
16. "... ubi quot et quanta vicissim viderimus, in aula praesertim Reginae, rarissimae virtutis Elizabethae, supersedeo dicere," in Kathona, *Fejezetek,* 113.
17. Church of England, *A Fourme to be used in Commom Prayer* (London: Richard Jugge and John Cawood, 1566).
18. Klaniczay corrects Quinn and Cheshire's reference to a student list of Heidelberg in "Jegyzetek Budai Parmenius Istvánról," 230.
19. A rare example is Vulpe Johannes, who appears at Cambridge in 1562 and later became a physician to the Earl of Sussex and a clergyman writing his will in London in 1590. György Gömöri, *Magyarországi diákok angol és skót egyetemeken 1526–1789: Hungarian Students in England and Scotland 1526–1789* (Budapest: Eötvös Loránd Tudományegyetem Levéltára, 2005), 5.
20. John Marshall, *John Locke, Toleration and Early Enlightenment Culture: Religious Intoleranceand Arguments for Religious Toleration in Early Modern and 'Early Enlightenment' Europe* (Cambridge: Cambridge University Press, 2010), 255.
21. Both Henry Unton and his brother Edward were in Italy sometime around 1579–81. Quinn and Cheshire eds., *The New Found Land,* 17.
22. Quinn and Cheshire eds., *The New Found Land,* 77. ("... multas etiam sapienter institutas respublicas, multarum ecclesiarum probatissimas administrationes introspeximus ..." Ibid, 76).

23. *De navigatione.* Quinn and Cheshire eds., *The New Found Land*, 93. ("Sed me fata vetant, memoraturumque canora / Inclyta facta tuba ad clades miserabilis Istri / Invitum retrabunt ..." Ibid, 92).
24. Quinn and Cheshire eds., *The New Found Land*, 8.
25. Quinn and Cheshire eds., *The New Found Land*, 47, 58–61.
26. Richard Hakluyt, *Principall Navigations, Voiages and Discoveries of the English Nation* (London: Christopher Baker, 1589), 692.
27. Peter C. Mancall, *Hakluyt's Promise: An Elizabethan's Obsession for an English America* (New Haven and London: Yale University Press, 2007), 76.
28. Hakluyt, *Principall Navigations*, 2^r.
29. About Dee's imperial vision see Frances A. Yates, *Astrea: The Imperial Theme in the Sixteenth Century* (London: Routledge & Kegan Paul, 1975), 48–50.
30. John Dee, *General and Rare Memorials Pertayning to the Perfect Arte of Navigation* (London: John Day, 1577), 54.
31. Dee, *General and Rare Memorials*, 53.
32. Humphrey Gilbert, *A Discourse of a Discoverie for a New Passage to Cataia* (London: Henry Middleton, 1576), H1^v.
33. Dee already praised Gilbert as a "Couragous Capitaine" who was ready to venture on discovery in his preface to his translation of Euclid's *The Elements of Geometry* (London: John Day, 1570), A1^r.
34. The poems were annexed to his *A Discourse of the Queenes Majesties Entertainment in Suffolk and Norfolk* (London: Henry Binneman, 1578), H2^r–L4^v.
35. Churchyard, *Discourse of the Queenes Majesties Entertainment*, I1^v I2^r.
36. Churchyard, *Discourse of the Queenes Majesties Entertainment*, K3^r.
37. Howard Mumford Jones, "The Colonial Impulse: An Analysis of the 'Promotion' Literature of Colonization Author(s)," *Proceedings of the American Philosophical Society* 90.2 (1946): 131–161.
38. Thomas Churchyard, *A Prayse and Reporte of Maister Martyne Forboishers Voyage to Meta Incognita* (London: Andrew Maunsell, 1578), no pag.
39. Thomas Ellis, *A True Report of the Third and Last Voyage into Meta Incognita* (London: Thomas Dawson, 1578), C1^r.
40. Ellis, *A True Report*, A3^r.
41. See also Fitzmaurice, *Humanism and America*, 10–16.
42. George Best, *Discoverie A True Discourse of the Late Voyages of Discoverie for the Finding of a Passage to Cathaya* (London: Henry Bynnyman, 1578), Bi^v.
43. Churchyard, *Prayse and Reporte*, no pag.
44. Best, *A True Discourse*, N4^r; Dionyse Settle, *A True Reporte of the Laste Voyage into the West and Northwest Regions* (London: Henry Middleton, 1577), A4^v.

45. Jacques Cartier, *A Shorte and Briefe Narration of the Two Navigations and Discoveries to the Northweast Partes Called New France* (London: H. Bynneman, 1580), B1ʳ.
46. Richard Hakluyt, *Divers Voyages Touching the Discoverie of America* (London: Thomas Woodcock, 1582), 2ᵛ.
47. Elizabeth Heale, "The *De navigatione* of Stephen Parmenius of Buda: Old World Barbarism and the Spanish 'Black Legend,'" in *Writing the Other: Tudor Humanism / Barbarism*, eds. Michael Pincombe and Zsolt Almási (Newcastle: Cambridge Scholars Publishing, 2008), 136–158.
48. Nathan Probasco points out that Parmenius's work is part of an exceptional group of six promotional documents all produced by Humphrey Gilbert's circle to advertise his 1583 voyage. See Nathan Probasco, *Researching North America: Sir Humphrey Gilbert's 1583 Expedition and a Reexamination of Early Modern English Colonization in the North Atlantic World* (Ph.D. Thesis, Unpublished, University of Nebraska-Lincoln, 2013), 23–25, 89–90.
49. "I conceive great hope, that the time approaches and now is, that we of England may share and part stakes [if we will ourselves] both with the Spaniard and the Portingale, in part of America and other regions as yet undiscovered." Hakluyt, *Divers Voyages*, 1ʳ.
50. "If wee woulde beholde with the eye of pitie howe al our Prisons are pestered and filled with able men to serve their Countrie, which for small robberies are dayly hanged up in great numbers eveb twentie at a clappe out of one iayle (as was seene at the last assises at Rochester) wee woulde hasten and further every man to his power the deducting some Colonies of our superfluous people into those temperate and fertile partes of America." Hakluyt, *Divers Voyages*, 1ʳ.
51. Hakluyt, *Divers Voyages*, 2ᵛ.
52. Parmenius, *De navigatione*, 85, lines 61–64. ("… quam non Babylonia sceptra, / Non Macedum invictae vires, non Persica virtus / Attigit aut unquam Latiae feriere secures." Ibid. 84, lines 46–48).
53. Michael Householder, "Eden's Translations: Women and Temptation in Early America,"(*Huntington Library Quarterly* 70.1 (2007): 11–13.
54. Qtd. in Householder, "Eden's Translations," 24.
55. Michel de Montaigne, "Of Cannibals," translated by Charles Cotton, in *Essays*, edited by William Carew Hazlitt (London: Reeves and Turner, 1877), 254.
56. Parmenius, *De navigatione*, 85, lines 49–50. ("… tibi per tot secula soli Servata est region nullis regnata Monarchis." Ibid. 84, lines 37–38).
57. Parmenius, *De navigatione*, 83, lines 17–25. The Latin original contains the enumeration of benevolent gods and nature between lines 13–23. Ibid. 82, 84.

58. Parmenius, *De navigatione*, 88, lines 90–104. The English translation does not render precisely this formal poetic device of Parmenius.
59. Parmenius, *De navigatione*, 93, lines 185–188, 191–192, 194–202. The corresponding Latin original is at lines 140–156.
60. See also the argument of Elizabeth Heale who contrasts Parmenius's envisioned learned and talented population of America with other contemporary tracts planning to transport the poor and vagrant to the new colonies. Heale, "The *De navigatione*," 152–154.
61. On the entertainments at Kenilworth see Susan Fry, *Elizabeth I: Competition for Representation* (Oxford: Oxford University Press, 1993), 56–96; on the Woodstock entertainments see Erzsébet Stróbl, "Entertaining the Queen at Woodstock, 1575," in *The Oxford Handbook of Tudor Drama*, eds. Thomas Betteridge and Greg Walker (Oxford: Oxford University Press, 2012), 428–445.
62. Parmenius, *De navigatione*, 88, lines 93–95. The corresponding English lines are at 120–123.
63. Parmenius, *De navigatione*, 97, lines 266–279, 287–289. The corresponding Latin original is at lines 206–207, 220–223.
64. Parmenius, *De navigatione*, 85, lines 61–64. ("… quam non Babylonia sceptra, / Non Macedum invictae vires, non Persica virtus / Attigit aut unquam Latiae feriere secures." Ibid. 84, lines 46–48.)
65. Parmenius, *De navigatione*, 99, lines 318–319. ("Et numquid lacrymas, inquit, soror Anglia, nostras Respicis, et dura nobiscum in *sorte gemiscis*." *Ibid, 98, lines 246–247*).
66. Parmenius, *De navigatione*, 99, lines 320–325, 33–333. In the Latin original the lines are at 248–251 and 254–256.
67. Parmenius, *De navigatione*, 105, lines 416–423. In the Latin original the lines are at 325–330.
68. George Peckham, *A True Report of the Late Discoveries and Possessions Taken In the Right of the Crowne of England* (London: John Charlewood, 1583), B3^v.
69. Peckham, *A True Report*, B3^v–B4^r.

Bibliography

Primary Sources

Cartier, Jacques. *A Shorte and Briefe Narration of the Two Navigations and Discoveries to the Northweast Partes Called New France*. London: H. Bynneman, 1580.

Church of England. *A Fourme to be used in Commom Prayer*. London: Richard Jugge and John Cawood, 1566.

Churchyard, Thomas. *A Discourse of the Queenes Majesties Entertainment in Suffolk and Norfolk.* London: Henry Binneman, 1578.
Churchyard, Thomas. *A Prayse and Reporte of Maister Martyne Forboishers Voyage to Meta Incognita.* London: Andrew Maunsell, 1578.
Dee, John. *General and Rare Memorials Pertayning to the Perfect Arte of Navigation.* London: John Day, 1577.
Ellis, Thomas. *A True Report of the Third and Last Voyage into Meta Incognita.* London: Thomas Dawson, 1578.
Gilbert, Humphrey. *A Discourse of a Discoverie for a New Passage to Cataia.* London: Henry Middleton, 1576.
Hakluyt, Richard. *Divers Voyages Touching the Discoverie of America.* London: Thomas Woodcock, 1582.
Hakluyt, Richard. *Principall Navigations, Voiages and Discoveries of the English Nation.* London: Christopher Baker, 1589.
Parmenius, Stephanus. *De navigatione illustris et magnanimi equitis aurati Humfredi Gilberti, adducendam in novum orbem coloniam susceptá, carmen epibatikos Stephani Parmenii Budeii.* London: Thomas Purfoot, 1582.
Peckham, George. *A True Report of the Late Discoveries and Possessions Taken In the Right of the Crowne of England.* London: John Charlewood, 1583.

Secondary Sources

Ács, Tivadar. "Egy tengerbe veszett magyar humanista költő a XVI. Században" ("A Sixteenth Century Hungarian Humanist Poet Who Drowned at Sea"). In *Filológiai Közlöny* 8. (1962): 115–122.
Almási, Gábor. *The Uses of Humanism: Johannes Sambucus (1531–1584), Andreas Dudith (1533–1589), and the Republic of Letters in East Central Europe.* Leiden: Brill, 2009.
Cartledge, Bryan. *The Will to Survive: A History of Hungary.* London: Hurst & Company, 2011.
Balázs, Mihály."About a copy of De falsa et vera unius Dei... cognitione: Additional data to the history of the English connections of the Antitrinitarians of Transylvania." In *Odrodzenie i Reformacja w Polsce XLVII.* (2003): 53–64.
Faragó, Tamás. *Bevezetés a történeti demográfiába (Introduction to Historical Demography).* Budapest: Corvinus Egyetem, 2011.
Fitzmaurice, Andrew. *Humanism and America: An Intellectual History of English Colonisation, 1500–1625.* Cambridge: Cambridge University Press, 2007.
Fry, Susan. *Elizabeth I: Competition for Representation.* Oxford: Oxford University Press, 1993.
Heale, Elizabeth. "The *De navigatione* of Stephen Parmenius of Buda: Old World Barbarism and the Spanish 'Black Legend.'" In *Writing the Other:*

Tudor Humanism/Barbarism. Edited by Michael Pincombe and Zsolt Almási, 136–158. Newcastle: Cambridge Scholars Publishing, 2008.

Jambrek, Stanko. "Stephen Kis of Szeged: A Baranyan Reformer with a European Influence." In *KAIROS—Evangelical Journal of Theology* 4.1. (2012): 77–98.

Kathona, Géza. *Fejezetek a török hódoltsági reformáció történetéből (Chapters from the History of the Reformation under Turkish Occupation)*. Budapest: Akadémia, 1974.

Klaniczay, Tibor. "Jegyzetek Budai Parmenius Istvánról" ("Notes on Stephen Parmenius of Buda"). In *Hagyományok ébresztése*. Budapest: Szépirodalmi Könyvkiadó, 1976.

Mancall, Peter C. *Hakluyt's Promise: An Elizabethan's Obsession for an English America*. New Haven and London: Yale University Press, 2007.

Péter, Katalin. *Magyarország története: 1526–1686*. Budapest, Akadémia, 1987.

Pettegree, Andrew, Duke, Alastair and Lewis, Gillian. *Calvinism in Europe, 1540–1620*. Cambridge: Cambrige Universtity Press, 1996.

Probasco, Nate. *Researching North America: Sir Humphrey Gilbert's 1583 Expedition and a Reexamination of Early Modern English Colonization in the North Atlantic World*. Ph.D. Thesis, Unpublished. University of Nebraska-Lincoln, 2013.

Quinn, David B. and Cheshire, Neil M. *The New Found Land of Stephen Parmenius*. Toronto and Buffalo: University of Toronto Press, 1972.

Stróbl, Erzsébet. "Entertaining the Queen at Woodstock, 1575." In *The Oxford Handbook of Tudor Drama*. Edited by Thomas Betteridge and Greg Walker, 426–445. Oxford: Oxford University Press, 2012.

Szabó, András. "Coetus-Natio-Respublica-Politica-Societas-Congregatio-Collegium-Gens: A wittenbergi magyar diákegyesület au újabb kutatások fényében, 1555–1613" ("The Wittenberg Coetus of Hungarian Students in the light of New Research, 1555-1613"). In *Irodalomtörténeti Közlemények* 115.2. (2011): 229–234.

Szögi, László. *Budai, pesti, és óbudai diákok külföldi egyetemjárása I. 1526–1867 (The Peregrination of Students from Buda, Pest and Óbuda I: 1526–1867)*. Budapest: Budapest Főváros Levéltára, 2004.

Yates, Frances A. *Astrea: The Imperial Theme in the Sixteenth Century*. London: Routledge & Kegan Paul, 1975.

CHAPTER 10

Captains, Kings, Queens: Politics, Piracy, and the Sea in Middleton's The Phoenix (c.1603–04)

Claire Jowitt

UNDERSTANDING EARLY MODERN SEA CAPTAINS

This chapter focuses on the ideological uses of the figure of the sea captain in Thomas Middleton's play *The Phoenix* (1603–04). It examines whether this drama used its piratical sea captain as a vehicle to express or question particular actual or imagined English national characteristics and, if it did, then in what ways? The Captain (he has no other name) in *The Phoenix* is a particularly striking and culturally telling figure, though he is little-known to audiences today because the play is rarely performed, and scholars, when they discuss the text at all, tend to focus on the "disguised ruler" plotline. The chapter explores the ways that the Captain in Middleton's play is isolated from, and at odds with, the values and relationships the play sets up as orthodox, and how the consequences of this isolation are played out. Though *The Phoenix* is not read as solely about regime change, the chapter explores whether the alteration from a female to a male monarch in England in 1603 impacts on the play's gender politics.

C. Jowitt (✉)
University of East Anglia, Norwich, UK

© The Author(s) 2017
E. Paranque et al. (eds.), *Colonization, Piracy, and Trade in Early Modern Europe*, Queenship and Power, DOI 10.1007/978-3-319-57159-1_10

In *Crowds and Power* (1960), Elias Canetti wrote powerfully about the symbolic character of the English nation: "Everyone knows what the *sea* means to an Englishman; what is not sufficiently known is the precise form of the connection between his relationship to the sea and his famous individualism. The Englishman sees himself as a captain on board a ship with a small group of people, the sea around and beneath him. He is almost alone; as captain he is in many ways isolated from his crew."[1] For Englishmen, according to Canetti, the fantasy figure of the sea captain was a "remarkably stable" national self-identity. He describes how this isolated male figure personified his ship, sought to impose his "absolute" and "undisputed" "power of command" on a sea that is "there to be ruled," and provided a powerful collective vision of how to behave and interact with others that endured for generations. It is easy to see, of course, how this model is reflected in triumphalist accounts of English colonial and imperial history with, for instance, the nineteenth-century historian John A. Froude describing Richard Hakluyt's collection of "English" exploration, trade, and travel, *The Principal Navigations* (1589; 2nd rev. edn 1598–1600) as "the prose epic of the modern English nation."[2] Froude is right to suggest that Hakluyt made great claims for England's nautical history and for the central role of the nation's sea captains such as Sir Francis Drake, Sir Walter Raleigh, and Sir Thomas Cavendish, amongst others, in supporting Elizabethan expansionist policies abroad, defending the nation in times of war, and providing a model of patriotic manhood.[3] Accounts of English male fortitude and individual heroism are noticeably prominent in *The Principal Navigations*, for instance, and even when the sea refused to be "ruled" by a particular sea captain's "power of command" and he died in service at sea, his tragedy is often turned to achievement in Hakluyt's retelling of the explorer's story. Hakluyt's account of Humphrey Gilbert's death by drowning on September 9, 1583, when his ship, the *Squirrel*, was lost at sea on the return leg of his colonizing voyage to Newfoundland, is one of the most well-known examples of tragic failure gloriously re-purposed. Gilbert refused to abandon his pinnace and transfer to the relative safety of the larger *Golden Hind* when the fleet encountered a violent storm near the Azores and, according to the eyewitness report of Edward Hayes, captain of the *Golden Hind*, Gilbert was last seen on deck reading a book, probably Thomas More's *Utopia*. Hayes alleged that his final words were "We are as near to heaven, by sea as by land."[4] The remarkable circumstances of Gilbert's death led to this particular sea captain being much admired and, more importantly, being seen as an exemplar of the type of spirit and character required to build an English empire, even though the voyage failed to establish a colony in Newfoundland (which did not happen until 1610). The language of patriarchal political power and the idea of a sea captain's isolation overlap in Canetti's interpretation of the model and combined with religious conviction in Hakluyt's version of Hayes' account of Gilbert's death. The lone sea captain is shown managing his crew and the sea and, when this goes badly, as a Protestant Englishman, he expresses confidence concerning his place in the kingdom of heaven.

This chapter focuses on the figure of the sea captain in a different early modern literary form: popular public drama, specifically the genre of voyage drama.[5] Plays about new or foreign lands and unfamiliar or exotic people and objects were in vogue in the late sixteenth and early seventeenth centuries. Englishmen and women not only read their copies of Hakluyt, but also were themselves in motion across lands and seas to distances and on scales scarcely imagined a hundred years before and able to buy an exciting range of new imported goods and commodities. Drama became the most easily accessible source of information about this newly envisage-able wider world for a nation of armchair travelers, with scores of plays—extant and "lost"—engaging with the theme and practice of journeying.[6] In particular, this chapter explores the ideological uses of what I suggest was emerging as a particularly important character in early modern drama, the sea captain, as he appears in Thomas Middleton's play *The Phoenix* in order to test how this genre treated this figure. I first explore whether early modern drama also used sea captains as vehicles to express or celebrate particular actual or imagined English national characteristics; the essay, then, goes onto consider the significance of the ways in which this negotiation occurred. The sea captain in *The Phoenix*, which most probably dates to 1603–04, is a particularly striking and culturally telling figure, I suggest, though he is largely unknown to audiences today because the play is performed rarely, and scholars, when they discuss the text at all, tend to focus on the "disguised ruler" plotline, and hence overlook his startling bravura. Most spectacularly, nearly three hundred years before the notorious wife-selling scene of Thomas Hardy's *The Mayor of Casterbridge* (1886) where Henchard sells Susan to a sailor, in *The Phoenix*, it is the sailor that marts his wife as a sexual object for money. This chapter explores the ways that the Captain in Middleton's play is isolated from, and at odds with, the values and relationships the play sets up as orthodox, and how the consequences of this isolation play out. Indeed, the Captain's isolation, I shall argue, contains complex cultural and political markers. In Hakluyt's account of Gilbert in *The Principal Navigations*, the sea captain's isolation is described in positive terms as a type of individualism that acts as proxy for a heroic spirit, yet drama often treats these characteristics differently, I suggest. In drama, a captain's individualism is rendered more negatively as isolation and is seen as a marker of perilous and risky characteristics, signaling someone who is a social or sexual misfit. Though I do not wish to read *The Phoenix* as solely about regime change, a significant part of my argument is about how the play engages with the alteration from a female to a male monarch in England in 1603. I suggest it is reflected in both the Captain's complex and conflicted psychosexual drama and in the play's debate about his status as pirate or privateer. In other words, I argue that *The Phoenix* engages with a major policy shift between Tudor and Stuart regimes, concerning state-sponsored violence at sea, and in so doing, Middleton's play is a culturally important marker of conflicted, and gendered, responses to the Jacobean clampdown on privateering.

I first want to explore Middleton's Captain's place in the history of the development of the stage figure of a sea captain in early modern drama. According to Christopher W. Brooks, Middleton's Captain is "the first pirate (or privateering) captain of any importance" to appear on the English stage. He continues "the ambiguity of the Captain's status may well be a reflection of the ambiguity of the privateering captain's status in 1603 [...] still retain[ing] in the popular mind some of the reflected glory of Elizabethan times, of the Drakes and Hawkinses and Raleighs, but was officially no longer approved of."[7] These claims indicate that Middleton's Captain is a significant individual example within the development of this character type and suggest that the status of his activities as piratical, hence illicit, or as privateering, therefore licit, is important. However, it also needs to be acknowledged that Brooks' first statement about the Captain in *The Phoenix* fails to take account of a range of sixteenth-century plays that include in their *dramatis personae* important pirate and/or privateering captains. These characters include, for instance, the heroine "Captain" Bess Bridges in Thomas Heywood's *The Fair Maid of the West Part 1* (c.1596–1603), the title character of the anonymous play *The Life and Death of the Famous*

Captaine Thomas Stukeley (first performed c.1596/97, entered in the Stationers' Register August 11, 1600, and published 1605),[8] and sea captain and "pirate" Antonio in William Shakespeare's *Twelfth Night* (c.1600–01). It is important to assess the individualism or isolationism of these earlier versions of this stage figure. Indeed, these characters, amongst others, suggest that the figure of the pirate/privateering captain was utilized to significant effect by dramatists before Middleton used it.[9] All these "Captains" are, in some ways, isolated figures. Bess is isolated by her gender and the resemblance the play invokes between her and the singular figure of Elizabeth I.[10] Stukeley is isolated from his friends, family, wife, and countrymen by his restless search for honor which means he relentlessly moves from one situation and geographic location to another ("I must have honor, honor is the thing/Stukeley doth thirst for" he says early in the play as he abandons his wife).[11] Finally Antonio, beached in what is to him an unfriendly Illyria, is isolated by his homoerotic desire for the castaway Sebastian, standing alone on stage at the end of the play whilst all other characters find mates (except the other "misfits," the fool Feste, the foolish Sir Andrew Aguecheek, and the "mad" Malvolio).[12] The characters of Bess and Stukeley, in particular, intersect with late Elizabethan amphibious and expansionist policies, though Antonio too has done notable service at sea for his country: "I have many enemies in Orsino's court" he says, as a result of his bravery in a sea fight, alternately seen by Orsino as worthy of "fame and honor" and as marking him out as a "[n]otable pirate" and "salt-water thief."[13] Bess, in her ship *the Negro*, fights better than the seamen who surround her. She is also more successful in gaining plunder, and she seems, as Canetti suggests, to show "the power of command" as she describes enemy shipping acknowledging her authority: "It did me good/To see the Spanish carvel vail her top/ Unto my maiden flag" she says.[14] Both a land and sea captain (that is, a soldier and sailor), Stukeley is shown as courageous and resourceful, yet becomes increasingly alienated and unruly, and his treason and abdication of English national identity represent a lost opportunity to harness his skills in the national interest at a time of increasing European political tensions.[15] The depiction of these three captains shows isolation to be an ambiguous, troubling force, and as something that connects to whether their activities are described as full-blown piracy or as licit amphibious aggression (i.e., privateering), which would, therefore, make a sea captain both redeemable and capable of being re-incorporated into

English society. In Captain Bess Bridges' case, this is clearly how her behavior is supposed to be interpreted, since the play explicitly ends her isolation through marriage with Spenser (though, it should be noted, her personal activity and vigor are much diminished as a result). In Captain Antonio's case, his place in the main action appears marginalized at the end of *Twelfth Night*, yet he remains partially connected to the heteronormative dominant group through the mutually held bonds of affection between him and Sebastian (and indeed by the relationship between "Cesario" and Orsino as they hold hands on stage at the end of the play).[16] Even Captain Stukeley's traitorous and mercenary "real-life" story[17] is somewhat moderated in the dramatic version: he appears brave and charismatic in a braggartly way, though increasingly flawed and excessive in his political and religious affiliations.

Brooks' second statement is useful for clarifying the terms of my argument: "the ambiguity of the privateering captain's status in 1603" indicates that Middleton's character of the Captain can be seen as an indicator of a major cultural shift, appearing on stage at a moment of political sea change as a result of the death of Elizabeth I on March 24. Simply put, if Middleton was writing in response to the policy shift of James's crackdown on privateering, by addressing how and why he constructs the stage figure of the sea captain, it becomes possible to rethink the trajectory of drama about exploration and voyaging across the two regimes. Brooks' analysis presupposes that the dating of *The Phoenix* to 1603 is straightforward, but this is not the case. It is important, therefore, for my argument concerning the larger cultural and political dimensions of Middleton's Captain to summarize the surviving evidence concerning when the play was composed and/or first performed. Its date crucially affects the range and direction of both its allegorical and topical meanings, and to an assessment of its claims to be seen as important because metonymic of a wider shift that is detectable across the cultural forms of the period.

Much of the criticism on *The Phoenix* focuses on its use of the "disguised ruler" plotline, and the play is commonly dated to the beginning of James I's reign due to what Leonard Tennenhouse has called its depiction of "a textbook figure of sagacious majesty."[18] Indeed, as its most recent editors Lawrence Danson and Ivo Kamps confidently state, "in various senses [it is] a Jacobean play: it was written in the first year of James's reign; it was performed at court in James's presence; and [...] it is imbued with the anxiety and optimism of that time of political transition." Martin Wiggins also dates it to 1603–04, with his "best guess" being February 1604.[19] Firm evidence in support of this dating is quite slight: though *The Phoenix* is believed to have been performed on February 20, 1604, most probably in front of James I, this has never been conclusively proved.[20] "A Booke called The Phenix" was entered in the Stationers' Register on May 9, 1607, and the play was printed in quarto that year, making this the *terminus ad quem* for the play. I use 1607 as marking the outer limit for the play's political–allegorical meanings. The title page's statement that the play "hath beene sundry times Acted by the *Children of Paules, And presented before his Maiestie*," and a Chamber Accounts entry describing an unknown Paul's play being performed before the king on February 20, 1604 has led Edmund K. Chambers to describe this date as the "only available" one for the court performance.[21] In other words, though current scholarship cannot be entirely certain from the performance and publication history whether Middleton wrote the play in the last years or months of Elizabeth I's reign or early in James I's reign, the balance of the evidence strongly suggests that the play is Jacobean. There is also no reason to doubt the claim on the title page of the 1607 edition that the play was performed before the king, and it is, therefore, unsurprising to find that a young and ambitious playwright uses his work to contain a fairly explicit and heavy-handed allegory in praise of either a new or newish ruler.[22] Finding a definitive answer to the question of the play's date is not the intended goal of my analysis, except as it affects the ways the Captain's depiction is shaped by alterations in foreign and domestic policies between regimes and by the new monarch's gender. Brooks' comment about changes in the treatment of privateering between administrations signals that this is a key issue for determining the play's date since, for sea captains, the end of the war with Spain meant large-scale unemployment or underemployment.[23] Its emphasis on supporting the processes of political transition is most strikingly revealed in the central plotline of Phoenix, son and heir of the aged and fading King of Ferrara, who at the request of his father and his father's chief advisor Count Proditor (the name being Italian for "traitor") agrees to undertake educative travel abroad with Fidelio, his friend (and, on one level, a version of Middleton himself). If Middleton wrote the play in 1603, then Elizabeth I, like the King of Ferrara, had also been on the throne for 45 years. Despite his father's instruction to go abroad, Phoenix decides instead to travel in disguise in his homeland (much like the Duke in Shakespeare's

Measure for Measure (c.1601–06), the play with which *The Phoenix* is most frequently compared), "look[ing] into the heart and bowels of the dukedom [for] abuses ready for reformation or punishment."[24]

Sex, Captains, and the Politics of Isolation

Middleton's character of the Captain—he has no other name and is only known by his profession—appears only in the first half of the play, but his importance is plainly signaled by the number of lines he is given—231—with only three characters in the play (Phoenix, and the two lawyers, Falso and Tangle) having more to say. The Captain has recently married Fidelio's mother Castiza, Italian for "pure" or "chaste," but quickly regrets the marriage, now seeking to be rid of her in any way he can, intending to return to the sea and his life there. "What lustful passion came aboard of me that I should marry–was I drunk?" he questions bitterly when alone.[25] That his plans for getting rid of her involve pandering, human trafficking, and even murder, indicates how thoroughly disreputable a character Middleton intended his version of a captain to be. Mark Eccles, Peter G. Phialas, and John Brooks have argued that one way to understand the Captain plotline is as a satire on Middleton's hated stepfather, Thomas Harvey, a self-styled "captain" whose attempts to gain the estate of Anne Middleton, and abuse of her, led to a number of bitter lawsuits.[26] In court records from 1600, for instance, Harvey testified that mother and son had spread a rumor that Harvey was "deade beyonde the seas" to serve their own financial ends.[27] Though Middleton's mother was dead by 1603, Harvey was still alive—the last year he was recorded to have paid his dues to the Grocers' Company was 1605–06—so the play may have been Middleton's way of paying back his stepfather for his mother's mistreatment (which—like the Captain's fantasy—allegedly included an attempt to poison her).[28] However, the richness of the Captain's depiction in *The Phoenix* goes beyond providing a lens on to Middleton's troubled family history.

From his first entrance, the status of the Captain's occupation as licit or illicit is of paramount concern. He is shown being tempted by three "soldiering fellows" to seek "noble purchase," that is rich booty in what is clearly a piratical venture in pursuit of "Three ships, not a poop less," and in his first soliloquy, he explicitly describes himself as a "salt-thief," or a pirate.[29] His presence on land, as well as that of the soldiering fellows—that is specifically the soldiers from on board a ship rather than sailors, useful in times of war or for voyages likely to involve hand-to-hand combat—in search of occupation, has a particular significance in dating the play from just after the end of the war. Wide-scale piracy was a particular issue amongst demobbed and underemployed sailors returning to England. Captain John Smith's *The True Travels, Adventures and Observations of Captain John Smith* (1630), written late in life, is an apologist's account of how "piracy" proliferated at the start of James's reign:

> After the death of our most gracious Queene *Elizabeth*, of blessed memory, our Royall King *Iames*, who from his infancy had reigned in peace with all Nations; had no imployment for those men of warre, so that those that were rich rested with that they had; those that were poore and had nothing but from hand to mouth, turned Pirats; some, because they became sleighted of those for whom they had got much wealth; some, for that they could not get their due; some, that had lived bravely, would not abase themselves to poverty; some vainly, only to get a name; others for revenge, covetousnesse, or as ill; and as they found themselves more and more oppressed, their passions increasing with discontent, made them turne Pirats.[30]

Smith has, it is apparent, more than a degree of sympathy with these unemployed "men of warre"—the double meaning of the term as a ship is apt—who with "no imployment" "turne pirats," but other commentators and the state were more hostile in their condemnation. In one of the king's first proclamations on June 23, 1603, for instance, the new policy against piracy was made apparent: "men of warre" "having no sufficient commission as aforesaid" who "shal take any the ships or goods of any Prince in league, or amitie with us, shall be reputed and taken as Pirates" and "shall suffer death as Pirates."[31] The entire scene between the demobbed soldiering fellows and the carousing bored land-ridden sea captain, who married by mistake when almost drunk, after having "sworn all heaven over and over" "ne'er have married," is only meaningful if the play was written after the end of the wars in Ireland and with Spain. Under Elizabeth, with the nation at war since 1585, the state had attempted to draw a somewhat rough and ready distinction between the nation's commissioned and outlaw pirates, however difficult in practice those differences were to maintain.[32] James made no distinction between seaborne attacks on Spain or on other nations: all piracy was a capital crime. Middleton's disreputable, piratical Captain seems, on one level, a textbook case in support of this more draconian attitude and the dynamics of this scene, together with the publication and likely performance history, provide further supporting evidence that the play dates to 1603–04.

The Captain repeatedly uses particularly intense and graphic sexual images and metaphors to express himself, his current situation, and his aspirations. Sex and the sea are linked closely in his language. As his first line in soliloquy reveals ("what lustful passion …"), the Captain explains his marriage as the result of a momentary sexual attraction for Castiza. Her plaintive complaint to him that "For love to you did I neglect my state,/Chide better fortunes from me,/Gave the world talk, laid all my friends at waste," confirms the sexually motivated nature of their marriage on both sides and, indeed, undermines her identification as "chaste" implied by her name.[33] It seems that is actually Castiza's active and appetitive sexuality that is the real focus of anxiety as the Captain fears being made impotent by his new wife. In despair, and full of self-loathing and disgust, the Captain worries he is unable to either satisfy her sexually when on land ("Why didst thou marry me?/You think, as most of your insatiate widows,/That captains can do wonders, when,'las,/the name does often prove the better man"), or control her sexually—or escape the effects of her imagined over-active sexuality on his own person—when away at sea ("what a horrible thing'twould be to have horns/brought me at sea").[34] His solution to his dilemma is to be rid of her anyway he can. Indeed, as we shall see, Phoenix's later scathing, disgusted, and sexualized remark about Castiza's behavior that "she was a beast/to marry him" noticeably echoes the Captain's view of her. The Captain's antifeminism extends to even the play's most heroic figure, and thus serves to connect the two men in a shared value system that implies fear of, and disgust with, women.[35] The Captain, having quickly agreed to the soldiering fellows' invitation that he return to his life at sea, and to piracy, where women are described as transitory sexual objects who do not constrain him or make him feel inadequate, determines to divorce Castiza and sell her to the lustful Count Proditor, his "Lord," for "five hundred crowns."[36] In structural terms, then, the Captain is a particularly crucial figure, since it is his relationships with Proditor, his long-standing financial backer, and Fidelio, his new stepson, that provide a key connection between the play's main and subplots. Proditor, as the Captain's "chapman" or merchant, is the outlet for the pirate/privateer's booty; as a courtier, he provides the protection and influence in high places that the Captain requires. In keeping with the established transactional terms of their relationship, it is to Proditor that the Captain seeks to sell his unwanted wife.

Proditor, the corrupt and predatory, and significantly treasonous, nobleman is clearly supposed to invoke the controversial and charismatic courtier, poet, adventurer, and "pirate" Sir Walter Raleigh, "last of the Elizabethans," as Hugh R. Trevor-Roper memorably commented in a 1957 essay.[37] Crimes of piracy were so notorious and high profile in the early seventeenth century, with James I well known for holding strongly hostile views about the crime and those that committed it.[38] My larger argument, then, is that the figure of the pirate Captain, and his relationship with his "chapman" Proditor, offers a particularly charged means to evaluate and assess political meaning in these years. It is important likewise to emphasize Raleigh's importance as a cultural and political figure in the early seventeenth century.[39] Anna R. Beer sums up Raleigh's significance when she writes that he "should not have mattered in the seventeenth century" due to his political marginalization through imprisonment and popular vilification, yet he was in fact the principal man the Stuart state was unable "to silence."[40] The scope of this article is considerably more limited than Beer's whole-century assessment, as it focuses on the way the figure of Raleigh/Proditor acts as a prominent and recognizable means to punish the man who challenged the authority of, specifically, the early Stuart state. On James's accession, Raleigh wrote *A Discourse touching a War with Spain*, which aggressively recommended the continuation of the war. Neither the tone nor the content of this "martial" paper found favor with the new king, leading to Raleigh's imprisonment and trial on the November 17, 1603 for his alleged involvement with Lord Cobham in plots to secure the succession for James's cousin and Englishwoman Lady Arbella Stuart. It was claimed at Raleigh's trial that for his part in the plot he would receive 8000 crowns and a pension from Spain. Cobham was interrogated and signed a sworn confession (later recanted), which served as the chief evidence of Raleigh's treason.[41] He received the following sentence upon his first conviction for treason in 1603: "yow shalbe drawne upon a hurdle through the streetes to the place of execution and ther to be hanged and cut down above, and your body shalbe opened and your privye members cut off, and your hart and bowells pulled out and throwne into the fire before your eyes, then your head to be strecken of from your body, your body shalbe divided into fower quarters, to be disposed at the kinges pleasure."[42] Though condemned to the full punishment of a traitor's castration, heart removal, disemboweling, and quartering, the sentence was commuted and Raleigh was imprisoned. If, as is highly likely, the play was written in 1603–04, and first performed on February 20, 1604, then the spectacular fall of Raleigh was a recent, and riveting, event. Thus, Proditor's exposure for treasonously conspiring the murder of the Duke at home and Phoenix abroad, his prostration "Behold, the serpent on his belly creeps" and punishment of "everlasting banishment" because his "life is too bad to end" each resonate with aspects of Raleigh's disgrace and imprisonment.[43] Proditor's behavior in the play also matches the descriptions of Raleigh presented by Attorney General Edward Coke in the case for the prosecution at the trial. Coke rehearsed at length Raleigh's past failings and dubious reputation, especially for false friendship and duplicity, caricaturing him as a "viper" and "monster" and "the rankest traitor in all England."[44] Raleigh's sentence was commuted in December 1603, and for some months, there was a widespread expectation that he might be exiled, similar to both Sir Griffin Markham—who was banished notwithstanding his central role in the Bye Plot—and to the outcast Proditor.[45]

Just as the Captain is associated with Proditor in *The Phoenix*, Middleton's stepfather knew Raleigh well. Harvey had been employed in the 1580s as chief factor at Raleigh's failed colony Roanoke and had returned to London penniless with Sir Francis Drake in 1586. It was the disaster at Roanoke which led to Harvey's pressing need to recapitalize through his marriage to the rich widow Anne Middleton.[46] In the play, the Captain is bested and exposed by Fidelio and Phoenix and then sent to sea, and Proditor's treason is uncovered and he is banished. The traitor Proditor can thus be seen to represent Raleigh to King James's jaundiced eye, with the roles of Proditor and the Captain reversed since Proditor is "the 'chapman' or purchaser of the Captain's wife, whereas in real life, Harvey was chief factor for Raleigh's colony. The play seems intending to celebrate, in a rather heavy-handed fashion, the new king's perspicacity at the expense of his discarded and disgraced courtier. In the Captain's failures and inadequacies, the play likewise expresses cynicism about the qualities of the nation's fighting men and implicitly praises the new king's pacific policies through the end of the long war with Spain.

However, in the course of the Captain's scenes it becomes apparent that sex and the sea link in both more specific senses and in politically intriguing ways, and that the Captain's relationship with Proditor is itself highly charged sexually. The Captain describes himself as a "salt-water thief" as we have seen, but "salt water" elsewhere in the play repeatedly connects to sex. For instance, the Captain fears that he will "have my wife dance at home, and my ship at sea, and both take in salt water together."[47] Danson and Camps gloss the line "In the wife's case, salt water alludes to her lover's semen."[48] Yet the First Soldier's remark about the Captain's out-of-character marriage to Castiza only ten lines earlier, "Of a man that has tasted salt water to commit such a fresh trick," which uses the same terminology, reveals the ambiguous and complex nature of the sexual identity of the Captain himself.[49] If salt water means semen (its homophone "seamen" further confirms the connection),[50] then the Captain's "taste" for it rather than fresh water (i.e., his wife), coupled with a metonymic identification between him and his ship, which also "takes in" salt water, is clearly intended to indicate that his sexuality at sea is orientated toward other men. Certainly, Patrick J. Cook emphasizes what he calls the "complications of gender identity" in his reading of *The Phoenix*, arguing for an oedipal and neurotic reading of the Captain: "[f]ailure to resolve an unsatisfactory oedipal relationship has left him ill-equipped to perform the phallic functions that accompany and symbolize the Law of the Father."[51] In particular, the Captain's complex relationship with his father, who was (the Captain reveals) "too ruttish to let me thrive under him" leads to "a profound ambiguity" in the character's sexuality ("it is unclear whether the Captain regrets his father's failure to bugger him while he beggared him, or the selfish failure to satisfy him sexually in their incestuous act").[52] Cook's reading of the play as "sodomitical competition" between a range of male characters including, most prominently, the lawyers, Tangle and Falso, is useful in highlighting how sexual orientation is a key to the play's power politics, but my focus is more specific. Primarily, I focus on the depiction of the sexuality of the characters associated with the sea, especially the relationship between the Captain and Proditor, and how this engages the play's larger political attitudes about leadership and good governance, and what, as we saw earlier, Canetti called the "power of command," when discussing the isolation of a captain at sea.

If the Captain's sexuality in the past was conditioned by his relationship with his father, in the present of the play's action his sexual focus is shown to be fixed on the homosocial/homoerotic world of the soldiering fellows at sea and on Lord Proditor. The close friendship between the two men thus links the courtier to the homosocial/homosexual world occupied by the Captain and his maritime circle. If, on one level, Proditor shadows the recently disgraced Raleigh, then the latter's well-known and celebrated connections with the ocean further establish the link. Edmund Spenser had called Raleigh "The Shepherd of the Ocean" in 1591, and Raleigh also took to calling himself "the Ocean" in reference to his, now lost, poem "The Ocean's Love to Cynthia," or, "The Ocean, to Cynthia," a long elegy written to celebrate Elizabeth as Cynthia—which is thought to have contained nearly 15,000 lines of verse (Figs. 10.1, 10.2).

Watery sentiments of devotion were also expressed in portraiture. A 1588 portrait of Raleigh, for instance, contains an allegorical expression of loyalty in maritime imagery in the left-hand corner. Comprising just a few wavy lines of dark blue underneath the crescent moon, they symbolize Raleigh's constancy to Elizabeth, who is represented by the moon. Just as the moon controls the tides, the queen controls Raleigh who is naturally content to be swayed by her irresistible influence. The association between Elizabeth and the moon was widespread at the time and Raleigh, of course, was a famous sailor whose first name "Walter" is only one letter away from "water."[53]

When Proditor enters to tell his friend the Captain the "news" of Phoenix's apparent departure abroad with Fidelio, the dialogue describes a kiss between the courtier and *either* Castiza *or* the Captain.[54] Modern editors add the stage direction "kisses Castiza" to heterosexualize the interaction and indicate its recipient when Proditor says, "I'll come to you/in order, captain." But neither the timing of the kiss nor the moment when Castiza should leave the stage is specified in the dialogue—as a result, it is not certain that she is even still present at this point.[55] Consequently, the kiss's intended recipient is not clear-cut in the 1607 printed edition of the play. Without the inserted stage directions, the interchange reads quite differently, as the intimacy is far more centrally focused on the relationship between Proditor and the Captain:

Cap: what, my worthy lord;
Proditor: Ile come to you in order Captaine
Cap: Oh that's in order: a kisse is the gammoth to pricksong.
Prod: Let me salute you Captaine.
Captain: My deere esteemed Count, I have a life for you.[56]

Fig. 10.1 *Sir Walter Raleigh*, by unknown English artist, oil on panel, 1588 © National Portrait Gallery, London

Fig. 10.2 Detail, *Sir Walter Raleigh*, by unknown English artist, oil on panel, 1588 © National Portrait Gallery, London

If Castiza has already exited (it is only made explicit in the printed text thirty lines later that she is no longer present on stage when Proditor says "the Lady's removed," and she may have left at any point before then),[57] then the "order" of salute that Proditor speaks of might refer to a plan for an encounter with Castiza later. Alternatively, it may simply be that, even with Castiza still present on stage, the first kiss from Proditor is aimed at her husband. Certainly, the Captain's "I have a life for you" and, later, the extremity of his hurt and humiliated response to Proditor's rejection of him after he sells Castiza "I love the pearl thou sold'st, hate thee the seller./Go, to sea, the end of thee–is lousy," indicates a significant depth of feeling on the Captain's part.[58] He appears discomfited and upset by the double-entendre insult, and by Proditor's betrayal. His reaction prompts further ribald phallocentric remarks, including the unsympathetic remark from his antagonist Fidelio "What, drooping?"[59]

Proditor's connections with the Captain serve to connect him to an anti-establishment seaborne world where sexual identity and sexual orientation, and definitions of, and distinctions between, types of maritime violence, appear both fluid and unstable. *The Phoenix* explicitly condemns these anti-establishment patterns of behavior as the Captain and Proditor are exposed and punished in line with James I's hostility to, as Smith put it, "men of warre" such as Raleigh who argued for vigorous prosecution of the war with Spain and who, according to a confession taken in 1603 as part of the state's investigation of the Bye plot, sought to take control of the navy (the alleged plan was "for the betraying a parte of the Navie into Sir Walter Raleigh his hands").[60] Yet, it is important to question whether the play's imagined seaborne world of sexual deviance and piracy is a discrete and separate sphere? In other words, can anti-establishment maritime patterns of behavior, which King James notoriously despised, and which are unmasked and condemned in *The Phoenix*, be distinguished from supposedly orthodox, land-based patterns of behavior that the play would need to present to finish the allegory in praise of the new king? Are Fidelio and Phoenix, the play's land-locked protagonists different from its seaborne antagonists Proditor and the Captain, or are there troubling similarities between the pairs of men?

In fact, the two pairs of men parallel, echo, and mirror each other in important ways in the action. It is Proditor, of course, who orchestrates Phoenix's (apparent) departure to travel abroad at the beginning of the play, just as he appears to underwrite the Captain's voyages of privateering and piracy. Phoenix's decision to "stay at home, and travel," and to trick the Captain through impersonating a gullible country gentleman and "easy-affecting venturer" who wishes to invest in the seaman's next voyage, brings the parallels between the two men into even greater focus.[61] By appearing as "a farmer's son," Phoenix's rustic play-acting restages the Captain's revealing earlier account of the discontents of his own boyhood where the envied fantasy figure of a "rammish plowman's" son spending his father's money on indulging in tobacco, sex, and fine clothes was used to contrast to his own dissatisfactions under his "ruttish" father.[62] In other words, the Captain's jealousy of this alternative boyhood, *and* the boy who had enjoyed it, adds a frisson to his desire to accept Phoenix-in-disguises' financial investment in his next voyage since the latter appears to be that desired other boy. The supposedly worlds-apart antagonist and protagonist mirror and echo each other. Though explicitly and repeatedly Phoenix makes clear his disparagement and detestation of "such an ugly land- and sea-monster" as this "counterfeit captain," his impersonation of the son of the father the Captain wished he had been and had had, as well as Phoenix's promised investment, like Proditor, in the Captain's voyages, clearly problematizes any discrete separation between the characters.[63] Indeed, when Phoenix discusses the terms of his investment, it is apparent that he understands the level of risk, and type of voyage, the Captain is likely to undertake and this is the attraction. "I have a certain generous itch, sir, to lose a few angels in the way of profit:'tis but a game at tennis, Where, if the ship keep above line,'tis three to one; If not, there's but three hundred angels gone," he says.[64] Danson and Kamps gloss these lines as "a complicated image which refers, first, to the line on an Elizabethan tennis court wall (the ball had to hit above the line to remain in play), and second, to shipping (where the 'line' refers to the proper line of flotation, the 'water line,' when the ship is fully laden)."[65] But there is a third meaning here, piracy, since if a ship ventured "beyond the line" it referred to it crossing the meridian into Iberian waters, established as such by the Treaty of Tordesillas in 1494 which carved the newly discovered New World and still-to-be-discovered lands into spheres of influence for Spain and Portugal, and which all other European colonial nations disputed (see Fig. 10.3). In other words, in disguise, Phoenix demonstrates the desire to invest in a voyage "beyond the line" where the financial return is imagined to be more than the three to one of the legitimate mercantile venture, though of course a piratical voyage is a correspondingly riskier investment more likely to founder. Though Elizabethan privateers did, of course, suffer a few "resounding failures," these voyages were frequently very profitable indeed with "a good voyage, but not an exceptional one" making a "clear profit of £1000 on a fixed capital of £200."[66] The Captain's reply "here's a voyage toward will make us all" indicates his understanding of the type of investment Phoenix seeks, and that he can accommodate it.

What, then, are the implications of the resemblances between the two pairs of characters in Middleton's *The Phoenix*? It is easy to read this play as opportunistic prentice work to catch a popular mood. An aspirant dramatist denigrates, marginalizes, and then exposes an apparently "chaste" woman as a fraud at a point in history where, as Bishop Godfrey Goodman put it when reflecting on the end of Elizabeth's reign from the time of Charles I, the kingdom was "generally weary

Fig. 10.3 Cantino World Map, 1502. Western half of the Cantino map of the world, 1502, showing (at left) the Tordesillas Treaty demarcation line of 1494, which divided the non-Christian "new" lands between Spain and Portugal, 370 leagues west of Cape Verde Islands. Granger Historical Picture Archive/Alamy Stock Photo

of an old woman's government."[67] The Lincolnshire rector Henry Hooke expressed notably similar antifeminist sentiments c. 1601 in "Of the succession of the Crowne of England." He wrote, "that what corruptions in justice, what blemishes in religion, the infirmitie, the inconveniency of woemenhead, would not permit to discover and discerne, the vigor, and conveniency of man sytting as king in the throne of aucthoritie; maye diligently search out, and speedilye refrorme."[68] It is

Hooke, too, who preached a sermon before King James in Whitehall in 1604 that spoke of the new king as a "rare Phoenix" where the queen's "aged infirmities [were] repaired in the perfection of his [the king's] strength."[69] Yet, the play is far less secure in Phoenix's perfection than Hooke. Distinctions between nautical antagonist and terrestrial protagonist break down as the venality and dissident sexuality of the pirate Captain are clearly also present in Phoenix. Both characters are isolated by their position as captain of their domain, and the mimicry between the two supposedly antithetical individuals and spheres suggests *The Phoenix* offers a surprisingly critical approach to a new regime and new king. It seems that in early modern drama, *contra* Hakluyt's account of Gilbert, the singularity associated with captaincy possessed negative political dimensions, as the captain's individualism resembled the troubling singularity, or even more worryingly, the arbitrary power of a divine right monarch. In neither land nor sea domains in *The Phoenix* is the role and situation of captain—with its responsibility of the "power of command"—optimally performed. Perhaps Middleton's Captain, with his fragile and devalued ("drooping") masculinity, was supposed to contrast to Phoenix's soaringly resurgent position as king-in-waiting, but the play's persistent undercutting of the distinctions between the two men suggests otherwise.

What then is *The Phoenix's* broader significance? One marker of its importance is that the play's emphasis on the political threat and inherent vice under the Jacobean policy shift on privateering contrasts to the understanding in travel writing of the sea captain's individualism as a more positive virtue. In this regard, the play is metonymic of a wider shift and so represents something more significant than itself. The way *The Phoenix* invokes Raleigh, however, also means that the play is significant in itself, since it is not only reflective but also constitutive of its moment. This layering of meaning is apparent too in the way it both lines up with the dominant ideology as it supports James's outlawing of the privateer in contrast to Elizabeth's state-funded pirates, yet also warns about the dangers of individualism in the figure of the ruler and hence simultaneously criticizes that same ideology. It is in its articulation of these unresolved, perhaps unresolvable, conflicts that Janus-faced look simultaneously backwards to the Tudor regime mournfully and acknowledges relief concerning its end, and look forwards hopefully but with concern to the new king's rule, that the play's real importance rests.

Notes

1. Elias Canetti, *Crowds and Power*, trans. Carol Stewart (London: Phoenix Press, 2000), 171.
2. John A. Froude, *Short Studies in Great Subjects*, 4 vols (London: Longmans, Green, and Co., 1891), I, 446.
3. For discussion see Richard Helgerson, *Forms of Nationhood: The Elizabethan Writing of England* (Chicago: University of Chicago Press, 1992); Bruce R. Smith, *Shakespeare and Masculinity* (Oxford: Oxford University Press, 2000), 39–66.
4. See David B. Quinn, ed. *Voyages and Colonizing Enterprises of Sir Humphrey Gilbert*, 2 vols (London: Hakluyt Society, 1940); Claire Jowitt, "Humphrey Gilbert," in *The Encyclopedia of English Renaissance Literature*, Gen. Eds. Garrett A. Sullivan, Jr and Alan Stewart, 3 vols (Oxford: Wiley-Blackwell, 2012), I, 381–3. See also Philip Edwards, "Edward Hayes Explains away Sir Humphrey Gilbert," *Renaissance Studies* 6, no. 3–4 (1992): 270–86; Steve Mentz, "Hakluyt's Oceans: Maritime Rhetoric in *The Principal Navigations*," in *Richard Hakluyt and Travel Writing in Early Modern Europe*, eds. Daniel Carey and Claire Jowitt (Farnham: Ashgate, 2012), 283–94.
5. For a definition of the genre of voyage drama see Claire Jowitt and David McInnis "Introduction; Understanding the Journeying Play," in *The Journeying Play: Travel and Drama in Early Modern England*, eds. Claire Jowitt and David McInnis (forthcoming).
6. For discussion of the range of plays in the genre see *The Journeying Play: Travel and Drama in Early Modern England*.
7. Christopher W. Brooks, *Pettyfoggers and Vipers of the Commonwealth* (Cambridge: Cambridge University Press, 1986), 115, 117.
8. See Charles Edelman, "Introduction," *The Stukeley Plays* (Manchester: Manchester University Press, 2005), 34.
9. For discussion of these pirate/privateering characters, as well as consideration of the likely date of each play's composition, see Claire Jowitt, *The Culture of Piracy, 1580–1630: English Literature and Seaborne Crime* (Farnham: Ashgate, 2010), 110–35.
10. See in particular Jean E. Howard, "An English Lass Amid the Moors: Gender, Race, Sexuality and National Identity in Heywood's *The Fair Maid of the West*," in *Women, "Race" and Writing in the Early Modern Period*, eds. Margo Hendricks and Patricia Parker (London and New York: Routledge, 1994), 101–17.
11. Anon., *The Famous History of the Life and Death of Captain Thomas Stukeley*, ed. Edelman, *The Stukeley Plays*, Scene 6, 48–9. The possible authorship of the play has been frequently discussed by critics; for a

summary of the debate see Edelman, "Introduction," 38–42, who argues that the first half of the play was written by Thomas Heywood.
12. Valerie Traub suggests that the "homoerotic energies of Viola, Olivia and Orsino are displaced onto Antonio, whose relation to Sebastian is finally sacrificed for the maintenance of institutionalized heterosexuality and generational continuity." See *Desire and Anxiety: Circulations of Sexuality in Shakespearean Drama* (London, Routledge, 1992), 123.
13. William Shakespeare, *Twelfth Night or What You Will*, ed. Keir Elam, The Arden Shakespeare. Third Series (London: Cengage Learning, 2008), 1.41, 5.1.55, 62.
14. Thomas Heywood, *The Fair Maid of the West Part I*, ed. Robert K. Turner, *The Fair Maid of the West Parts I and II* (London: Edward Arnold, 1968), IV, iv, 3–4.
15. For a consideration Stukeley's depiction as traitor and/or hero see Claire Jowitt, *Voyage Drama and Gender Politics, 1589–1642: Real and Imagined Worlds* (Manchester: Manchester University Press, 2002), 80–99.
16. Shakespeare, *Twelfth Night*, 5.1.250.
17. See Juan E. Tazón, *The Life and Times of Thomas Stukeley* (Ashgate: Aldershot, 2003).
18. On the "disguised ruler" plot-line see, for instance, Marilyn L. Williamson, "*The Phoenix*: Middleton's Comedy *de Regimine Principium*," *Renaissance News*, 10 (1957), 183-7. Leonard Tennenhouse, *Power on Display: The Politics of Shakespeare's Genres* (London: Methuen, 1986), 157.
19. See Thomas Middleton, *The Phoenix*, eds. Lawrence Danson and Ivo Kamps, in *Thomas Middleton: The Collected Works*, Gen. Eds. Gary Taylor and John Lavagnino (Oxford: Clarendon, 2007), 91. Martin Wiggins and Catherine Richardson, "1420. *The Phoenix*," in *British Drama 1533–1642: A Catalogue*, 6 vols (Oxford: Oxford University Press, 2015), V, 75–9.
20. See Thomas Middleton, *The Phoenix* (London: E[dward] A[llde] for A[rthur] I[ohnson], 1607); Edmund K. Chambers, *The Elizabethan Stage*, 4 vols (Oxford: Clarendon Press, 1923), IV, 169. For a full discussion see Kevin A. Quarmby, *The Disguised Ruler in Shakespeare and His Contemporaries* (Farnham: Ashgate, 2012), 139–47.
21. Quarmby, *The Disguised Ruler*, 142.
22. For discussion, see James Goldberg, *James I and the Politics of Literature: Jonson, Shakespeare, Donne and Their Contemporaries* (Baltimore: John Hopkins University Press, 1983).
23. See Kenneth R. Andrews, *Elizabethan Privateering: English Privateering During the Spanish War, 1585–1603* (Cambridge: Cambridge University Press, 1964).

24. Middleton, *The Phoenix*, 1.102–4.
25. Middleton, *The Phoenix*, 2.42–3.
26. Mark Eccles, "Middleton's Birth and Education," *RES* 7 (1931): 431–41; Peter G. Phialas, "Middleton's Early Contact with the Law," *SP* 52 (1955): 187–93; John B. Brooks, "Middleton's Stepfather and the Captain of 'The Phoenix'," *Notes and Queries* n.s. 8 (1961): 382–4.
27. Phialas,"Middleton's Early Contact with the Law," 193.
28. *The Phoenix*'s satire on the corruption of lawyers and the legal profession may also have been part of Middleton's response to his family's bitter legal wrangling. See Gary Taylor, "Thomas Middleton: Lives and Afterlives," in *Thomas Middleton: The Collected Works*, Gen. Eds Gary Taylor and John Lavagnino (Oxford: Clarendon, 2007), 25–58, especially 31, 49.
29. Middleton, *The Phoenix*, 2.1, 2.6, 2.56.
30. John Smith, *The Complete Works of Capt. John Smith*, ed. Philip L. Barbour, 3 vols (Chapel Hill: University of North Carolina Press, 1986), II, 914.
31. Quoted by Christopher Lee, *1603: The Death of Queen Elizabeth I* (New York: St. Martin's Press, 2003), 328.
32. Kenneth R. Andrews analyzes three different forms of private maritime violence: "the indiscriminate, persistent and criminal pursuit of maritime robbery [piracy]; officially authorised reprisals by merchants for loss of ships or goods [reprisals]; and government commissioned but privately promoted action against enemy shipping and goods in time of war [privateering]." For further details, see Andrews, "The expansion of English privateering and piracy in the Atlantic, c.1540–1625," in *Course et Piraterie*, ed. Michel Mollat, 2 vols (Paris: Centre National de la Recherche Scientifique, 1975), I, 196–230, 200. See also Andrews, *Elizabethan Privateering*, 22–31. In practice, the boundary between piracy, reprisal, and privateering was a permeable one. As Peter Earle describes "[p]rivateering or reprisal commissions were frequently dubious in their legitimacy and the privateers had few fears of discipline from the commissioning authorities [...] the temptation to exceed the commission, turn pirate and ransack neutral shipping was ever-present." See Earle, *The Pirate Wars* (London: Methuen, 2003), 22.
33. Middleton, *The Phoenix*, 2.82–4.
34. Middleton, *The Phoenix*, 2.91–4, 2.50–1.
35. Middleton, *The Phoenix*, 4.282–3.
36. Middleton, *The Phoenix*, 4.250.
37. Hugh R. Trevor-Roper, "The Last Elizabethan: Sir Walter Raleigh," *Historical Essays* (London: Macmillan, 1957), 103–7.

38. For an account of the history of piracy in the early seventeenth century, including James I's views, see Clive M. Senior, *A Nation of Pirates: English Piracy in its Heyday* (New York: David and Charles, 1976); Kenneth R. Andrews, "The expansion of English privateering," 196–230; Earle, *The Pirate Wars*.
39. The literature on Raleigh's life, and his significance in history, is immense, but see in particular: S. J. Greenblatt, *Sir Walter Raleigh: the Renaissance Man and his Roles* (New Haven: Yale University Press, 1973); Anna R. Beer, *Sir Walter Ralegh and his Readers in the Seventeenth Century* (Basingstoke: Macmillan 1997); Mark Nicholls and Penry Williams, *Sir Walter Raleigh in Life and Legend* (London: Continuum, 1997).
40. Beer, *Sir Walter Ralegh*, 8.
41. See Rosalind Davies, "'The Great Day of Mart': Returning to Texts at the Trial of Sir Walter Ralegh in 1603," *Renaissance Forum*, 4 (1999), 12 pages; http://www.hull.ac.uk/renforum/v4no1/davies.htm.
42. John W. Shirley, *Thomas Harriott: A Biography* (Oxford: Clarendon, 1983), 317.
43. Middleton, *The Phoenix*, 15.167; 199; 201.
44. See Nicholls and Williams, *Sir Walter Raleigh*, 206.
45. See Nicholls and Williams, *Sir Walter Raleigh*, 225–6.
46. Phialas, "Middleton's Early Contact," 193.
47. Middleton, *The Phoenix*, 2.28–30.
48. Middleton, *The Phoenix*, 2.30n.
49. Middleton, *The Phoenix*, 2.18–19.
50. See *OED* "seaman" 1.b (c.1478) in Hary, *Actis & Deidis Schir William Wallace*, "Semen he feyt and gaiff thaim gudlye wage."
51. Patrick J. Cook, "Beggary/Buggery and Oedipal Conflict in Thomas Middleton's *The Phoenix*," *EMLS* 12.2 (2006), 1–19, at 9, 8 [http://purl.oclc.org/emls/12-2/cookphoe.htm].
52. Middleton, *The Phoenix*, 2.68–9; Cook, "Beggary/Buggery," 8.
53. For discussion see http://www.npg.org.uk/whatson/elizabethi/film.php.
54. Middleton, *The Phoenix*, 2.108.
55. Middleton, *The Phoenix*, 2.103–8. Danson and Kamps, following the convention established by nineteenth-century editors for heavier use of stage directions, direct Proditor's salute to Castiza. For discussion, see Cook, "Beggary/Buggery," 9.
56. Middleton, *The Phoenix* (London, 1607) B2r–v.
57. Middleton, *The Phoenix*, 2.133.
58. Middleton, *The Phoenix*, 8.234.
59. Middleton, *The Phoenix*, 8.272.
60. M. Nicholls, "Treason's Reward: The Punishment of Conspirators in the Bye Plot of 1603," *Historical Journal* 38 (1985): 821–42, at 833.

61. Middleton, *The Phoenix*, 1.89; 7.4.
62. Middleton, *The Phoenix*, 8.60; 2.58, 69.
63. Middleton, *The Phoenix*, 8.15–16.
64. Middleton, *The Phoenix*, 8.68–72.
65. Middleton, *The Phoenix*, 8.71n.
66. Andrews, *Elizabethan Privateering*, 124–49, at 146, 137. See also John C. Appleby, *Under the Bloody Flag: Pirates of the Tudor Age* (Stroud: The History Press, 2009).
67. Godfrey Goodman, *The Court of King James I*, 2 vols (London: R. Bentley, 1839), I, 96. See also John Guy, ed., *The Reign of Elizabeth I: Court and Culture in the Last Decade* (Cambridge: Cambridge University Press, 1995).
68. Quoted by Katherine Eggert, *Showing Like a Queen: Female Authority and Literary Experiment in Spenser, Shakespeare, and Milton* (Philadelphia: University of Pennsylvania Press, 2000), 82.
69. Quoted by Curtis Perry, *The Making of Jacobean Culture: James I and the Renegotiation of Elizabethan Literary Culture* (Cambridge: Cambridge University Press, 1997) 56–7. See Alan R. Young, "The Phoenix Reborn: The Jacobean Appropriation of an Elizabethan Symbol," in *Resurrecting Elizabeth I in Seventeenth-Century England*, eds. Elizabeth H. Hageman and Katherine Conway (Maddison: Farleigh Dickinson University Press, 2007), 68–81.

Bibliography

Andrews, Kenneth A. *Elizabethan Privateering: English Privateering During the Spanish War, 1585–1603*. Cambridge: Cambridge University Press, 1964.

Andrews, Kenneth R. "The expansion of English privateering and piracy in the Atlantic, c.1540–1625." In *Course et Piraterie*. Edited by Michel Mollat. 2 vols. Paris: Centre National de la Recherche Scientifique, 1975.

Appleby, John C. *Under the Bloody Flag: Pirates of the Tudor Age*. Stroud: the History Press, 2009.

Beer, Anna R. *Sir Walter Ralegh and his Readers in the Seventeenth Century*. Basingstoke: Macmillan 1997.

Brooks, Christopher W. *Pettyfoggers and Vipers of the Commonwealth*. Cambridge: Cambridge University Press, 1986.

Brooks, John B. "Middleton's Stepfather and the Captain of 'The Phoenix'." In *Notes and Queries* n.s. 8. (1961): 382–4.

Canetti, Elias. *Crowds and Power*. trans. Carol Stewart. London: Phoenix Press, 2000.

Chambers, Edmund K. *The Elizabethan Stage*. 4 vols. Oxford: Clarendon Press, 1923.

Cook, Patrick J. "Beggary/Buggery and Oedipal Conflict in Thomas Middleton's *The Phoenix*," In *EMLS* 12.2. (2006): 1–19. http://purl.oclc.org/emls/12-2/cookphoe.htm.

Davies, Rosalind. "'The Great Day of Mart': Returning to Texts at the Trial of Sir Walter Ralegh in 1603." *Renaissance Forum* 4. (1999): 12 p.

Earle, Peter. *The Pirate Wars*. London: Methuen, 2003.

Eccles, Mark. "Middleton's Birth and Education." *RES* 7 (1931): 431–41.

Edelman, Charles. *The Stukeley Plays*. Manchester: Manchester University Press, 2005.

Edwards, Philip. "Edward Hayes Explains away Sir Humphrey Gilbert." In *Renaissance Studies* 6, no. 3–4. (1992): 270–86.

Eggert, Katherine. *Showing Like a Queen: Female Authority and Literary Experiment in Spenser, Shakespeare, and Milton*. Philadelphia: University of Pennsylvania Press, 2000.

Froude, John A. *Short Studies in Great Subjects*. 4 vols. London: Longmans, Green, and Co., 1891.

Goldberg, James. *James I and the Politics of Literature: Jonson, Shakespeare, Donne and Their Contemporaries*. Baltimore: John Hopkins University Press, 1983.

Goodman, Godfrey. *The Court of King James I*. 2 vols. London: R. Bentley, 1839.

Greenblatt, Stephen J. *Sir Walter Raleigh: the Renaissance Man and his Roles*. New Haven: Yale University Press, 1973.

Guy, John. ed. *The Reign of Elizabeth I: Court and Culture in the Last Decade*. Cambridge: Cambridge University Press, 1995.

Helgerson, Richard. *Forms of Nationhood: The Elizabethan Writing of England*. Chicago: University of Chicago Press, 1992.

Heywood, Thomas. *The Fair Maid of the West Part I*. Edited by Robert K. Turner. *The Fair Maid of the West Parts I and II*. London: Edward Arnold, 1968.

Howard, Jean E. "An English Lass Amid the Moors: Gender, Race, Sexuality and National Identity in Heywood's *The Fair Maid of the West*." In *Women, "Race" and Writing in the Early Modern Period*. Edited by Margo Hendricks and Patricia Parker. London and New York: Routledge, 1994.

Jowitt, Claire. *Voyage Drama and Gender Politics, 1589–1642: Real and Imagined Worlds*. Manchester: Manchester University Press, 2002.

Jowitt, Claire. *The Culture of Piracy, 1580–1630: English Literature and Seaborne Crime*. Farnham: Ashgate, 2010.

Jowitt, Claire. "Humphrey Gilbert." In *The Encyclopedia of English Renaissance Literature*. Edited by Garrett A. Sullivan, Jnr and Alan Stewart. 3 vols. Oxford: Wiley-Blackwell, 2012.

Jowitt, Claire and McInnis, David. "Introduction; Understanding the Journeying Play." In *The Journeying Play: Travel and Drama in Early Modern England*. Edited by Claire Jowitt and David McInnis.
Lee, Christopher. *1603: The Death of Queen Elizabeth I*. New York: St. Martin's Press, 2003.
Mentz, Steve. "Hakluyt's Oceans: Maritime Rhetoric in *The Principal Navigations*." In *Richard Hakluyt and Travel Writing in Early Modern Europe*. Edited by Daniel Carey and Claire Jowitt. Farnham: Ashgate, 2012.
Middleton, Thomas. *The Phoenix*. London: E[dward] A[llde] for A[rthur] I[ohnson], 1607.
Middleton, Thomas. *The Phoenix*. Edited by Lawrence Danson and Ivo Kamps. In *Thomas Middleton: The Collected Works*. Edited by Gary Taylor and John Lavagnino. Oxford: Clarendon, 2007.
Nicholls, M. "Treason's Reward: The Punishment of Conspirators in the Bye Plot of 1603." In *Historical Journal* 38 (1985): 821–42.
Nicholls, Mark and Williams, Penny. *Sir Walter Raleigh in Life and Legend*. London: Continuum, 1997.
Perry, Curtis. *The Making of Jacobean Culture: James I and the Renegotiation of Elizabethan Literary Culture*. Cambridge: Cambridge University Press, 1997.
Phialas, Peter G. "Middleton's Early Contact with the Law." In *SP* 52. (1955): 187–193.
Quarmby, Kevin A. *The Disguised Ruler in Shakespeare and His Contemporaries*. Farnham: Ashgate, 2012.
Quinn, David B. ed. *Voyages and Colonizing Enterprises of Sir Humphrey Gilbert*. 2 vols. London: Hakluyt Society, 1940.
Senior, Clive M. *A Nation of Pirates: English Piracy in its Heyday*. New York: David and Charles, 1976.
Shakespeare, William. *Twelfth Night or What You Will*. Edited by Keir Elam. The Arden Shakespeare. Third Series. London: Cengage Learning, 2008.
Shirley, John W. *Thomas Harriott: A Biography*. Oxford: Clarendon, 1983.
Smith, Bruce R. *Shakespeare and Masculinity*. Oxford: Oxford University Press, 2000.
Smith, John. *The Complete Works of Capt. John Smith*. Edited by Philip L. Barbour. 3 vols. Chapel Hill: University of North Carolina Press, 1986.
Taylor, Gary. "Thomas Middleton: Lives and Afterlives." In *Thomas Middleton: The Collected Works*. Edited by Gary Taylor and John Lavagnino. Oxford: Clarendon, 2007.
Tazón, Juan E. *The Life and Times of Thomas Stukeley*. Ashgate: Aldershot, 2003.
Tennenhouse, Leonard. *Power on Display: The Politics of Shakespeare's Genres*. London: Methuen, 1986.
Traub, Valerie. *Desire and Anxiety: Circulations of Sexuality in Shakespearean Drama*. London: Routledge, 1992.

Trevor-Roper, Hugh R. "The Last Elizabethan: Sir Walter Raleigh." *Historical Essays*. London: Macmillan, 1957.

Wiggins, Martin and Catherine Richardson. *British Drama 1533–1642: A Catalogue*. 8 vols. Oxford: Oxford University Press, 2011.

Williamson, Marilyn L. "*The Phoenix*: Middleton's Comedy *de Regimine Principium*." In *Renaissance News* 10 (1957): 183–7.

Young, Alan R. The Phoenix Reborn: The Jacobean Appropriation of an Elizabethan Symbol." In *Resurrecting Elizabeth I in Seventeenth-Century England*. Edited by Elizabeth H. Hageman and Katherine Conway. Maddison: Farleigh Dickinson University Press, 2007.

Index

A
Adrianople (Edirne), 146
Africanus, Cornelia, 98
Africanus, Scipio, 107
Albert VII, Archduke of Austria, 7
Aleppo, 141, 146, 152, 153
Alexandretta, 141, 142
Alexandria, 99, 100, 106
Alvarez de Toledo, Fernando, Duke of Alva, 55, 56
Anglo-Scottish Diplomacy, 22
Anne Boleyn, Queen of England, 176
Anne of Brittany, Queen of France, 176
Anne of Denmark, Queen of England, 118
Antonio, 170, 172, 173, 227, 228
Antwerp, 175
Asolo, 100, 106, 112
Astraea, 211

B
Basse, William, 178
Beg, Qoli, 153, 154
Beza, Theodore, 199
Black Plague, 1

Boaistuau, Pierre, 178, 180
Bothwell, Earl of, 25
Bovolini, Taddeo, 106
Boyd, Robert, 25
Brisset of Antrim, Margaret, 19
Browne, Thomas, 177, 178
Buda, 195–198, 200, 201
Bullokar, John, 177

C
Cabot, John, 54, 202
Cadiz, 83
Camden, William, 196
Campbells of Argyll, 19
Captain, The, 21, 223, 226, 230, 232, 234–236
Cartier, Jacques, 51, 201, 206
Castiza, 230, 232, 235, 236, 238
Cataro, Anne, 141
Caterina Cornaro, Queen of Cyprus, 6, 97, 98, 108, 110, 111
Catherine de Medici, Queen Regent of France, 6, 7, 41
Catherine of Aragon, Queen of England, 118, 125, 176

© The Editor(s) (if applicable) and The Author(s) 2017
E. Paranque et al. (eds.), *Colonization, Piracy, and Trade in Early Modern Europe*, Queenship and Power, DOI 10.1007/978-3-319-57159-1

Index

Catherine of Braganza, Queen of England, 130
Catholic Reformation, 1
Challoner, Thomas, 22, 23
Charla, 97, 101, 106, 111
Charlesfort, 53–56
Charles I of England, 77, 240
Charles V, Holy Roman Emperor, 2
Charles IX of France, 42
Christ Church, Oxford, 200, 201
Churchyard, Thomas, 204–206
Clarke, Samuel, 180
Colbert, Jean-Baptiste, 144, 145, 156
Colbert, Jean-Baptiste Antoine, 144
Coligny, Gaspard, 44, 45, 52–55, 57, 58, 62
Colonization, 3, 4, 6–9, 42, 50, 52, 59, 112, 195, 201, 203, 205, 206, 212–215
Condé, Louis, 44, 45, 47, 51, 61, 62
Constantinople, 2, 59, 141–144, 146–148, 150, 152, 155
Count of Gondomar, 77
Count of Onate, Inigo Vélez de Guevara, 79
Count Proditor, 229, 232
Croft, James, 20, 120
Cromwell, Thomas, 175, 176
Cypris, 109
Cyprus, 8, 97–103, 105–112, 142, 146

D

de Berhes, Henri, 84
de Boot, Anselmus, 174
de Consaloveris, John Baptista, 175
de Cordoba, Gonzalès, 84
Dee, John, 202, 206, 208, 212
de Enjeva, Gabriel, 55
de Ferriol, Charles, 143, 150, 152
de Gourgues, Dominique, 58
de Grandchamp de Grantrie, Guillaume, 60
de Guzman, Gaspar, Duke of Olivares, 79
de la Primaudaye, Pierre, 109, 177, 179
de Lavergne, Gabriel-Joseph, Vicomte de Guilleragues, 148
de Lusignan, Carlotta, 97
de Mansfeld, Ernest, 82
de Montaigne, Michel, 219
de Nassau, Jean, 84
de Navaz, Antonio, 79
de Richelieu, Cardinal, 144
Deshayes de Courmenin, Louis, 147
de Toledo, Pedro, 128
de Zagly, Philippe, 145, 153, 154, 161
Diana, 107, 175, 211
Dido, 107
Digby, John, 121
Donne, John, 179
Drake, Sir Francis, 5, 195, 214, 224, 234
Dubies, Pierre, 142

E

East India Company, 123, 127, 128
Elisabeth, Henry II of France's daughter, Queen of Spain, 50, 55
Elizabeth of Austria, Queen of France, 57
Elizabeth I of England, 3, 9, 30, 42, 104, 110, 118, 120, 170, 183, 195, 227–229
Ellis, Thomas, 205
Exotic, 6, 9, 170, 173, 174, 180, 225

F

Fabre, Jean-Baptiste, 8, 141–143, 145, 146, 148, 149
Fabre, Jourdan, 146
Fabre, Louis-Marseille, 146
Fabre, Matthieu, 146, 147
Fabyan, Robert, 175

Father Maunier, 149
Ferdinand II, King of Aragon, 2, 78, 80
Fiorenza Sanudo, 106
Fort Caroline, 55, 56, 58
Fort San Augustín, 56
Fort San Felipe, 56
Fort San Mateo, 56, 58
Foxe, John, 199, 200
Francis I, King of France, 2, 51, 59
Frederick I of Bohemia, 121
Frederick V, Elector Palatine, 121
Frobisher, Martin, 201, 204, 205, 214

G

Gascoigne, George, 204, 210
Gilbert, Sir Humphrey, 9, 195, 196, 200, 203–205, 207, 209, 212, 214, 215, 224, 225, 242
Glens, 19, 23, 26, 30
Gracchus, Gaius, 98
Gracchus, Tiberius, 98
Guises, The, 44

H

Hakluyt, Richard, 119, 196, 200, 201, 206, 207, 215, 224
Hardy, Thomas, 225
Hawkins, John, 201, 214
Helena Paleologa, 102, 107
Henrietta Maria of France, 8
Henry, Lord Darnley, 182
Henry II of France, 50
Henry III of France, 42
Henry VII of England, 202
Henry VIII of England, 7, 118, 119, 125, 175, 176, 182
Herbert, Thomas, 180
Holbein, Hans, 175
Holland, 76–78, 80, 85, 147
Holy Roman Emperor, Ferdinand II, 2, 18, 60, 78

Holy Roman Emperor Maximilian II, 60
Horton, John, 175
Howard, Thomas, Earl of Surrey, 176
Huguenots, 7, 42, 44–53, 55, 58, 60–63

I

Isabel Clara Eugenia
  Co-Sovereign of the Spanish Netherlands, 74
  Governor of the Spanish Netherlands, 7, 73, 74, 76, 80, 82, 84
  Infant of Spain, 73
Italian wars, 59

J

James I of England, 50, 77, 120
James II of Cyprus, 98
James III of Cyprus, 97, 105
James IV of Scotland, 176
Jessica, 169–174, 179, 183, 184
John Sigismund of Hungaria, 198
Juana II of Naples, Queen of Jerusalem, 108

K

Katherine Howard, Queen of England, 182
Kenilworth Castle, 210
Khan of Yerevan, 142, 149, 150
Knights Hospitaller, 100, 101, 103, 107
Knights of St John, 102, 112
Knox, John, 79
Komnenos, Isaac, 98
Kyrenia, 100, 103

L

Laois, 26, 27
Laudonnière, René, 53–55, 57, 58

Le Grand, Antoine, 177
Leopold V, Archduke of Austria, 82
L'Hospital, Michel, 45, 46, 48, 62
Liliani, Giambattista, 107
Lily, John, 60
Limassol, 98, 102
Louis XII of France, 176
Louis XIV of France, 8, 63, 141–144, 146–148, 152, 153, 155–157, 160

M
Mabbe, John, 183
MacDonalds of Dunyvaig, 19
Mameluke Egypt, 100
Maplet, John, 178, 180
Margaret, Countess of Lennox, 182
Maria Ana, Infant of Spain, 8
Marseille, 144, 146–148, 153, 157
Martin, Richard, 177, 180, 201
Mary I of England, 6, 7, 17, 18, 20, 22, 23, 25, 27, 28, 119, 170
Mary of Guise, 7, 22, 23
Mary Stuart, Queen of Scotland, 24, 79, 118, 171, 182, 183
Massacre of Wassy, 47, 54
McOneboye, Coll, 21, 22
Menéndez de Avilés, Pedro, 56
Merchant of Venice, The, 169–171, 174
Michel, Pierre-Victor, 142
Middleton, Thomas, 9, 223, 225
More, Thomas, 177, 224
Moulins, 56, 158

N
Naples, 59, 81, 98, 101, 111, 147
Naxos, 99, 101
Nichols, Thomas, 179
Nicot, Jean, 144

O
O'Donnell, Calvagh, 20, 22, 23, 29
O'Donnells of Tyrconnel, 19
Offaly, 26, 27
Olivares, 79
O'Neill, Eugene, 83
O'Neills of Tyrone, 19, 29
Ottoman, 2, 59–61, 100, 101, 142, 144, 146–148, 151, 155, 157, 161, 181, 197

P
Parmenius, Stephen, 9, 195, 196, 200, 215
Peace of Amasya, The, 155
Peckham, George, 214
Persia, 8, 141–156, 158, 160, 180, 181
Petit, Marie, 8, 141, 142, 155
Phélypeaux, Jérôme, Comte de Pontchartrain, 141
Philip II of Spain, 7, 50, 73, 85
Philip III of Spain, 120
Philip IV of Spain, 7, 73–75, 82
Philip the Good, Duke of Burgundy, 104
Phoenix, The, 9, 223, 225, 226, 228–230, 234, 235, 239, 240, 242
Piracy, 2–6, 8–10
Plantagenet, Honor, Viscountess Lisle, 176
Pope Clement VII, 118
Pope Pius II, 102
Popular public drama, 225
Privateering, 5, 154, 226, 227, 229, 242
Protestant Reformation, 1

Q
Queenship, 3, 5, 6, 8, 98, 169

INDEX

R
Ráckeve, 198
Radcliffe, Thomas, Baron Fitzwalter, Earl of Sussex, 18
Raleigh, Sir Walter, 122, 224, 239
Renaissance England, 170
Reynolds, John, 119
Reza Beg, Mohamed, 143
Rhodes, 100, 102, 142
Ribault, Jean, 52–56, 58
Richard the Lionheart, 98
Ridolfi Plot, 183
Rings, 170, 171, 174, 175, 182, 183
Roberts, Lewes, 177
Rudolph II, Emperor, 174

S
Safavid Shah, 123
Safavid Shah Sultan Hosayn, 141
Salic Laws (also *Lex Salicas*), 43, 44
San Thomé, 123
Savary, Jacques, 145
Savile, Thomas, 196
Scot, Michael, 178
Seymour, Edward, 176
Shah Quli Khan, 156
Shah Tahmasp, 155
Shakespeare, William, 227
Shylock, 170–175, 178, 181, 183, 184
Sidney, Sir Philip, 205
Silk trade, 142
Skaricza, Máté, 198, 199
Smith, Thomas, 205
Spencer, Edmund, 210
Spinola, Ambrogio, 84
Strelley, Jane, 175
Stuarts, The, 123, 125, 126
Sueyro, Emmanuel, 77
Sulkhan Saba Orbeliani, 156
Sultan Selim II, 60, 61
Sultan Murad III, 59
Sultan Suleiman the Magnificent, 59, 144, 155
Szegedi Kis, István, 198, 199

T
Thirty Years War, 80, 120
Trade, 2, 3, 6–10, 59, 61, 74–77, 86, 98, 99, 107, 119, 122, 128, 142, 144, 146, 147, 156, 157, 161, 180, 205, 224
Tubal, 172, 173
Tudors, The, 7, 18, 126
Turkey, 144, 146, 161, 180, 181
Turquoise, 9, 170, 171, 173–184

U
Ulster, 17–20, 22, 23, 26, 27, 29, 30
Ulster Scots, 18, 21
Unton, Henry, 196, 200
Uzbek, 146

V
Vakhtang VI, Georgian Regent, 145, 155, 156
Venetian Republic, 97, 102
Venice, 8, 97–103, 105–107, 110–112
Venus, 100, 102, 104, 105, 107, 109
Voyage drama, 225

W
Wolsey, Cardinal, 176

Y
Yerevan, 142, 152, 155

Z
Zorzi of Cornaro, 111, 112